THE OTHER EUROPEAN COMMUNITY

Barents Sea

Akureyri
ICELAND
Reykjavík

0 100 km

FAEROES

Norwegian Sea

Arctic Circle

Tromsø

Murmansk

Kiruna

White Sea

Luleå

Oulu
Kuopio

Trondheim

Sundsvall

Gulf
of
Bothnia

60°

Bergen

Oslo

Gävle

Tampere

Helsinki

Uppsala

Gulf of Finland

Leningrad

Stavanger
Kristiansand

Skagerrak

Jönköping

Stockholm
Norrköping

SOVIET

North
Sea

Ålborg
Århus
Copenhagen

Gothenburg

Kattegat

UNION

55°

Malmö

Baltic
Sea

DENMARK

Hamburg

NETHER-
LANDS

WEST
GERMANY

Berlin

EAST
GERMANY

POLAND

Warsaw

Miles
0   200

0   300
Kilometres

THE OTHER EUROPEAN COMMUNITY

Integration and co-operation
in Nordic Europe

BARRY TURNER
with Gunilla Nordquist

St. Martin's Press
New York

All rights reserved. For information, write:
St. Martin's Press, Inc., 175 Fifth Avenue, New York, NY 10010
Printed in Great Britain
First published in the United States of America in 1982

ISBN 0-312-58946-8

Library of Congress Cataloging in Publication Data

Turner, Barry.
    The Other European community.

    Bibliography: p.
    Includes index.
        1. Scandinavian cooperation.   2. Finland—Relations—
Scandinavia.   3. Scandinavia—Relations—Finland.
4. Nordic Council.   I. Nordquist, Gunilla.   II. Title.
DL57.T85   1982   948   81-23330
ISBN 0-312-58946-8   AACR2

Contents

DL
57
T85
1982

Preface

This book would not have been possible without the generous help and advice of friends who spend their lives in the mainstream of Nordic democracy. In giving their time and attention to persistent interrogators, who, after one or two interviews, frequently returned to renew the punishment, they brought to life events which might otherwise have remained petrified in official documents.

Our particular thanks must go to Klas Olofsson and to his colleagues at the Nordic Cultural Secretariat. It was Klas who conceived the idea of the book and, having launched the project, never once failed to give practical assistance or encouragement on the many occasions that both were needed. We also owe much to Sven Dahlin, one of the most experienced practitioners in Nordic co-operation, who took an interest in the work throughout and at manuscript stage acted as a friendly but constructive critic.

We have not used footnotes; all explanations are in the text. But a word of caution should be added on the interpretation of currency exchange rates. The Swedish Krona and the Norwegian and Danish Krone are not of equal value, and all of these are to be distinguished from the Finnish Mark. At the time of writing, the Swedish Krona is valued at approximately 5.5 to the dollar and 10 to the pound; the Danish Krone at 7 to the dollar and 11 to the pound, and the Finnish Mark at 4.5 to the dollar and 9 to the pound. Unless otherwise indicated in the text the Nordic currency used for government figures is the Swedish Krona.

Introduction

Straddling the top of Europe, the Nordic races have been for much of their history culturally sheltered on the south and west by the sea and on the east by the forests and swamps which separated Finland from the inhabited parts of Russia. Naturally, they tended to look inwards and, irrespective of political differences, to develop a common set of values. Down the centuries, the achievements of one country – from the Icelandic sagas to the Swedish invention of the ball-bearing – were adopted by the others as part of the Nordic creative genius. So, today, a Swede will take pride in a piece of Finnish design, a Norwegian looks to Swedish technology to multiply the wealth from North Sea oil and a Dane acknowledges the midnight sun as part of his heritage, even though geographically he is ill-suited ever to see it.

This book is an attempt to identify more closely what is essentially Nordic by exploring the political, economic and cultural development of the five countries and their attempts to work together in pursuit of shared ideals. Relationships have not always been amicable. Nationalist sentiment, nurtured by the fear that small countries, once the easy victims of military adventure, are now just as vulnerable to the economic forces of their more powerful neighbours, has thwarted attempts to engage in some form of union on the lines, say, of the European Community. Instead there has evolved a more loosely organized system of inter-governmental consultation, with the Nordic Council acting as the main forum for debate.

Yet even without the trappings of centralized rule, co-operation has progressed so far as to make real the concept of Nordic citizenship. That a similar claim cannot be made for Europe as a whole must surely be accounted for by the strong cultural affinity between the Nordic countries. Though impossible to

I

reproduce artificially, there is perhaps a lesson to be learned from the Scandinavian experience: that economic and strategic interests are not the sole determinants of a constructive alliance. The Treaty of Rome might have provided a stronger foundation for European unity if greater allowance had been made for encouraging mutual understanding and sympathy between ordinary people.

If reason is needed for devoting most of the book to the modern period it is because in this century Scandinavia – or, more accurately, Norden – has really come into its own, notably in the achievement of a form of advanced democracy which combines a remarkable sense of equality with a high level of material prosperity, a permutation that has eluded other countries professing a strong commitment to social change. But what has been called 'the middle way', the title Childs gave to his interwar best-seller on Sweden, and, more recently, 'socialism without pain', has recently suffered crises of self-confidence which some judge to be terminal. International recession and what appears to be a permanent downturn in the relative fortunes of the Western economies has provoked a powerful reaction against the Nordic style of egalitarian politics. It is said to have encouraged at all levels a mood of complacency which militates against painful but essential changes in the industrial and commercial fabric. The immediate response from the left has been defensive in a way that suggests there might well be something in the argument. But this is not the end of the story. New ideas for extending the concept of democracy without abandoning radical traditions or sacrificing living standards are beginning to take root. With the emphasis shifting towards changes in the work environment, the extension of educational opportunities, and the wider delegation of responsibility, and all this coming together in the first tentative concept of cultural democracy, the Nordic countries may soon be in for another quiet but trend-setting revolution.

1
The making of Norden

Omitting Iceland, the lonely outpost in the North Atlantic which is farther away from mainland Norden than Britain, the other four Scandinavian countries form a territorial entity which extends 1,200 miles from the Danish–German frontier to the northernmost part of Norway. Their land area (excluding Greenland) is about 450,000 square miles, greater than Britain, France and Spain put together. But the balance changes dramatically when people, not acres, are counted. Vast expanses of northern Finland, Norway and Sweden are given over to mountains and forest ('Europe's last wilderness'), while most of volcanic Iceland is uninhabitable. Those who can properly call themselves Nordic number just under twenty-two million and are to be found living mostly along the coasts or in the rich agricultural areas of the south where nearly all the big towns are located.

As the country best situated to make productive use of its land, Denmark is the most densely populated, with 5 million inhabitants or 261 per square mile. (Even so, this last figure is considerably less than the 530 per square mile for the United Kingdom.) At the other extreme is Iceland, barely registering 5 to a square mile. Most of her 220,000 population lives in the capital, Reykjavík, which thus, by European standards, qualifies as a small town. In between come Sweden (8.2 million, 46 per square mile), Finland (4.7 million, 34 per square mile) and Norway (4 million, 32 per square mile). Excluded from those figures are The Faeroes, an outcrop of rocky islands in the Atlantic north of the Shetlands, and Greenland. Both come under Danish jurisdiction but enjoy a large measure of home rule. Greenland is distinguished by being the world's largest island but since in defiance of its name most of it is covered in ice, it also has one of the smallest proportions of habitable land. The Arctic Svalbard island group is administered by Norway and certain Antarctic territories are also Norwegian possessions.

The climate of Norden is by no means as inhospitable as its latitudes might seem to indicate. The Gulf Stream and the south-westerly winds from the Atlantic take some of the edge off winter and the average temperature for January is about the same as for central Europe. The summers may not measure up to Mediterranean standards, but the bright sunshine creates a pleasant dry warmth from late May to mid-August when the Scandinavians abandon the towns for their country and seaside cottages.

When the glaciers finally retreated from Norden some fifteen thousand years ago they left behind a landscape that was, at best, patchy in quality. The soil was at its most fertile in Denmark and in southern Sweden but over the rest of Sweden and in Finland and Norway it was too stony to be of great potential value to farmers. Even today Norway has only three per cent of its land under cultivation while three-quarters of Denmark is given over to agriculture. The intensive and highly productive farming which is characteristic of Denmark has developed in response to the shortage of other resources. It is only post-war, with the skilled and imaginative application of imported raw materials, that manufacturing industry has come to play a major role in the economy.

This is not to say that the rest of Norden enjoys an abundance of natural riches. The forests of Norway, Sweden and Finland were the first, and until well into this century, the only great source of wealth. Starting as a supplier of planks and props for European manufacturers, the timber industry has consistently expanded its range of products so that today paper in all its varieties, building materials and furniture figure prominently in the table of Nordic exports. Sweden had a further initial advantage in possessing rich deposits of iron ore on which she based her steel and engineering industry.

But throughout Nordic history more natural wealth has been extracted from the sea than from land. This is as true today as at any other time, though in the modern scheme of things the emphasis has extended from fish to oil. The rich harvests from the Lofoten fishing grounds off northern Norway have sustained the coastal communities for centuries while the great fishing banks near Iceland are still the mainstay of that country's economy. Each of the big four has a high ranking in the league of shipbuilding nations and the Norwegian merchant fleet is the fifth largest in the world.

Until this century the entire Nordic region was virtually devoid of energy resources. It was only when advantage was taken of the numerous rivers and waterfalls to create hydro-electric power and a secure foundation for commercial expansions that the potential for developing a prosperous and advanced society was finally realized. By the Second World War, Norway was the world's second largest user per capita of hydro-electric power, with Sweden and Finland not far behind. Since then, of course, the tapping of North Sea oil has once again transformed that Norwegian economy.

Danish and Swedish hopes of sharing in the North Sea bonanza have so far been disappointed, though Denmark has found sizeable reserves of natural gas, and exploration continues off the Greenland coast. Until recently Norway has not bestowed any great favours on her neighbours, choosing instead to try to build up her industrial base by bargaining oil supplies against the provision of technical know-how, an objective which, as we shall see later, has encountered unexpected obstacles.

Undoubtedly the most remarkable source of energy in Norden is also the oldest, Iceland's hot springs. Ever since the war, Reykjavík has been heated by water pumped in from these springs and when major developments in the south-west and north are completed, over seventy per cent of Icelanders will have geothermal heating in their homes.

The progressive industrialization of Norden has been accompanied by an internal migration from north to south and from the rural to urban areas. While a century ago only ten to twenty per cent lived in towns, this proportion has risen to fifty to eighty per cent. Belated recognition of the social risks of over-centralization has produced massive aid programmes for the depopulated districts but with what effect it is impossible at this stage to estimate. While the problem is usually debated in a context of rural crisis the pressure on the urban environment is also a matter for concern. This may sound incredible given the size of population relative to land area, but some of the biggest cities are in the richest agricultural region and strong conflicting interests are at work.

Copenhagen is a case in point. The city dominates Zealand, by far the largest of the hundred or so inhabited islands which crowd the entrance to the Baltic. The neighbouring island, Funen, has its own growth centre in Odense, the country's third largest city, while on the Swedish side, just a forty-minute hovercraft journey away, is Malmö. The well-established prosperity of the region based on industries as diverse as shipbuilding, vehicle assembly, brewing and food processing, together with easy communications to the wealthiest parts of Germany, make this part of Norden a natural focal point for economic growth in northern Europe. But can its environment's resources take the strain?

The sceptics point to what has happened to Amager, the tiny pear-shaped island just to the south of Copenhagen. Once the market garden for the capital, it is now the site for the international airport. No one believes that its few remaining green acres will long survive against urban sprawl and the demand for second homes by the sea. The fear of creating an environmentalist's nightmare, an urban conglomeration across the Danish–Swedish border which would absorb the smaller towns of southern Norden or sap them of their commercial strength, was one of the arguments for not going ahead with the projected Öresund bridge linking Copenhagen and Malmö.

That the bridge was a serious proposition in the early seventies – indeed, was promoted as a major exercise in Nordic co-operation for which there was powerful business support on both sides of the water – warns against attaching too much significance to political boundaries. The people of Copenhagen and Malmö have as much if not more in common with each other than with fellow citizens further north. Nor is it difficult to find other examples of social-economic and cultural overlaps which transcend national identities. The farmers who work the flat, fertile and highly cultivated areas of Denmark feel a strong affinity with their colleagues in the extreme south of Sweden. They developed their agriculture in almost exactly the same way from feudal strip-farming and three-field rotation to enclosure and more intensive forms of husbandry in the late eighteenth and early nineteenth centuries. The technique of building timber-framed houses was developed in this part of Scandinavia and, outside the new industrial areas, the region is still characterized by neat villages set against a backdrop of gently rolling, well-tended farmland.

Although Denmark is often seen as a country naturally suited to arable farming, the north and west was at one time dominated by vast tracts of sand and heath. Fishing was then the predominant occupation, with some cattle and sheep breeding. It was not until the late nineteenth century that successful efforts were made to create the conditions for highly productive agriculture. The historical contact, then, is not so much with the fertile south as with the Atlantic cultural region which comprises Iceland, The Faeroes and western Norway. Fishing is still the leading industry, and the Atlantic region is neither industrialized nor urbanized to any great extent. Geographical features vary widely from the flat stretches of sand and heath in western Denmark to the steep grass-covered fells of western Norway, while Iceland and The Faeroes display a combination of steep craggy cliffs and broad island plains covered with scrub and grass. A characteristic shared by them all is the almost total absence of woods which gives the landscape a stark and often lunar appearance. The social bond is weakened by distance and the Icelanders' acknowledged claim to cultural uniqueness. However, as both Iceland and The Faeroes were colonized from west Norway, shared origins must be acknowledged even if today it is economic rather than ethnological factors which are the chief binding force.

The central Scandinavian region, which stretches from the Oslo fjord across central Sweden to south-west Finland, takes in three capitals and has a high concentration of industry. It has always been an area of innovation, open to new ideas from the cultures of both northern and eastern Europe. But the importance of cross-boundary urban links noted earlier with Copenhagen and Malmö and emphasized in this case by the predominance of Swedish speakers in the coastal 'golden horseshoe' of Finland must not be allowed to detract from the significance of the rural heritage based on fishing, forestry and animal husbandry. Agriculture and fishing are still fundamental to the economy of the thousands of islands crowded into the Swedish and Finnish archipelagos. The Åland islands on the half-way point between the two countries enjoy a wide measure of self-government, a concession from Finland to a largely Swedish-speaking population.

The forestry industry is concentrated on an area extending from eastern Norway across the bottom half of northern Sweden to the west coast of Finland. This was one of the earliest sectors of Norden to be industrialized and the rapid growth of timber exports in the nineteenth century has left an indelible mark on the towns with their mills and factories, pervaded by the unmistakable smell of sawdust and pulp. But to take the longer view of its history, the region has derived its character as much from its particular style of farming as from forestry. Until the industrial revolution the sparse population led a peripatetic existence with cattle-breeding as its central activity. The best grazing grounds were on the mountain sides and in the vast forests of east Norway and the neighbouring parts of Sweden, where the peasant farmers took no note of lines of political demarcation in their periodic movement of the herds from one pasture to another. The society they created put great emphasis on independence and individual freedom.

The vast forest landscape of east Finland must be taken on its own, its cultural overlap being more apparent in the strength of Slavic rather than Nordic influences. Until the timber industry came into its own the region offered little except a subsistence living to scattered peasant farmers and unlimited hunting to visitors from the south. But increasing demand for a vital raw material attracted migrants from the east, who brought with them elements of Slavic lifestyle such as the sauna and the log cabin, which have long since been absorbed into the Nordic culture. Today with forestry no longer a labour-intensive industry east Finland is the part of Scandinavia worst hit by depopulation. History seems to be repeating itself in that the greatest attraction of the lakes and forests is for visitors from the south in search of sport and recreation.

The sub-Arctic region of Norway, Sweden and Finland, home of the Samia or Lappish people, is one of the clearest examples of geographical and cultural bonds outweighing political definitions of nationality. There are less than 45,000 Lapps: 22,000 in Norway, 17,000 in Sweden, 3,500 in Finland and less than 2,000 in northern Russia just over the Finnish border. But though few in number and widely dispersed, they have a distinctive culture nurtured by their own language, and they are deeply conscious of a history which can be traced back to the time of the Romans. Originally a coastal people, the Lapps turned inland when they found they could get food, clothing and shelter by staying close to the wild reindeer herds. Reindeer hides were draped around poles to make simple tents; skins were turned into shoes, furs and bags; reindeer horn made buckles and knife handles and the animals were killed for their meat. It was a way of life which kept the Lapps on the move following the herds from their winter grazing in the forests to the summer pasture on the mountains. As practised Arctic travellers they pioneered the use of skis, a word which derives from Skridfinrna, the old Scandinavian word for Lapland; *skrid* or *skrida* meaning to slide.

Few Lapps now lead a genuinely nomadic existence. The minority who still engage in reindeer breeding often drive and some even fly to check on their wandering herds. But their sense of identity remains strong and their strenuous appeal for the protection of their traditional rights, including the free occupation of vast grazing areas, has met with a sympathetic response from governments in the south. They share a sense of guilt for an uncaring past when exploitation by hunters and mineral prospectors threatened the very existence of the Lappish people. The Nordic Lapp Council, a creation of the 1950s, and the Nordic Lapp Institute at Kautokeino, Norway, founded in 1973, are responsible for collaboration between Sweden, Norway and Finland on matters affecting the Lapps, including the encouragement of tourism, now the region's major source of income.

Although Greenland is not strictly speaking part of Europe, she has strong cultural and political links with Scandinavia. The first inhabitants were Eskimos from north America, but Nordic settlement started in the tenth century when a group of Icelanders found their way to the fertile fjords of south-west Greenland, the only part of the island that really justified its name. Though in theory it owed allegiance to the Dano-Norwegian kingdom, distance and the absence of exploitable resources permitted the colony almost complete independence. It survived for about five hundred years and was then unaccountably wiped out, possibly by an epidemic or by clashes with the

Eskimos. Nordic communications with Greenland were not resumed until the beginning of the eighteenth century when a Norwegian missionary initiated a new period of colonization. Intermarriage with migrants from the American continent created a mixed race identified by its Mongolian features. But the prevailing religious and social influences were from Scandinavia which meant that Greenland again became part of the Dano-Norwegian state and remained with Denmark along with Iceland and The Faeroes after 1814 when Norway was ceded to Sweden.

Having divided and subdivided Norden to show that there are more ways of looking at the region than through the eyes of a cartographer, what is it, apart from geographical proximity, that binds the five countries together, making them distinct from the rest of Europe? A large part of the answer is in language and history.

Danes, Norwegians, Icelanders and Swedes all speak north Teutonic languages related to the German and Anglo-Saxon tongues and derived from a common language which was still spoken about a thousand years ago. This was the time of the Vikings, a collective term used to describe those intrepid Scandinavians who left their homes to seek their fortunes in distant lands. From Sweden, the Vikings ventured eastwards following the rivers into Russia to establish a short-lived colony in the region of Novgorod. The Norwegian Vikings sailed to the Atlantic islands, Scotland and Ireland, and also colonized Iceland which had become an independent state by the middle of the tenth century. The Danes conquered England, and for a short time under Canute the Great the Anglo-Danish kingdom was one of the leading European powers.

To associate the non-aggressive and somewhat introspective nature of the latest Nordic generation with the death and glory adventures of their Viking ancestors, even at this distance in history, is a challenge to the imagination. But not all Scandinavians were Vikings. To equate the two is, as Thor Heyerdahl has pointed out, as simplistic as referring to all seventeenth-century Englishmen as buccaneers. Moreover, not all Vikings were plunderers. Contemporary sources give a lurid portrait of savage marauders, their minds set on rape and pillage. But there is increasing evidence to show that where trade or settlement

could be achieved, the Vikings were not slow to take up the
peaceful option.

What has never been in dispute was their brave determination to beat formidable odds in their overseas excursions. One
of the many whose exploits were faithfully recorded by the saga
writers was Eric the Red who discovered Greenland and, with
a promoter's eye to attracting settlers from Iceland, gave the
island its name. His son, Leif Erikson, combined piety with
great courage, the first part of his reputation being acquired by
his missionary zeal on behalf of Christianity (Greenland remained the last outpost of Nordic paganism), the second by his
voyage of discovery across the Davis Strait, to America. The
expedition was entirely peaceful, motivated by the desire to set
up trading posts for timber and fur and to find new land for
cattle farming; that it failed cannot detract from the vision and
bravery of those who were inspired to set out in their open boats.

Achievement of a different sort distinguished Iceland when
the first democratic national assembly, the Althing, was founded
in about 930. In this tiny but scattered community the sturdy
and often aggressive individualism of the early Vikings was
contained by the sure knowledge that to survive in a part of the
world where nature gave little away, there was a need to work
with instead of against each other. Soon after their arrival, the
Norwegian colonists set up local *things* or assemblies of freemen
to resolve disputes. Then, in about 927, one of their number
returned to Norway to study law and to prepare a code for all
of Iceland. The adjudicating body was the Althing, the only
national *thing* to be created by the northern peoples. It served
also as a legislature and as 'a fair, a marriage mart, and a
national celebration in which a large proportion of the Icelandic
population participated for two weeks each June' (Tomasson,
1980, p. 15). If the Althing is accepted as the birthplace of
Nordic democracy, then the first notable event in its history
occurred in 1000 when, by majority decision, Christianity was
adopted as Iceland's official religion.

In the end, the Vikings overextended their military resources.
This was inevitable when occasional defeats deprived them
of their superhuman status and invited retaliation from their
victims. Those who were ready to attack at the heart of the
Scandinavian homelands found them weakened by internecine

warfare and by the absence overseas of many of the best fighters. The need for security supported by the desire for personal aggrandizement led some nobles towards attempting a more centralized form of government.

The pattern was set by Harold Fairhair who determined to create a kingdom of the coastal region of Norway. A series of battles with rival chieftains culminated in about 900 in his proclamation as king of the Norwegians. His successors, who were not without their achievements, lacked his personal authority, and by the mid-tenth century, though the Norway kingdom had extended further north, the country was effectively under the suzerainty of Harold Bluetooth, king of Denmark and Skåne. It was Bluetooth's grandson, Canute the Great, proclaimed king in 1014, who fought successfully to consolidate England into his North Sea Empire and directed his expansionist ambitions towards Sweden, then the most backward of the Scandinavian countries.

Of course, the territorial division was nowhere so simple and straightforward as this brief summary might imply. With competitors always on hand to challenge the central ruler there was a constant risk of imperial disintegration. The true frailty of royal authority was shown on the death of Canute when the English, unchallenged, simply chose their own king while the Danish and Norwegian nobles decided that whichever of their own monarchs lived longest should take power in both countries, an agreement which for a time resulted in a Norwegian ruler for Denmark.

But, however unsettled the style of government, the later Viking kings created a form of patchwork nationalism. In this they were strongly supported by the Church, a vital force in the process of unification. By 1200 Norway, Denmark and Sweden had developed into clearly defined if loosely organized kingdoms with largely the same borders as they have today except that Skåne, Halland and Blekinge in the south of Sweden formed part of Denmark while Jämtland, Härjedalen and Bohuslän in the west of Sweden belonged to Norway, and the southern border of Denmark was at the Eider in what now is northern Germany. Though there remained a large measure of linguistic overlap, Danish, Swedish and Norwegian henceforth developed their own forms of dialect and spelling while the Icelanders, culturally marooned in the Atlantic, kept to the ancient speech which today is incomprehensible to other Scandinavians.

The thirteenth century was a period of intense economic and cultural activity. The expansion of fishing to satisfy the demand from Catholic Europe in turn stimulated agriculture and other basic industries. This new-found prosperity brought with it a passion for building – particularly churches and cathedrals – and a desire by the wealthy to copy the fashions of the German and French aristocracy. A growing national self-confidence was evidenced in Denmark's attempt to gain domination over the Baltic with a succession of conquests in north Germany and the annexation of Estonia in the Gulf of Finland. But imperialist ambitions could not be sustained, and the Danish grip on the Baltic provinces weakened just at the time when they were beginning to emerge as great commercial centres.

With an influx of population from the more advanced states in the south of Germany, coastal towns like Danzig, Königsberg and Lübeck grew rich and domineering on the profits of the Baltic trade. Under the protection of a monopolistic association known as the Hanseatic League, the German entrepreneurs secured important trade concessions for herring, salt and grain from Denmark and played a leading role in that country's turbulent political affairs.

German influence was also strong in Norway. To maintain the supply of corn, of which there was nearly always a shortage, the port of Bergen was allowed to become a Hanseatic base for controlling the north-Atlantic trade routes. But unlike Denmark the political fabric of the country was held together by support for the monarch (the scarcity of fertile land counted against the creation of semi-independent feudal estates), who was able to provide his authority by reasserting Norwegian control over Iceland and Greenland.

As the least developed of the three central Scandinavian countries, Sweden had relatively amicable relations with the German traders, who were welcomed by successive rulers as a valuable source of investment and tax revenue. Stockholm contained a large German population, and further down on the south-east coast Kalmar and the offshore island of Gotland were virtually run by German immigrants who imposed their own form of local government, the burgomaster and council, and their own language for all official business. Gotland was the last link in the chain of Hanseatic trading posts to the east. This included Finland, which by a gradual process of colonization, legitimized by crusades against the heathen, was brought into the Swedish kingdom. That she remained there for almost five hundred years fully justifies her inclusion in the Nordic sphere of influence even though the origins of the Finns are anything but Scandinavian. Finnish is not related to any of the great European languages but together with Estonian and Hungarian forms part of the Finno-Ugrian group. Early Swedish influence, however, established a second line of cultural development, so that even today Swedish retains the status of a second official language and six per cent of the population use it as their first language.

With the growing power of centralized government it was only a matter of time before a Scandinavian monarch challenged the privileges of the Hanseatic League. When the moment came the Germans were doubly discomfited because it was one of their own who struck the blow. In pursuing this claim to be the 'true heir to the throne of Denmark', Valdemar Atterdag had the advantage of an upbringing in the Imperial German court which gave him the blessing of the emperor and of the leading princes. But Atterdag was soon to prove he was his own man, prepared to devote his considerable energy and tactical skills to uniting Denmark under his leadership.

Success inevitably brought him into conflict with Sweden over the disputed southern provinces of Skåne, Halland and Blekinge. His solution to the problem was to attack Gotland, hoping thereby to secure a base for further assaults on the Swedish mainland, if these proved to be necessary, and at the same time to show the Hanseatic League who was master in Scandinavia. In 1361 Gotland was taken in one of the sharpest and bloodiest battles in Nordic history. Safe within their walled city of Visby, the Hanseatic merchants watched the massacre of the Goths and afterwards made haste to buy protection with a large donation to the Danish exchequer. Retaliation came in the form of an unsuccessful rebellion against Atterdag and a Hanseatic assault on Danish positions along the Sound which consolidated German control over the approaches to the Baltic. But even if Atterdag could not claim outright victory, he showed what could be achieved and so prepared the way for important changes in the Scandinavian power structure.

Valdemar Atterdag had no obvious male successor but he did have a very able and ambitious daughter, Margaret, who was married to Håkon of Norway. When the Danish king died in 1375 she was quick to put in a claim to the throne on behalf of her five-year-old son, Olav. It was the first in a set of skilled political manoeuvres to establish her personal rule over all three Scandinavian kingdoms. The prospect was not unrealistic. National identities were not yet so strong as to preclude acceptance of a single royal authority. Marriage and inheritance forged links between governing families which often took precedence over loyalty to the state. But even where these connections did not exist, fear of further encroachment by the Germans, the real outsiders, offered a cause for unity. After the ravages of the Black Death, which took off between a third and a half of the population, Scandinavia was particularly vulnerable. Naturally, thoughts turned towards achieving security by concerted action.

Acting for her son, Margaret became regent of Denmark and, on the death of Håkon, regent also of Norway. By then she had gained a reputation for standing up to the Hanseatic League which endeared her to that section of the Swedish nobility who had opposed the election of a German claimant, Albrecht of Mecklenburg, to the Swedish throne. Such was her authority that plans for an armed uprising assisted by Danish forces were not seriously impeded by the unexpected death of her son. She was confirmed as regent of Denmark and Norway and, after the defeat and capture of Albrecht and her acknowledgement of the privileges of the Swedish nobility, saw her way clear to achieving a Nordic union.

Though unable to take the triple crown for herself she ensured the continuation of her power by nominating her five-year-old nephew, Erik of Pomerania, as king of all three countries. His election was formalized by a convention of the nobility at Kalmar in 1397. But Margaret did not have it all her own way. While the coronation seemed to confirm the general desire for a strong central monarchy, the document formalizing the union allowed the state councils of the individual countries to make the final decision on all important matters.

Margaret worked hard to cement the union. While there was never any doubt that Denmark ranked first in the territorial hierarchy, she was careful not to over-exploit her Danish connections. Duties and privileges were distributed with a strict regard for provincial sensibilities as well as for loyal and efficient service. Nonetheless, it needed more than a generation of enlightened rule to create a single Scandinavian state.

Soon after Margaret's death in 1412 Erik found himself in trouble with the Swedish nobles, who resented being taxed to finance Danish wars in north Germany. But even if Erik had lived up to his aunt's standards of diplomacy it is doubtful if the Kalmar pact could have long survived the shift in the centre of power from Denmark to Sweden, by now a rapidly developing country strong enough to resist Danish efforts to drain her of revenue. Erik finally abdicated and was succeeded by another union king, but after 1450 Denmark was only able to impose her will on Sweden sporadically.

As the first in a long line of nationalist leaders, a young nobleman, Sten Sture, who was made regent in 1470, defeated the Danes at Brunkeberg just outside old Stockholm. The battle is one of the most memorable in Swedish history because it shattered any remaining illusions of Danish hegemony. Following his success Sten Sture worked on Swedish nationalist sentiment with grand and defiant gestures like the public display of a huge wood carving of St George slaying the dragon (now on view in Stockholm cathedral) or, of more lasting influence, the setting up of the first Swedish university, at Uppsala. The union came to be seen by nobility and commoners alike as the instrument of Danish imperialism used to crush the country and to exploit it economically.

Norway on the other hand had no choice but to remain part of the kingdom of Denmark, even after the disintegration of the Kalmar union. Her economy was weak, and though adventurers were prepared to try their chances against the Danes, the country lacked an upper class strong enough to sustain the claims of sovereignty.

It has been said that if, at the time of the Kalmar pact, all Scandinavians had been required to read a single translation of the Bible, the union would have endured. Whatever the truth of this, it is a hypothesis which relies more on the binding force of language than of religion. After the Reformation, however, when all five countries were converted to Lutheranism, it was religion that was expected to take the lead in promoting unity. That there were as many quarrels and rivalries between church-men as between temporal leaders militated against any dramatic manifestation of Nordic brotherhood, but it is argu-able that over the years a shared religious philosophy has brought the Nordic countries closer together.

Values engendered by the Church introduced a high degree of uniformity into the development of state administrations and legal systems while facilitating the exchange of social and poli-tical ideas. And in contemporary Norden, though interest in formal religion has declined except in some rural areas (Scan-dinavians are said to 'have made spiritual reticence a virtue'), the puritan ethic remains dominant. It can be seen in the respect for work as an activity good in itself that carries over into a suspicion of leisure pursuits which are largely passive. (Nordic people seem never to be entirely relaxed when they are simply watching something.) Protestant belief in the individual as the maker of his own salvation underlies the lasting influence of the popular movements in education and social reform. The vitality of the temperance groups, which first came to prominence in the closing decades of the nineteenth century, is a case in point.

But to return to the chronological narrative, by the sixteenth century Europe was accustomed to thinking of Norden as two states, Denmark–Norway (including Iceland and Greenland) and Sweden–Finland. The languages of the ruling class were Danish in the west and Swedish in the east. Finland was so permeated by Swedish culture at this period that it became an integral part of Scandinavia.

The two sides were fairly evenly balanced but relations were seldom amicable. Sweden–Finland felt herself to be hedged in between Denmark and Norway and the two nations were rivals for control of Russian trade in the Baltic. Intermittent fighting in the second half of the century resulted in few territorial changes, but Sweden was weak and vulnerable when Gustavus Adolphus, 'the Dragon King', inherited the crown in 1611. A leader who combined military prowess with outstanding intel-lectual abilities, Gustavus set about raising his country to the status of a great power first by consolidating his hold on strategic points on the Russian side of the Baltic and later by taking his armies into northern Europe to play a critical role in holding back the Catholic advance in the Thirty Years War. This enterprise cost him his life but gained for Sweden large possessions in the north of Germany.

The fortunes of Denmark, meanwhile, had shifted into reverse with the loss of Gotland and the Norwegian territories of Jämtland and Härjedalen to her old enemy. In 1660 Sweden finally conquered Skåne, Halland and Blekinge which nowadays are thought to be intrinsically Swedish but then were just as naturally part of Denmark. Further Swedish gains in Norway included the province of Bohuslän in the south-east just below Oslo, an acquisition which tidied up the border to give Sweden the overwhelming strategic advantage if she resolved on further dismemberment of Denmark or Norway. In fact, this was probably what Charles x, the warrior king, had in mind, but even if his ambitions had not been cut short by fatal illness, Britain and Holland's interest in Baltic trade would have counted decisively against Swedish dominance of the Scandinavian peninsula.

By now the internal boundaries of Norden were set firm, though the political division was still between Denmark–Norway and Sweden–Finland. Sweden went on to further military glories but her days as a great power were numbered by the emergence of Russia as a formidable rival. In the early part of the eighteenth century Sweden was forced to give up her Baltic territories including a part of Finland and all her north-German possessions except west Pomerania.

The restoration of the balance of power in Norden brought a lull in dynastic rivalry and even encouraged thoughts of cooperation in the interests of Scandinavian security. As a foretaste of things to come, the two monarchies joined in a policy of armed neutrality to defend their merchant shipping from the contenders in the Seven Years War. But it was not the time for any serious weight to be given to the concept of unity on the Kalmar model. The early striving of popular reaction against royal despotism and the claims of national minorities caused more than enough concern to rulers whose first instinct was to try to protect what they had. Though Sweden was reasonably secure in her possession of Finland, at least in so far as the Finns themselves showed no enthusiasm for transferring their allegiance to a Russian master, there were dangerous tensions within Denmark–Norway created by the build up of German nationalism on the southern border and by the growing confidence of a Norwegian middle class who resented the privileges of the Copenhagen business élite. There was even talk in Oslo of union with Sweden as an alternative offering better prospects of gaining freedom without losing the military protection of a powerful neighbour. The opportunity to test this thesis came sooner than the Norwegians might have expected with the dramatic rejuggling of Scandinavian allegiances caused by the Napoleonic wars.

Undeterred by the Franco-Russian alliance of 1807, Sweden held to a policy of co-operation with Britain while that same year, Denmark, smarting under the British bombardment of Copenhagen, allied herself to Napoleon. Accordingly, Sweden was trapped in a Baltic pincer movement, and after an inglorious campaign which led to a coup in Stockholm and the overthrow of the Gustavian monarchy, Finland was ceded to Russia. The terms, for the Finns, were generous, a pledge being made by Tsar Alexander to govern as Grand Duke and to protect their established laws and liberties. In accepting the new arrangements with equanimity – a reaction which made the blow all the more terrible to the prestige-conscious Swedes – the Finns were not showing disloyalty to the Scandinavian connection but were simply registering a transfer of power to which many of their leaders had long been reconciled.

Sweden now looked towards Norway for compensation for her losses in the east, and the choice of a new ruler, a cousin of the Danish king, was partly determined by his influence with those Norwegians who were sympathetic to a transfer of allegiance. But within a year Christian August had died of a stroke and the succession was open once again. This time it was complicated by the need to take into account the wishes of Napoleon with whom Sweden had lately made peace. After some curious machinations involving the duplication of couriers dispatched to sound out views in Paris, the choice fell on one of Napoleon's marshals, Bernadotte, who became king under the name of Karl Johan in 1810.

So entered one of the most remarkable of Nordic leaders,

who, though never learning Swedish or Norwegian, identified immediately with the interests of his adopted country. When Napoleon punished Sweden for engaging in an extensive but illicit trade with the British by annexing Swedish Pomerania, Karl Johan used the excuse to line up with the enemies of France. He was in powerful company, because now the Russians were also in league against Napoleon. Karl Johan's first objective was to win Russian agreement for the return of Finland but when this proved unacceptable he settled for a promise that if their joint enterprise was successful, the Tsar would support a union of Sweden and Norway. This was the price Denmark was forced to pay for clinging to her alliance with France. By the treaty of Kiel, 1814, King Frederik signed away his rights in Norway, although he was allowed to retain Iceland, Greenland and The Faeroes and even made some small gains in Germany by way of compensation.

But because no one thought to take account of the wishes of the Norwegians the transfer of power on the Scandinavian peninsula went less smoothly than the main protagonists anticipated. The frustration of being treated as a backward province found expression in a bid for independence and the proclamation of a liberal constitution which centred power on an elected Storting. The outside chance of success depended on support from the great powers, but while Britain sympathized with the Norwegian claim for self-government, there were stronger demands for the fulfilment of treaty obligations to Sweden. Pushing home his advantage Karl Johan sent his army across the border to hasten a submission. In November 1814, the king of Sweden was 'unanimously elected and recognized' by the Storting as the king of Norway. But the constitution remained to ensure that government from Stockholm was less obtrusive than government from Copenhagen.

Finland too managed to keep her rulers at arm's length. In theory the Grand Duke could direct affairs as he wished, but in practice the Finns were generally left to their own devices. That most official business continued to be carried out in Swedish helped in otherwise unfavourable circumstances to maintain links with the Scandinavian peninsula.

Just as the German- and Italian-speaking peoples began to move towards unification after the Napoleonic wars, so also a

Scandinavian movement started in the north of Europe. The inspiration came largely from academic and professional groups, precisely those people who thrived on wider contacts and who recognized that the Nordic countries had more in common than the modern record of political intrigue and violence might have suggested. To prove the point the historical perspective was shifted to a distant Nordic past when territorial divisions were barely in evidence and the exploits of the fearless Vikings were forging a sense of pride in the wider Scandinavian heritage. The mix of romanticism and idealism caught the imagination of the educated young, and in the 1840s it was the students who were the driving force for numerous public demonstrations in favour of Nordic unity.

Of a more mundane but also more substantial character were the early inter-Nordic professional conferences. That the lawyers first got together in 1872 and have been meeting regularly ever since goes a long way to explaining the high degree of coordination between the Nordic judicial systems. Conventions of economists and bankers starting in the sixties led to a Scandinavian currency and a common rate of exchange for Norway, Sweden and Denmark which lasted up to the First World War. In 1875 the three states adopted the metric system. Nordic free trade was another much discussed proposition, but though some tariffs were reduced or abolished the movement went into reverse when protectionism spread over Europe in the 1880s.

The trouble with Scandinavianism was not, as is so often claimed, that it was over-romantic or impracticable or that it was supported by the wrong people (the young intellectuals were, after all, the next generation of opinion leaders). It failed because the timing was wrong. To build up the confidence to work together the countries of Norden had first to indulge in a more localized form of nationalism. The Norwegians and Finns were having problems reconciling their cultural ties with Denmark and Sweden with their new political affiliations. Not surprisingly they sought the answer in trying to establish their own clear identities. They did so by fostering their national languages and by rediscovering a pride in their origins, popularizing the study of history and folk culture (see Chapter 7). Denmark and Sweden too needed a period of recovery from the humiliation of what was clearly a demotion in the ranks of European power politics and time to reassess their role in Norden where old loyalties could no longer be taken for granted.

Not that the politicians had too much time for philosophical reflection. Denmark was particularly under attack as she faced the prospect of further territorial losses, this time in the south, where German nationalism was pressing hard against Schleswig-Holstein. The duchies had been attached to Denmark for four hundred years but the official language was German, and Holstein was actually a member of the German confederation. A revolution in 1848 was contained by the great powers acting in concert against the Germans. Sweden did not participate directly but a limited mobilization in support of Denmark gave some substance to the idea of a Scandinavian alliance. That it did not get beyond a few well-publicized royal appeals for unity was because both countries set their expectations too high. Sweden wanted support in deflecting Russian efforts to secure an ice-free harbour in the north and in keeping alive the hope of one day regaining Finland. Denmark, on the other hand, believed that Russian friendship was essential to the protection of her German possessions. She therefore expected Sweden to tone down her eastern policy while throwing her energies into a joint defence of Schleswig and, more improbably, the German-leaning Holstein.

The decisive test for Scandinavianism came in 1863 when Denmark quietly conceded the impracticability of holding on to Holstein by giving the duchy its own constitution and cutting it out of Danish affairs. At the same time Schleswig was bound more closely to Denmark. The German confederation objected, Prussian and Austrian troops went on the offensive, the greater powers stood aside and Schleswig and Holstein were both lost. The spirit of Scandinavianism was barely kept alive by the rallying of a few hundred Swedish and Norwegian volunteers.

The consequences of the war for Denmark can be measured in the loss of two-fifths of her territory, most of its rich agricultural land, and nearly a million inhabitants. For a time there was some doubt as to whether Denmark had any future at all as an independent state. And yet within a few years the country managed to pull itself back from one of the lowest points in its history. The economy benefited from a huge land-reclamation programme in the sandy region of Jutland which increased the acreage under cultivation until it fully compensated for that ceded to the Germans in Schleswig. As impressive was the adaptation of farming to meet the challenge of the drop in grain prices caused by cheap imports from America. In a concerted gamble which paid off handsomely, Danish agriculture turned from arable to animal products, for which there was a lively demand in the industrial centres of Britain.

This remarkable assertion of national will was in large measure inspired by the teachings of Bishop Grundtvig, founder of the folk high-schools. In the winter months the children of farmers and smallholders extended their learning beyond basic literacy by engaging in what Grundtvig called 'the living word'. Stories and songs from Denmark's great past inspired a sense of pride in the country's achievements and idealism for the future. But unlike most other nationalist propaganda it was not pure chauvinism that Grundtvig was imparting. His greatest accomplishment was to reconcile patriotism with a reduced status for Denmark in European affairs. If he did not go so far as to claim that small is beautiful, he at least got across the message that it is not necessary to be big to be virtuous. Denmark still had much to contribute to the world but her people needed faith in their own genius. The lesson was not lost on the subject countries of Norden. As they moved towards greater freedom in their internal political organizations so also they sought freedom from absentee sovereigns, confident now that they could make their own way in the world without the help of big brother.

The independence movement in Norway found a response, if not a whole-hearted one, from the liberal parliamentary democracy in Sweden. Successive steps towards self-government within the union culminated in a referendum in which the overwhelming majority of Norwegians voted for separation. In October 1905 Oscar II renounced his title to the western provinces and a month later a Danish prince was confirmed as Haakon VII of free Norway. The Icelanders too built up a formidable campaign for independence, but though near complete home rule was conceded at the beginning of the century, the country remained part of the kingdom of Denmark until the Second World War. That both settlements were achieved peacefully was a tribute to Nordic political good sense. It was

also fortunate that other nations did not feel their interests
threatened by changes in the Scandinavian power structure. In
this respect Finland was less fortunate. As recounted later, her
path to independence was bloody and protracted.

2
Norden: the beginnings of social democracy

The history of twentieth-century Norden is the advance of social democracy. This is not to deny the impact of opposing ideologies or the influence of other political parties. The strength of social democracy has been its ability to draw on a wide spectrum of ideas including those of the centre and right without compromising the belief in equality as the ultimate objective. It is one of the great ironies of politics that the Nordic rejection of doctrinaire socialism in favour of a widely supported policy of social reform linked to broadly capitalist notions of economic expansion has taken the Scandinavians closer to egalitarianism than any other people in Europe. And this without any of the violent disruptions associated elsewhere with attempts from the left, always unsuccessful, to make a quick dash for Utopia.

How was it that Norden was able to diverge so dramatically from the Western pattern of social and political evolution? To begin with, all five countries were late industrial developers. A shortage of minerals, especially coal, meant that for most of the nineteenth century their overseas trade was founded on the supply of primary products to the more commercially advanced nations. Timber was the leading revenue-earner. Demand was such that in Norway it led to the virtual denudation of the most accessible forests along the southern coastline.

Conditions changed radically towards the end of the century when there was a great burst of economic activity. Of a number of contributory factors, the early utilization of hydro-electric power, and the first hint of what it could mean for the growth of a manufacturing sector, were probably the most important. But the increasing wealth of the leading European powers had its overspill effect on Norden. The improvement in communications achieved by the railways and steam-driven ships brought boom markets within easy reach of industries like pulp,

---

paper, agriculture and fishing. A rapid increase in population created the pool of labour that was essential to the growth economy.

Sweden was in the best position to exploit the opportunities. She already had a small but sturdy industrial base centred on a modest output of iron-ore. Shipbuilding and textiles were well established and, with other infant enterprises, supported a thriving banking system. As with the other Nordic countries the priority given to education made for an intelligent labour force capable of adapting to new skills.

The introduction of the steam-driven sawmill to Sweden coincided with an increase in British demand for timber products from tar and resin to telegraph poles and pit props, which Norway and Canada, the traditional suppliers, were unable to satisfy. As a result an impressive boost to exports was achieved at the cost of decimating the northern landscape. But by the end of the century, when timber accounted for almost half of the country's total exports, the development of a chemical process for converting wood into good quality paper had ensured a less wasteful yet more profitable exploitation of Sweden's forests. The first chemical pulp factory was set up in Bergvik in 1872. By the First World War, Sweden sold more pulp than any other country.

Mining also benefited from new industrial techniques. The Bessemer process, partly developed in Sweden, stimulated domestic production of good-quality steel, while the Gilchrist method, which brought into productive use iron-ore of high phosphoric content, opened up the prospect of mining in the far north, around Kiruna and beyond the Arctic Circle. Engineering came to lead the growth industries, its reputation for quality products nourished by an enthusiasm for innovation and a gift for invention. To the Swedes goes credit for making the first ball-bearing, the first adjustable spanner, the first cream separator and the first primus stove, not to mention the first safety match and, somehow linked to it in the imagination if not in strict historical fact, the first stick of dynamite.

The Danes sought prosperity in the expansion of agriculture, a brave decision after the 1864 war with Germany had deprived the country of some of its most productive land. No sooner had the loss been compensated for by reclamation in sandy Jutland, than the industry was dealt a potentially more damaging blow by the opening up of the North American prairies and the Russian wheatlands. With the easy transportation of cereals over long distances by rail and steamship, European prices collapsed and Danish farmers faced ruin. The only way to recovery was to adapt to animal husbandry and the export of perishable dairy products, for which there was an unsatisfied demand in the industrial conurbations of Britain and Germany. The success of this turnabout (within twenty years, Denmark was a net importer of grain) owed much to the co-operative movement, one of the precursors of social democracy. By joint investment in dairies, bacon factories and other support services, economies of scale were achieved without risk to the social cohesion of the small family farms. Urban industrial growth was at first heavily dependent on food products such as beet sugar and beer, but a healthy trade balance allowed for plentiful imports of coal and iron which in turn stimulated the growth of shipbuilding and high-grade engineering on the Swedish pattern.

With no agriculture surplus to speak of and limited timber resources the Norwegians put much of their effort into making a living from the sea. The fishing industry had several natural advantages: a long, ragged coastline afforded good harbours, the waters were ice-free and the continental shelf accommodated rich spawning grounds. When times were hard there were more volunteers for Arctic sealing and whaling expeditions, a hazardous but highly profitable occupation in which Norway established a world lead. The first floating factory whaler was launched from a Norwegian dock in 1905.

Young Norwegians found it difficult to avoid the sea. If they were not fishermen, likely as not they were merchant sailors. At more than one and a half million tons, the merchant fleet was bigger than all the other Nordic fleets put together. Conversion to steam was complete by 1900 when, notwithstanding the growth of shipbuilding and the pulp and paper industries, Norway still had more seamen than factory workers.

While Denmark, Sweden and Norway were in the throes of economic change, Finland was still locked into a pre-industrial social structure which was as primitive as it was poor. In terms of the Finnish national income, textiles was an industry of note but there were only three mills and these were almost exclusively at the service of the Russian market. Timber accounted for about two-thirds of the export trade. Most Finns lived on what they could get from the land, which generally was precious little. As late as 1867-8, bad harvests led to famine, which killed off eight per cent of the population.

The Icelanders were scarcely more prosperous. At the beginning of the century there was not a factory in the country, scarcely a passable road, no bridges, no man-made harbour and very few stone-built houses. The expectation of better times to come could be deduced from the adaptation of the fishing fleet from open rowing boats to decked vessels capable of venturing to more distant waters. The founding of a national bank and the progress of the co-operative movement also promised better trading opportunities.

For young Scandinavians caught up in the industrial revolution, a fortune was to be made in learning a craft, and with limited opportunities to do that at home the place to go was Germany. Those who migrated south for their apprenticeship returned imbued with ideas for getting together with fellow artisans to form craft unions. They were not trade unions in the modern sense, more voluntary societies dedicated to the principles of self-help such as insurance against sickness. But when the example was followed by unskilled workers it was not long before the unions were seen as having a function beyond that of self-improvement. Employers were suddenly faced with demands for better conditions backed by threats of strikes. In 1879 Sweden's first big labour dispute brought the troops to Sundsvall, where five thousand forestry workers protested against their subsistence-living in an industry noted for its high profits. Craftsmen too came to realize that unity gave them a stronger voice in their dealings with the employers. The three hundred Oslo typographers who went on strike for seventeen weeks in 1889 showed what could be done by way of demonstrations and publicity to capture the popular imagination.

One of the lessons gained at this time was that in small countries, still with relatively few industrial workers, it was not enough just to organize on a local level. It was too easy for employers to outmanœuvre one group of agitators by shifting work to other parts of the country or by bringing in strike-breakers. By the late 1880s, other unions were following the lead of the Norwegian typographers by setting up national organizations with powerful central bodies, a process facilitated by the relatively simple and homogeneous industrial structure. The next step, to bring all the unions into national federations, was taken in Denmark and Sweden in 1898 and in Norway the following year. Finnish unionists took longer to organize themselves at a national level because there were fewer of them, probably not more than twenty thousand in all when the federation was established in 1907. Support for centralization was by no means unanimous, but advocates of the local initiative consistently found themselves outflanked by the employers, who themselves were coming together to form central authorities capable, if necessary, of taking on the entire workers' movement.

It was only a matter of time before the antagonists joined in a trial of strength. It happened first in Denmark, where the unions' firm roots in the craft tradition gave them an advantage when it came to persuading workers of the benefits of holding together, and where at this stage Marxist ideas had a stronger appeal than elsewhere in Scandinavia. But hopes on either side of an outright victory were quickly disappointed. In 1899 a series of bitter strikes and lockouts served only to demonstrate that unions and employers were evenly matched. Without a commitment to revolution – which the workers' leaders were not ready to make – the only way of breaking the stalemate was to settle on a frame of reference within which disputes could be solved, if not amicably, at least with the minimum disruption. The logic was not lost on the other Nordic countries.

Put this way it does seem as if innate moderation and good sense, virtues so often attributed to the Scandinavians, were the prevailing factors in their advance towards maturity in industrial relations. But even allowing that the desire for consensus was second nature to people who were used to living in small and often isolated communities, the social environment in Norden had other distinctive features that set it apart from the mainstream movements for change in Europe and America.

With late industrialization some of the worst features of mass production were either avoided intentionally or simply not encountered because Scandinavian industry remained essentially a small-town affair. At the time the unions were beginning to canvass energetically for members, living standards were improving, and though feelings against employers and right-wing governments could run high (violence in labour disputes was by no means unknown), the biggest fear of the ordinary worker was that by pushing his masters too far he would drive himself into unemployment and poverty. The other powerful antidote to the threat of social disruption was the easy availability of a boat-ticket to the new world. From 1865-70 one in ten of United States immigrants was Scandinavian, and though the proportion was never to be so high again, the numbers of those departing increased sharply when times were really bad. The disastrous harvests of 1867-9 caused eighty thousand to leave from Sweden alone. It is with some justification that nineteenth-century emigration has been described as Scandinavia's social safety valve.

In the last year of the century Danish employers and unions put their signatures to what became known as the September Compromise, a comprehensive agreement on labour relations which the centralized power structure on both sides of industry quickly enforced throughout the country. The rules for keeping disputes within manageable proportions – for a strike to be officially recognized there had to be a two-week notice of intention – and the arbitration procedures which to begin with allowed the unions only a minority influence, seem in retrospect to have given a free hand to the employers. Certainly they were confirmed in their right to run their companies in the way they thought fit, and that included the freedom to hire and fire. But there was a joint commitment to strive for 'peaceful, stable and good working conditions', a responsibility employers took more seriously as they came to realize they had more to gain from a contented labour force. Gradually the terms of the agreement were changed to allow the unions a stronger voice (they secured equal representation on arbitration panels) and to open the way for government intervention in industrial bargaining. After 1910 a government mediator could step in when unions and employers failed to agree. He had power to postpone hostilities for at least one week whilst he came up with his own proposal for a settlement, the virtue of which was to be judged by an appeal to the industrial rank and file and to individual employers. A clear majority was needed to reject the mediator's solution but on anything less than a twenty-five per cent response the government view prevailed irrespective of the distribution of votes.

No one could have realized it at the time but the September Compromise was a formula for peaceful economic growth as much in the age of advanced technology as in the early phase of industrialization. It is still the *de facto* constitution of Danish labour relations and it has been copied in all the other Nordic countries. Norway was the first to follow, though here the politicians took the initiative. Legislation approved in 1915 introduced official mediators to interpret and enforce the regulations governing collective agreements. These unfortunate state representatives were pitched into the troubles of Norway's post-war phase of rapid industrialization when the unions regarded government and employers with equal distrust. They could barely keep up with the number of disputes, and time lost through strikes was far in excess of that recorded by any other Nordic country. The change came when labour and management began talking directly to each other. In 1935 the two sides negotiated a basis for settling grievances. A central labour court, supported by regional arbitration committees, was given the power to enforce nationwide collective agreements with fines for those who stepped out of line.

The principle was followed by Sweden three years later with the Saltsjöbaden Agreement between unions and employers, the basis for what today is probably the most comprehensive framework for centralized collective bargaining to be found anywhere in the Western world. After the unions' humiliating defeat in the 1909 general strike there was a long period in which employers and labour were hardly on speaking terms. But attitudes were modified as the political wing of unionism, in the shape of the social-democratic party, gained sufficient support to claim a share in government. The interests of the national economy demanded that the unions and employers should talk sensibly to each other, a precept which the 1932 social-democrat government was prepared, if necessary, to back up with legislation. Neither federation was prepared for this, with the result that they settled down to working out a mutually acceptable procedure for dealing with disputes.

Iceland adopted the Danish pattern of industrial relations

but with somewhat less power exercised by the central organizations, while Finland, with its slower economic development and sharper political differences between labour and capital, had to wait until the 1940s before national collective agreements were common for all important industries. A labour court on the Swedish model was introduced in 1946.

Today, the clearly identifiable features of Nordic industrial relations are the concentration of power at the centre of union and employer affairs, the enforcement of nationwide collective agreements and the involvement of government, originally as a mediator ready to act if all else failed, but latterly as the essential third partner in formulating wages policy. It is an association of principles which over the last half-century has led to some remarkable advances. Yet until very recently the freedom of managers to determine the composition of their labour force – in cruder terms, to hire and fire – was hardly ever seriously challenged. With this basic freedom went the right to invest in whatever project seemed to management to be potentially most profitable and the union recognition that profits were respectable, indeed vital, because they were the source of further investment and thus economic growth and higher living standards for union members.

To explain this remarkable faith in management requires more than the usual glib connection between Northern European peoples and their traditional respect for authority. The unions' insurance against defaulting employers was a powerful parliamentary contingent of social democrats, which if not actually in power was seldom far away from the centre of authority.

Social democracy had its start as the political offshoot of the trade unions. After the early efforts of idealists like Louis Pio – the Danish military officer who was inspired by the Paris Commune to set up a branch of the Marxist First International in Copenhagen and who was subsequently bribed by the police to emigrate to America – the movement was taken over by the craftsmen, the establishment of the working class. Their natural cautiousness in challenging the existing power structure was confirmed by their middle-class allies, the radical intellectuals whose leading spokesman was a distinguished Swedish scientist, Hjalmar Branting. Destined to be the first Scandinavian socialist prime minister, Branting had known all the best people since his schooldays, which he had shared with the reigning monarch. In 1886 he gave up his academic career to edit the newspaper *Socialdemokraten*, and in the following decade was elected to the Riksdag by which time he was the undisputed party leader.

As the early unionists had taken their ideas from Germany, Branting and his Nordic socialist colleagues looked to that country for inspiration in shaping a political programme. In so doing they were responding to more than cultural affiliations. The move towards free elections in Germany encouraged Marxists to eschew revolution in favour of what many hoped would be a peaceful parliamentary transition to socialism. German reformism corresponded closely to conditions in Norden where, if anything, a socialist democracy was more likely to emerge without violence because the class structure was less rigid. On the other hand the struggle in Russia against a corrupt autocratic regime had scarcely any bearing on the Scandinavian experience.

The exception, of course, was Finland, which lived in the shadow of Russian autocracy. Though it was almost entirely a rural economy and so, according to Marx, unpromising ground for the seeds of revolution, socialism took a strong hold in the first years of the century. By 1906 membership of the social-democrat party was over one hundred thousand. Finland's poverty, her antiquated and unrepresentative government and her backwardness in almost every aspect of social reform gave plenty of scope for radical politicians to make their appeal. But the driving force for change was the largely middle-class nationalist reaction against Russian attempts to bind the country more closely to the imperial administration.

Under Alexander II Finland had contrived to build on her status as a grand duchy, so that by the 1880s the measure of her independence was the lately acquired control over her own army. It was all too much for the Russian military, who feared that moves towards Finnish separatism could only make more difficult their task of defending the long western border. With the appointment of General Bobrikov as governor general in 1898 a start was made on bringing Finland back into the imperial fold. The army was put under Russian command, the Russian language was made compulsory for the civil service and for schools, and bureaucratic decision-making reverted to the Tsar's appointees.

Resistance first took the form of non-co-operation – less than half the Finns of military age responded to a general conscription – but as the Russian revolutionary movement gathered pace, their sympathizers in Finland gained the initiative. In June 1904 Bobrikov was assassinated. The following year news of the uprising in St Petersburg brought demonstrators out on to the Helsinki streets and stirred labour leaders to declare a general strike. But the promise of constitutional reforms, including a democratically elected assembly, gave a temporary respite to the lumbering dictatorship of Nicholas II and enabled Finnish moderates to reassert control over the social-democrat machine. Even when the failure of the Tsar to change the real nature of his government seemed to confirm the views of the Marxist hardliners, there was a reluctance to try further to speed up the revolutionary timetable by planting bombs or shooting down prominent reactionaries. For the mass of social-democrat supporters, most of whom were subsistence farmers, the obliteration of the Russian ruling class was secondary to purely domestic issues such as the wider ownership of land; issues which Marxist theorists were inclined to dismiss as capitalist preoccupations.

Though real gains were few prior to independence, the social democrats kept their following, and in 1916 gained distinction as the first Marxist party to win an absolute majority in a parliamentary election. It was a short-lived victory but one not without encouragement to the left in other Nordic countries where achievement by moderation was the ruling principle of social democracy.

With steadily increasing parliamentary representation, but without the immediate prospect of outranking all other parties and without a power base in the conservative-controlled second chambers, the young social-democrat parties found themselves allied to governments of more or less liberal persuasion in support of constitutional and social reforms. By these tactics the Danes secured state loans for smallholders wanting to buy their land, the Swedes brought in restrictions on child and female labour, and the Norwegians insured their merchant sailors and fishermen against accident. All three countries introduced old-age pensions and free elementary education. On the constitutional front, the advance towards universal suffrage and the reduction of the powers of second chambers held out the promise that before long the socialists would have their chance of governing alone.

Meanwhile, any attempt by the far left to accelerate the evolutionary process was stoutly resisted by the leadership. When in 1908 a riotous dispute in the Gothenburg docks escalated to a point where lockouts on a national scale were answered by the threat of a general strike, Branting was quick to urge restraint, offering as an alternative to revolutionary slogans the prospect of a peaceful solution by arbitration. It was a natural reaction from a parliamentarian whose thoughts were concentrated on the forthcoming election with the chance of a further widening of the suffrage turning on its outcome. The last thing Branting wanted was for social-democrat supporters to deprive themselves of work, and so reduce their income to a level where they would no longer be eligible to vote.

In securing his strategy but not his objective – the conservative government survived – Branting was soon faced with renewed demands for a general strike. This time the unions were less amenable to compromise but nonetheless held back on involving essential services like power and sanitation. The railwaymen too worked as normal. As servants of a nationalized industry it was said that their participation might have been seen as a direct attack on the state. When after five weeks the strike was called off – workers were taken back on condition they left their unions with the result that the federation (LO) temporarily lost half its membership – the left-wing extremists were surprised to find they were unable to capitalize on the failure. Instead, it was the moderates who were given credit for warning against the short cuts to socialism.

It would be a simple matter to build up further examples of the Nordic preference for moderation, or socialism by stealth, as some of the more impatient left-wingers chose to call it. But there was still some distance to go before Norden was secure in the reputation of always seeking the middle way. The social disruption caused by the 1914–18 war, even for the countries on the periphery of the conflict, counted heavily against those who sought a broad consensus for reform.

The guns of August were quickly followed by declarations of neutrality from Sweden, Norway, Denmark and Iceland. Aside from Finland, whose foreign policy was decided by her Russian masters, most Scandinavians did well in the early stages of the war. Free from the excesses of military expenditure they traded with both sides at inflated prices. But the diversion of interests was impossible to sustain. Before long there was pressure to favour one side at the expense of the other. When, for fear of retaliation, the Scandinavians demurred, they were punished anyway. A neutral flag at sea was no longer a guarantee against attack. The losses suffered by the Nordic carrying trade, including a million tons of Norwegian shipping, cut deeply into national income and led to shortages of food and raw materials. Inflation roared ahead, benefiting speculators and property owners but leaving the poor unprotected against a chaotic system of economics. By the end of the war, unemployment in Denmark was running at eighteen per cent and in Norway at twenty per cent.

Conditions favoured the growth of socialism but not the easy acceptance of change by the middle classes who saw the Russian revolution as a dreadful warning of what could happen to them. Events in Finland confirmed their worst fears. The collapse of the Russian autocracy in March 1917 brought about the immediate restoration of Finland's ancient constitutional rights but left open the question as to who should exercise them. The social democrats, who held a majority in the restored Eduskunta, were unequivocal in their demand for full internal independence and for a short time it looked as if the provisional government might accede, more or less gracefully, to their wishes. But the advance of the German armies in mid-1917 and the undoubted presence of Finnish volunteers among the invading forces soured the negotiations. A unilateral declaration of autonomy (except for defence and foreign policy) was thwarted by Kerensky when he dissolved the Eduskunta in July 1917. This left the socialist moderates in a quandary. With their ideological antipathy for the bourgeois state, their participation in government was conditional on winning through on major parts of their programme, central to which was independence. When the Russians refused to deliver, the social democrats were at a loss to know what to do next except to follow the extremists along the path of direct action.

They were pushed further in this direction by events in Russia where, in November, the Bolsheviks seized power. Unable now to contain their radicals who were in active collaboration with mutinous Russian troops, the social democrats barely resisted the lurch to the left. But even in joining trade unionists on a central revolutionary council, their objectives stopped well short of taking supreme power in the name of the working class. When demands for reform were blocked, the strongest action advocated was a general strike. And when this challenge succeeded in forcing concessions, including official recognition of the eight-hour day, the pressure was quickly turned down.

The anger and disappointment of the revolutionaries, or Red Guards, found release in gun-running and other preparations for taking power without the assistance of the social-democrat party machine. Following hard on the recognition by the Soviet government of Finnish independence, which Lenin saw as a step towards a new and closer relationship rooted in a shared Marxist destiny, the left was antagonized by the setting up of a police force and a national army. The intention of the non-socialist Eduskunta to restore order was taken to be a euphemism for obliterating the radical forces, a conviction supported by the appointment of General Mannerheim, a Finnish aristocrat who spoke no Finnish and who was a long-serving officer in the imperial Russian army, as military commander. In early 1918 he launched his campaign against the Reds with an enthusiasm and energy that convinced his opponents of the imminence of a bourgeois coup. In a quick counter-action, the social-democrat party council gave the signal for taking over the government. Finland was thrown into civil war.

In three months it was all over. The Reds, though supplied with arms and equipment by the Russians and controlling all the big industrial towns of the south, were no match for the professional White forces led by officers trained in the Swedish or Russian armies. As the enemies of Bolshevism the Whites gained sympathy and support abroad, while at home they succeeded in associating their cause with pride in Finland as an independent state. By contrast, however hard the Reds tried to show they were not Lenin's puppets, for example by demanding

37

further territorial concessions, they could not shake off the common conviction that a victory for socialism would bring with it a restoration of colonial rule.

The war, though short, was fought with terrible ferocity. To the seven thousand who were killed in open battle must be added at least as many who fell before the execution squads, and a similar number again who died of starvation or disease in detention camps. Yet in the immediate aftermath, creative political forces were quickly reasserted. In March 1919, with Mannerheim installed as regent, elections were held for a parliament whose first task was to draft a new constitution. Though virtually devoid of leadership and party activists, the social democrats won eighty seats, more than any other single party. But to make their influence felt they had to work together with the centre, whose representatives, mostly agrarians, held the balance between the socialists and the extreme right, the latter having campaigned on Finland's becoming a monarchy. The inevitable compromise was a constitution which combined the democratically elected assembly characteristic of the European parliamentary tradition with a strong president to perform the executive role, as in the United States.

The division of powers was a precaution against one party, always assumed to be the social democrats, bulldozing their programme through parliament. As it happened this fear was groundless, partly because the social democrats weakened their appeal by sustained and bitter internal conflicts, but more especially because they had to share the left-wing vote with the communists whose following remained stronger in Finland than anywhere else in Norden. Added to this, interpretation of the popular will by proportional representation gave a built-in guarantee that minority interests would not be ignored. But without the benefit of foresight, when in doubt the framers of the constitution gave the advantage to the president. He was to be elected for six years as against three – later, four – years for the legislature. There was no way in which he could be dismissed and no limitation on the number of terms he could serve. Legislation was the business of the Eduskunta but the president was allowed what amounted to a free hand in implementing the laws, and there was a wide area of government where he could act on his own prerogative. In placing foreign policy in this category, the architects of modern Finland, though recognizing the importance of the relationship with the Soviet Union, could not have guessed at the priority it would take in later years and the role the president was to assume in personifying the good faith of his country. For all these reasons Finland found herself with the most highly centralized and, in many ways, the most authoritarian government in Norden.

Though social divisions in the other Nordic countries were nowhere near so sharp as in Finland, dissatisfaction with the political and economic systems was frequently too strong to be pacified by social-democrat long-range forecasts of better things to come. In the last year of the war and the first year of the peace, most of the leading industrial centres experienced strikes and violent demonstrations which both sides in the class conflict judged to be the prelude to revolution. Tempers cooled with the first signs of post-war economic recovery, the defeat of the Reds in Finland and the advances made by the social democrats working in co-operation with the liberals and other broadly reformist groups.

Throughout this period, Branting, the Swedish social democratic leader, held fast to his belief that the place to work for lasting reforms was in a popularly elected parliament and that the achievement of universal suffrage was a necessary preliminary to the socialist control of the economy. This strategy naturally made no appeal to dedicated revolutionaries, but the average citizen was more inclined to judge by results. In this respect Branting scored a notable success when, in 1917, his party joined in coalition with the liberals to push through constitutional amendments to make the Riksdag more representative. But it was one thing to co-operate with the liberals on reforms which they had pioneered and quite another to persuade them, against all their political instincts, to co-operate in extending state control over the economy. The coalition fell in 1920 and though the social democrats continued in office as a minority government – the world's first elected socialist government – little was achieved in the mere six months it took to restore a right-of-centre administration. The twenties was a frustrating decade for the Swedish social democrats who formed two more governments (1921–3 and 1924–6) but found themselves implementing broadly liberal policies. Whenever they attempted socialist measures, by a direct attack on unemployment, for instance, they came up against the intransigence of the rural vote. But by now there was no going back along the constitutional path to find other routes to socialism. The lesson learned from the twenties was to try more seriously to attract the support of the centre, which really meant the farmers, for policies which could be clearly shown to benefit the entire nation. It was a tactic which, fortuitously, was ideally suited to the economic conditions of the following decade when social democracy really came into its own.

Danish social democrats went through a similar transformation. Having supported a radical government on extending the vote to all over twenty-five, they moved closer to that party in a successful effort to bring about the eight-hour day in industry and the civil service and, increasingly mindful of farming interests even when these did not accord with strict socialist ideology, to make it easier for would-be smallholders to acquire land without incurring heavy debts. Such was the relationship between the two parties that when the king forced prime minister Zahle out of office, the social democrats and trade unions threatened to mount a general strike unless he was reinstated. The Easter Crisis of 1920 was rooted in Zahle's failure to act more chauvinistically in reasserting Danish rights in north Schleswig (in a referendum administered by Germany's victors only half the province elected to return to Denmark), but the immediate cause of the government's downfall was the prime minister's refusal to hold an election before making proportional representation standard for all national elections. The king's intervention raised other potentially more explosive issues. Riding on a tide of labour unrest, the left multiplied its demands to include wage increases indexed to the cost of living, workers' rights to participate in management and an end to royal interference in national affairs.

It was clear to moderates on both sides that the general strike was turning into a political demonstration with objectives which went far beyond the official programme of the social democrats. With crowds outside the palace in Copenhagen calling for a republic and workers' committees planning the takeover of factories, fears were revived of imminent revolution. And so it might have been had not the king backed down, agreeing to a caretaker government acceptable to the main parties and to the immediate implementation of the new electoral law. This was the signal for the social democrats to pull back. In the subsequent election the liberals made gains, but more at the expense of the radicals than of the social democrats, who looked away as strike-breakers were brought in to clear the last pockets of worker resistance.

The liberal governments of the twenties were broadly reformist but more considerate of the needs of the small farmers and agricultural labourers than of the industrial workers. The social democrats were given their first chance to correct the balance when, in 1924, recession gave a powerful boost to their vote. Thorvald Stauning, a veteran socialist who became prime minister of a minority government, naturally looked to the radicals to give the same support as he had given them in the early post-war years. He was to be disappointed. At a time when unemployment was rising to twenty-five per cent, proposals for direct aid to industry, export credits and a shift in the tax burden from low to high earners were consistently rebuffed. The failure led to a temporary break-up in a long-standing political alliance, but out of power the social democrats and radicals formulated a policy on which they could work together without offending free-market economics. When Stauning returned as prime minister in 1929 it was to lead a coalition capable of uniting rural and urban interests in one of the most ambitious programmes of social reform ever mounted.

Norway was something else. There the leftist movement took a far stronger hold. First, it had an outstanding leader in Martin Transmael who emigrated to America at the beginning of the century and saw the face of capitalism in its toughest and most uncompromising phase. He returned to Norway convinced that his mission was not to ameliorate but to destroy the system that dehumanized labour. He urged miners who went on strike in 1912 to 'leave some dynamite in the boreholes' to deter strike-breakers, a piece of advice which came to symbolize the tactics of the left-wing unionists.

Conditions favoured Transmael's brand of politics. Of all the Nordic countries, Norway had experienced the most rapid transformation from a rural to an industrialized society. The huge majority of those working in the factories or on the new power-plants had been brought up in tiny villages or on isolated farms. They were unsettled, nervous about the future, resentful of change but at the same time wanting the higher standard of living that technology could bring. In the war it seemed that all their efforts were going into making a few individuals vastly rich. Profiteering was at its worst in shipping, where the owners benefited from the general scarcity of what they had to sell, which included the lives of merchant sailors, two thousand of whom died at sea.

The ill feeling built up against employers during the war was accentuated in the early twenties by the threat of unemployment. At the lowest point in the recession, one in four Norwegian workers was out of a job. Transmael's socialism was untried, but with the moderates clearly unable to offer any short-term solution, he attracted support as the only leader prepared to make the effort. In 1918 he forced out the labour old guard and was elected secretary of the party. Two years later his followers gained a majority on the congress of the trade union federation. So successful was Transmael in promoting Marxism that he was able to take the Norwegian socialists into the Third International.

It was all too much for the right wing, who broke away to form their own social-democrat organization. Though at the time it was hardly seen as a great disaster for the left, the split aroused fears in the ordinary voter as to where precisely Transmael was taking the party. The Norwegian spirit of independence, which only recently had found open expression, was hostile to political directions from abroad. When it was made clear that working-class unity required control from Moscow the Norwegians demurred and withdrew. There followed another party split, this time caused by the departure of the communists, who insisted on the inviolability of the Russian connection. Labour was still the dominant left-wing force (in the 1924 election Transmael's supporters won twenty-four seats as against the social democrats' eight and the communists' six), but the divided vote precluded the early possibility of gaining power by constitutional means, while a series of damaging strikes failed in their overall objective of rallying working-class support for a frontal assault on capitalism.

Opinion soon shifted decisively in favour of the Danish and

Swedish model for advancing socialism. The labour and social-democrat parties joined forces and in 1928 had their first if fleeting experience of power – they were out after two weeks. But the union held, and though the party stayed well to the left of Scandinavian politics, conditions in the thirties encouraged the evolution of a broad-based programme of reform.

By the early thirties the parallel evolution in the politics of the three central Scandinavian states was unmistakable. Having chosen to make their way by genuinely seeking a popular mandate, the parliamentary status of the social democrats gradually shifted from that of junior to senior partner in administrations aimed at holding the middle ground. Critical to this transformation was the toning-down of socialist policy to a point where such basic principles of capitalism as the right to private ownership were accepted without question (the nationalization of land was one of the earliest sacrifices to moderate opinion), and the appeal to the electorate rested in the claim that a government of the left could make capitalism work better for more people. Seeking to reconcile the aspirations of the urban worker with those of the farming community, the social democrats threatened to take votes from the centre parties, and so forced them to lend support to social and economic reforms which were not always strictly in accord with their free-market principles.

Added to this, the early acceptance of proportional representation as part of the package of electoral reforms made it easier for the social democrats to establish their parliamentary base. Ironically, it was the parties of the right who, fearing they would be squeezed out by the mass of new voters, fought hardest for a form of election which guaranteed their continuing presence in the legislature. But in achieving this limited objective they also protected the centre which, in turn, kept the social democrats in power. With single-member constituencies the electorate would almost certainly have polarized on the British model, causing the virtual annihilation of the liberal and agrarian parties. Any subsequent gains to the social democrats would have been counterbalanced by an equal number of, or more, votes shifting to the right, allowing the conservatives a better chance of developing a coherent and credible alternative government.

The common trend to be found in the political development of Norway, Sweden and Denmark in the thirties did not extend to Finland and Iceland.

As a tiny isolated country, Iceland's politics were bound to be a personalized affair with a few well-known leaders counting for more than party ideology. After the achievement of home rule, a nucleus of a modern party system started to emerge, but in the absence of a commercial middle class social conflict was rare, to say the least, and since unemployment was minimal (even at the height of the recession it was never above three per cent) the left was short of a theme on which to launch a crusade to reform. The social-democrat party, founded in 1916, was the first to be organized outside the Althing but it did not participate in government until 1934 when, matching experience elsewhere in Norden, an alliance was made with the farmers' party, the progressives. It did not last. Their problem was that they could seldom command sufficient support to govern alone, particularly after the social democrats lost half their number to the communists who advocated a popular front.

From 1929 the independence party, born of a merger between the liberals and conservatives, was the dominant political group, generally taking forty per cent or more of the popular vote. But it was, by its very nature, a pragmatic force, more radical than most centre-right parties, as evidenced by its willingness to enter coalition with anyone, including the social democrats. In the close family environment of Icelandic society conventional political behaviour was just not appropriate.

The twenties and early thirties were for Finland a period when the class antagonism inherited from the civil war remained in itself the dominant political issue. For the victorious Whites, communism was next to treachery and social democracy was next to communism. This made it all but impossible for the centre to work constructively with politicians on the moderate left. The reaction from the social democrats was to take refuge in determinism, hoping to achieve by the march of history what was, apparently, unattainable by working within the established political system. A few of their leaders like Väinö Tanner, who had always kept his distance from revolutionaries, even holding aloof during the civil war, were still willing to participate in government if the opportunity presented itself.

Tanner actually succeeded in forming a minority administration in 1926, but it was only one of fifteen governments to take office in the first ten years of independence. In most of these, the agrarians, the main party of the centre, played the leading role, and were responsible for the most constructive reform of this period, the provision of cheap loans to tenant farmers to enable them to buy their own holdings at pre-war prices.

The social democrats might have made more headway if they had not felt hemmed in by the communists. Though persecuted throughout the twenties the party continued as an effective electoral machine, operating from its strongholds in the poor rural districts of the north and east. The front-line power-base for the communists was the trade unions, which they all but dominated either openly or under the guise of social-democrat membership. This made it difficult to draw a clear line between left and far left, especially as labour unrest, though often politically motivated, stopped short of a direct challenge to the authorities. If the right was prepared for a frontal assault on what it clearly regarded as dangerous revolutionary elements, it was not always easy to identify the enemy. But the matter was simplified dramatically when some of the bolder spirits in the communist party took their crusade onto the streets.

In November 1929, the communist youth movement chose to hold a demonstration in Lapua, a deeply conservative small town in the heart of Österbotten, where Mannerheim had first rallied his supporters to fight the Red menace. Not surprisingly, the local inhabitants reacted with less than kindly tolerance, and the subsequent riot was the signal for other more serious acts of violence against communists – the smashing of a newspaper press in one town, the beating up of a left-wing sympathizer in another. The government prevaricated, with the result that the only official lead came from the president, who was openly sympathetic to the right. As the Lapua movement gathered pace, the government bowed to a demand to ban all communist newspapers before being replaced by an administration even more favourable to the Whites. In mid-1930 the communist members of the Eduskunta were arrested and a full catalogue of anti-communist laws approved. But still there was no sign of the right modifying its aggressive tactics.

Then, as the violence continued throughout the summer,

45

The Other European Community

politicians of the centre rediscovered their principles and their voices. The Lapua agitators were attacked as an ill-organized and disparate collection of extremists who were intolerant of any views but their own. Their call for a ban on the social-democrat party further damaged their credibility. Without a constructive policy or a leader of real stature the movement failed to attract popular support for what it hoped to be the climax of the anti-socialist campaign, a mass march on Helsinki. The event was inspired by the fascist march on Rome, but by comparison turned out to be a pathetic dénouement. Right-wing sentiment remained strong but it was no longer a threat to legitimate government.

The thirties recession revived hopes of an alliance between the centre and the social democrats, who steadily increased their representation to become the biggest single party. Their advance followed hard on the disappointment of the late twenties when, for a short while, timber and pulp exports had thrived and everyone had expected an economic breakthrough. When this failed to materialize interest refocused on the need to reform capitalism. Mainly as a result of Tanner's efforts to seek common ground with the moderate non-socialist parties, the social democrats, progressives and agrarians finally came together in 1937 to form a government led by a progressive prime minister, A. J. Cajander. But it was too late in a decade ending in war for the domestic achievements of the partnership to be anything but modest. A thin programme of social reforms headed by the introduction of paid annual holidays succumbed to an economic policy which was far departed from socialist ideas. Given more time the social democrats might have persuaded their allies to act more imaginatively. As it was, the traditional defensive measures against recession such as cuts in wages caused greater suffering in Finland than in any other of the Scandinavian countries.

The rest of Norden was not without its exponents of right-wing autocracy. A year after Lapua, Norwegian defence minister Vidkun Quisling was making his reputation as a man of impulsive action by sending in troops to enforce a mass lockout of workers who refused to accept wage cuts. The dispute, which centred on the employers' claim that the world recession called for sacrifices from the unions if businesses were to be saved and unemployment contained, was one of the most bitter in Nor-

46

wegian industrial history. But it did not lead, as many had expected, to a resurgence of right-wing agitation. The general acceptance of the basic tenets of social democracy allowed a better chance for compromise. In contrast to the Finnish experience, unions and employers quickly acknowledged the futility of hammering each other into the ground by negotiating a comprehensive 'basic agreement' on the future conduct of labour relations (see page 31).

The social democrats, meanwhile, abandoned their revolutionary slogans in favour of a carefully reasoned programme of economic development and reform which owed much to the conviction that efforts on the right to cure a deflationary recession by cutting investment and spending were about as effectual as trying to cure a cold by sitting out in the rain. With support coming in from the hard-pressed farmers and fishermen, the social-democrat vote jumped nine points to forty per cent in the 1933 election. The dramatic swing did not lead to outright victory but the failure of the liberal government to meet the challenge of unemployment led to its early demise. In 1935 the social-democrat leader Johan Nygaardsvold took over as prime minister but with the backing of the agrarians to whom he made substantial concessions.

The turning-point for the left in Denmark came at about the same time. Though in office since 1929, the party shared power with the radicals and faced a hostile majority in the upper house. Decisive action was therefore impossible. In the early part of 1933 unemployment was up to nearly forty-four per cent, and with the collapse of food prices even the most efficient farmers went in real fear of bankruptcy. The expiry of the national wage agreement in January was the signal for the employers to demand a twenty per cent reduction in wages and, when the unions resisted, to give notice of an immediate lockout. The social-democrat response was to ban all strikes and lockouts for a year, a strategy calculated to open the way for the peacemakers but also intended to help the workers since it was proposed to extend the life of the existing wage agreement by the same period. For this reason the radicals (the party of the small farmers) and liberals were less than sympathetic but, having their own ideas on economic recovery, they were prepared to bargain.

The Kanslergade agreement – so called because it was to his home there that Stauning, who masterminded the negotiations, invited the other party leaders – allowed for the industrial truce and measures to help the unemployed in return for a reduction of farm taxes and an immediate currency devaluation of ten per cent to boost food exports. This last item had previously run into opposition from those who feared that Britain would retaliate on behalf of her own farmers. But the gamble paid off and the social democrats, having taken the initiative, also took the credit for success. In the 1935 election the party gained over forty-six per cent of the popular vote, a figure unequalled before or since. In alliance with the radicals the left achieved what a few years earlier would have been unthinkable, an absolute majority in both houses.

The Swedish social democrats, who came to power in 1932 on suffrance of the agrarians, went through the same transformation of fortunes. A deal with the agricultural lobby allowed for restrictions on food imports in return for a sharp increase in public expenditure to help the unemployed. The prime minister, Per Albin Hansson, was a politician of moderate origins whose self-effacement and insistence on the simple life belied his skill as a power-broker and his grasp of political reality. He saw clearer than most that social democracy could only succeed if it was founded on consensus. But popular approval for reform required a strong economy and an end to the social divisions created by recession. As minister of finance, Ernst Wigforss believed he knew how to achieve this. A man of vision, he gave a socialist interpretation to the employment theories of Keynes and to the Swedish economist Knut Wicksell who, though less well known than his English contemporary, predated him in advancing many of the ideas that were to revolutionize the laws of capitalism. While on humanitarian grounds socialists elsewhere supported measures to ameliorate the suffering of the unemployed and opposed the lowering of wages as an ineffectual strategy, Wigforss was confidently positive in his claims, arguing that by creating jobs and paying high wages the purchasing power of society could be increased so that manufacturers would have more outlets for their products and unemployment would be eliminated.

The impact on Sweden's recovery of the public works programme mounted by the social-democrat government can be exaggerated by failing to give weight to the revival of international trade in the late thirties. Nevertheless, Hansson and Wigforss were the only political leaders in free Europe to make a serious attempt to inject life into the economy by such means as building new roads, hospitals and schools, electrifying the railways and improving housing conditions in country districts. By the same measure, Sweden's socialists were the first to increase appreciably the power of the state in economic life without revolution or large-scale nationalization.

It was still too early to talk of Nordic social democracy as a clearly identifiable political philosophy but that the parties drew mutual inspiration and support can be established from the records of the co-operative committee set up in 1932. The links between worker and farmer organizations was an early subject for discussion, and though the relationship between the two sides varied from one country to another – it was strongest in Sweden, where it even effected local politics, weakest in Finland, where a deal at government level had yet to be struck – the delegates agreed on the view that if farmers were dependent on workers' purchasing power there was a corresponding virtue in the farmers' being prosperous enough to buy industrial products. Social reform was also frequently discussed, but here again the relevant ministers had been meeting regularly since the early twenties.

When it got beyond broad strategy, there were marked differences on what were regarded as the priorities and on the pace at which each country believed it could advance towards equality. In the mid-thirties Denmark's social-security system was the model for all who believed in the state's responsibility for ensuring decent minimum living standards. Insurance schemes covering old age, disablement, health, unemployment and industrial injury were already well established when the Stauning government made it a matter of urgency to rationalize all the existing social laws into one comprehensive service. Financed partly by insurance, partly by taxation, the scheme was founded on the principle that the disadvantaged were to receive help as of right, not as an act of charity. The other Nordic countries followed with piecemeal legislation which, by the outbreak of war, brought them almost level with Denmark, at least on paper. But Finnish health and unemployment insurance was severely limited in its application, while in Iceland the law guaranteeing a minimum income to the out-of-work was passed in 1936 but not implemented until after the war. Most social legislation allowed the individual freedom to choose whether or not he wanted protection, an indication of the lasting strength of the voluntary societies. Even in Denmark health and unemployment insurance was only made compulsory after the war, by which time four-fifths of the population were covered.

The common background to social reform in the Nordic countries allowed for easy co-operation when it came to dealing with problems of cross-border migration. As early as 1911 Danish and Swedish health-insurance societies agreed that members could transfer from one to the other without loss of benefits. Full reciprocity for all Scandinavians had to wait until the 1950s when Finland caught up with health insurance but an early post-war reform enabled any citizen who had lived in one Nordic country for more than five years to receive a pension irrespective of his place of birth or his previous contributions.

The most disappointing aspect of social reform in the thirties was the slow pace of housing construction. Despite increased government support, there was a permanent shortage of accommodation in urban industrial areas, which was caused by the influx of workers from the countryside. When the social democrats took office in Sweden there were two and a half million citizens living more than two to a room. By 1939 solutions were still weighted more on promise than on fulfilment.

In the area of Nordic co-operation the notable failure was to make any real impact on the wider international community. The Oslo group which encompassed the Scandinavian countries together with Belgium, the Netherlands and Luxembourg met regularly but without achieving anything substantial. Even a moderate form of tariff co-ordination aimed at stimulating trade was dropped in the face of British opposition. In the family of nations the Scandinavians were still counted as poor relations even though their domestic achievements entitled them to a far higher status. A few independent observers tried to set the record straight by praising the changes taking place in Nordic society. Marquis Child's *Sweden, the Middle Way* became a best seller and introduced a new phrase into the language of politics.

Another admirer of the Nordic scene, the English politician
E. D. Simon, concluded, after a tour of Scandinavia, 'The mass
of the people are firm lovers of peace ... They are independent
people, loving and insisting on freedom ... they respect one
another's opinions and are tolerant of different views ... They
have the co-operative habit of working with and for others [and]
there is a steady approach to social equality.' But he added, 'A
European war might well shatter all these splendid attempts to
build a better social order.'

3
The quiet social revolution

The association of political ideas and interests that started to emerge in Norden in the thirties faced its severest test in the Second World War. Notwithstanding their common regard for neutrality, the five countries were ripped apart by conflicting loyalties and the irreconcilable demands of the belligerents. Sweden avoided the Nazi occupation suffered by Norway and Denmark by a form of diplomacy which, in the early stages of war, created bitterness among her friends by seeming to favour the German cause. Even when, later on, she was able to prove the wider advantages of keeping her independence by providing a refuge for thousands of Danish Jews and by giving military training to Norwegian and Danish exiles preparing for the day of liberation, the self-righteous feeling that somehow Sweden had opted out from her responsibilities came easily to the surface.

But if confusion of ideals is the measure of disruption caused by the war, then Finland must stand alone among the Nordic countries. At a time when Europe was still waiting for the central drama to begin, the Finns were taking up arms to resist Moscow's territorial demands aimed at bolstering Russian defences. Because they were outnumbered and outmatched in arms and equipment, their hopes were pinned on substantial foreign involvement. When this failed to materialize, there was nothing for it but to give the Russians all they wanted including the Karelian Isthmus. The 1940 treaty which ended the Winter War required the resettlement of no less than twelve per cent of the entire Finnish population. Not surprisingly, within the year Helsinki had opened up contacts with the Germans, allowing them transit for military traffic much as the Swedes were doing, and supply bases in return for much-needed food and armaments.

There followed the German invasion of Russia, an adventure which Mannerheim, in justifying the active participation of his army, described as a 'holy war' to restore Finnish borders. Having achieved this objective with remarkable ease, the Finns wanted out, a desire which became all the more determined as the German advance ground to a halt at Stalingrad and it began to look uncomfortably as if Hitler had over-reached himself. But there was no basis for a settlement that was not an outright surrender, and in refusing this the Finns could only wait for the inevitable Russian counter-attack. When it came, immediate retribution called for the expulsion of Finland's erstwhile allies. In retreating from the northern territory, the Germans took revenge by devastating everything in their path.

As for the rest of Scandinavia, Denmark's colonies fared better than the mother country. Though they too experienced occupation it was done peacefully and, broadly speaking, with the consent of the inhabitants. The Faeroes came under British protection, while the defence of Greenland and Iceland was taken over by America after that country entered the war in 1941. There were great implications here for the future of these Scandinavian minorities as witnessed by the degree of self-government, albeit on a provisional basis, conceded to them by the United States and Britain.

Sweden

As the Nordic country to emerge strongest from the war, Sweden was the first to rediscover her zeal for social reform. The emergency coalition was quietly dissolved and a purely social-democrat government took over with Per Albin Hansson remaining as prime minister. On the cabinet table was a programme for change, worked out and costed when Germany was still fighting but clearly beaten, anticipating a broad range of welfare measures from increased pensions to unemployment and sickness benefits. To bring the economy to a point where it could support those reforms, tighter management was advocated but without the prospect of large-scale nationalization (only oil distribution and insurance were nominated for takeover).

There was not the same urgency for revitalizing war-weary and undercapitalized industries which, for example, in the British context were incapable of attracting adequate private sector investment. By contrast, Sweden was well set to reopen for business. In six years her gross national product had risen by twenty per cent. Her industries were unscathed, her labour force well trained and her commercial leaders eager for further expansion. The unknown factor was the state of the European economy. To counteract the possibility of a post-war slump closing off the traditional export markets, the government took the lead in exploiting new growth areas – most notoriously by offering the Russians generous credits – and then took the knocks for bad judgement when instead of a slump there was a boom. In nearly every other respect the government loosened its hold on the economy. A start was made on dismantling the rationing system, import controls were lifted and even building regulations were liberalized. Only price controls and restrictions on capital movements were retained in their old form.

There were those on the left who complained that the government's programme fell somewhat short of a workers' revolution, but, with the full-blooded socialists relegated to the communist party, expecting otherwise would have been foolishly unrealistic. One or two in office wanted to push the country more to the left – Gunnar Myrdal as minister of commerce was all for going further, faster in that direction – but they were no match for prime minister Hansson, the gentle innovator and supreme mediator who was seen as the guarantor against political excesses.

The theory that moderation was bound to prevail sounded less convincing after Hansson's unexpected death in October 1946. Because there was no clearcut successor conservative nerves were set tingling by the thought that one of the old guard left – Gustav Möller, a guiding spirit of reform in the thirties and now minister of social affairs, or Ernst Wigforss, finance minister and chief architect of the latest party programme – might slip into the premiership. But a strong section of social-democrat opinion favoured a younger man for the job – someone who would brighten up the image of a government currently dominated by politicians whose ideas were moulded by pre-war

54

experience. As the youth campaign gathered momentum –
Wigforss helped it along by disclaiming any ambitions to be
leader – interest centred on Tage Erlander, one-time Möller's
under-secretary and now minister of education. He was of the
right generation, an intellectual with a feeling for practical
politics who had proved his administrative talents. The doubt-
ers counter-argued that his cabinet experience was limited to a
single year, he was virtually unknown outside the party and,
however level-headed he might seem to his immediate colleagues, there was no telling how he might respond to the heady
atmosphere of the prime minister's office. But with no serious
rival in sight reservations as to his capacity for leading party
and nation were set aside and Erlander was elected. It turned
out to be a wise choice, confirmed by a record twenty-three
years of unbroken power and a lasting reputation as one of the
great Nordic leaders of this century. At forty-five, however, the
fledgeling premier was diffident and cautious, still searching for
the easy, comfortable relationship with the voters that had been
the hallmark of Hansson's style of politics.

The opposition allowed him a short honeymoon. So strong
was opinion in favour of state welfare that legislation for child
allowances, free school meals and increased pensions quickly
entered the statute book. The principle of a free health service
was approved and a start was made on attuning the education
system to the spirit of equality. But when it came to financing
these reforms the government had a much harder time. The
1947 budget, which brought relief to low earners but increased
tax on high incomes and profits and introduced a wealth tax,
was anathema to the opposition who accused Wigforss of penal-
izing those whose enterprise was needed to make the country
prosperous.

If the finance minister took the brunt of the attack on the
budget, Erlander suffered heavy criticism on the broader issue
of managing the economy. With the unexpected but entirely
welcome trade boom in Europe, the benefit to Swedish exports
was matched by rapidly increasing imports, a balance of payments problem and inflation. A return to wartime controls was
supported by the argument that a high level of industrial investment could not be maintained if the resources of the country
were squandered in a bout of consumer spending. Once more

imports were cut back, building restricted and demand for non-essential products held down, while efforts were concentrated on expanding employment and increasing productivity in the export sector.

The case for the opposition was put most persuasively by Bertil Ohlin, the recently elected liberal leader and himself an economist of note. Government interference, he said, was distorting whole sectors of the economy which could not be expected to operate effectively without a free market. The other weak point of social-democrat economic policy was the failure to hold down inflation. In spite of controls, prices went up by eight per cent between 1945 and 1948—a gentle rise by today's standards but in the immediate post-war period it was enough to start rumours of imminent collapse of the currency. In its defence the government was able to show that the economy was expanding rapidly and that in adding substantially to the wealth of the country it had succeeded triumphantly in its central objective.

Ohlin's vigorous campaigning brought him substantial gains in the 1948 election, but since they were achieved largely at the expense of the conservatives the balance of power between left and right remained unchanged. With a majority of two over the non-socialists the social-democrat position, though precarious, was made tenable by the election of eight communists who could usually be relied upon to back the government in critical votes. But in the longer term Erlander feared the prospect of having to give way on some vital issue to keep the support of the far left. Like his predecessors he was no revolutionary. What he really wanted was to lead a reformist government based on the widest possible consensus of opinion. Only this way, he believed, could he bring the country to concentrate on the main job in hand – to expand and strengthen the economy to pay for the welfare society. It was not an unrealistic ambition. Behind the smoke-screen of election rhetoric the social democrats had much in common with the liberal and the agrarian parties both of which were committed to helping the underprivileged. The liberals' devotion to free-market forces was overdone by social-democrat standards and, in any case, Ohlin had stood out too strongly against Erlander's leadership for a coalition to appear credible. But the agrarians favoured a more pragmatic style of politics – they were used to working with the social democrats – and their leader Gunnar Hedlund got on well with Erlander. In 1951 the two parties came together in what was soon known as the red–green coalition. Four cabinet jobs went to the agrarians with Hedlund taking over at the ministry of internal affairs.

The new government was inspired by Erlander's ideal of progress by consultation and co-operation. For the first time, union and business leaders were given opportunities to put their views on major items of policy directly to the prime minister. A country house at Harpsund became their regular meeting place. To the opposition, these extra-parliamentary deliberations posed a threat to the principles of an elective government, but in the wider context of popular democracy which Erlander promoted, not least with the social-democrat organization, his was a brave attempt to educate the voters and at the same time to make government more responsive to their wishes.

Harpsund democracy removed the need for direct inter-ference in the running of the economy. While Erlander could get agreement by negotiation, what virtue was there in keeping the paraphernalia of state controls? When right-wing critics accused Hedlund of helping socialism, he was able to reply, 'It is strange to speak so much of government regulations at a time when one after another they are being abolished'.

Though much admired abroad it is doubtful if Erlander's strategy could at this time have worked in any European coun-try outside Norden. Sweden's small, homogeneous society was ideally suited to Erlander's political style of reaching out to the people. Their response, moreover, showed that they had some confidence in the future, a state of mind the citizens of the recently belligerent states had yet to recover.

Nowhere was this more apparent than in economic policy where the government kept up its drive for growth despite a high rate of inflation. The jump in prices in the early fifties – twenty per cent in 1951 alone – was partly in response to the increased cost of raw materials caused by the Korean War. But Sweden also suffered a scarcity of labour which pushed up wages by no less than twenty-five per cent between 1950 and 1952. Less startling figures elsewhere in Europe caused govern-ments to impose tight restrictions on spending and investment which in turn raised fears of an international recession. Erlander was not intimidated. He argued that the country was experiencing a 'once-and-for-all inflation' which was justified as part of a broad economic strategy guaranteeing increased productivity and full employment. As a practical demonstration of his belief he devalued the Krona by a massive thirty per cent, making Swedish exports more competitive but at the same time giving the inflationary spiral another twist by putting up the cost of imports.

The social democrats entered the 1952 election with the slogan 'two decades – from unemployment to full employment', a reminder that whatever the current economic problems they were infinitely preferable to the deprivations of the 1930s. Criticism of the government performance came chiefly from those who thought that more progress should have been made with improving social welfare: there was still a serious housing shortage and obligatory health insurance promised in 1946 had yet to be implemented. It was not immediately apparent that the solution to the other great talking point of the election – the stabilization of prices – would also offer a means of speeding up social reform. Yet curiously that is how it turned out. Middle-class fears of an ever-depreciating currency switched votes from the agrarians to the liberals and conservatives, and though the swing was not serious enough to threaten the coalition it was inevitable that Hedlund should demand more effort be put into holding back inflation. The question was, how? Direct controls were politically unacceptable and, in any case, increasingly difficult to implement given the trend towards freeing international trade. Restricting employment to soften the pressure on wages as advocated by the right was even less attractive. The only alternative was to take a firmer grip on money supply by fiscal measures including tax increases. The policy suited the social democrats ideally. Extending the boundaries of fiscal management smacked less of doctrinaire socialism than direct controls but was no less promising as a means of directing the economy to meet the needs of the welfare society. It was increasingly acknowledged that to achieve the reforms set out in the social-democrat programme, the state had to claim a bigger share of the national income. If the higher taxes necessary to achieve this could also be justified by reference to sound finance, then so much the better. Opposition might have been more vocal if voters had realized that Sweden was setting out to gain for herself a reputation as the most highly taxed country in the Western world. Including social insurance, the tax rate mounted from twenty-five per cent of gross national product in the mid-fifties to nearly fifty per cent in the early seventies as compared with a rise from twenty-nine per cent to thirty-five per cent for Europe as a whole. But as time went on the stock answer to those who wanted Sweden to be more in line with the other industrialized nations was that these countries had less-developed welfare systems and were, by and large, less successful in managing their economies.

As an example of how the government made good use of its fiscal powers, the social democrats achieved a long-standing objective to vary the level of investment so that more money could be channelled into industry and employment when times were hard. Some efforts had been made in this direction before the war but it was not until 1955 that a comprehensive scheme was introduced. It allowed for firms to allocate up to forty per cent of their profits to an investment reserve on which tax was not immediately payable. If these funds were released at a time approved by the government, outstanding tax on the sum withdrawn was cancelled, and a bonus tax-free allowance was set against current profits. The success in persuading firms to fight recession instead of submitting passively enabled Sweden to recover quickly from a succession of international economic crises which left other industrialized nations in total disarray.

On paper at least the coalition looked set for an overwhelming vote of confidence in the 1956 elections. The economy was booming, unemployment at a minimum, poverty almost eradicated. Sweden shared with Switzerland the distinction of being the richest country in Europe. Her welfare system was the envy of less affluent states. Even the rate of inflation was down to manageable proportions. But as the rest of Norden was soon to discover the very success of social democracy created its own opposition. In the forties and early fifties the attack had been led by the liberals, who were less critical to the aims of social democracy than of the means of achieving them. Now it was the turn of the conservatives to take the initiative. With the Swedish people enjoying a high and still rising living standard, ran the argument, the socialist state had outlived its usefulness. All that was on offer was more of the same. The conservatives, on the other hand, were on to something new – the creation of a property-owning democracy in which the accumulation of private capital was to be encouraged and ordinary citizens could feel that they had a personal stake in the future prosperity of their country. The conservative case was strengthened by the accusation by some social democrats that instead of thinking out its strategy for the sixties their party was relying on voters to register their gratitude for past achievements.

Matters were made more difficult for Erlander by tensions within the government which threatened to break up the coalition. With the decline of agriculture as a national industry (by 1960 only fourteen per cent of the working population was on the farms and in the following decade this proportion was to fall dramatically to less than five per cent) the agrarian party was in danger of losing the central core of its support. To correct the balance the idea was taken up of trying to appeal to the urban middle class, and in particular the small businessman, whose sense of values closely corresponded with that of the farmers. But that meant breaking with the social democrats, and Hedlund was not ready for such a dramatic move. His relationship with Erlander was close and he genuinely believed that the coalition was the best government Sweden had on offer. Pressure for change, particularly among the younger members of the party, increased sharply after the 1956 elections. Both parties lost ground but the agrarians suffered most, with a fall in representation to a mere nineteen seats.

The parting of the ways came a few months later when the social democrats introduced an earnings-related pension scheme. The proposal was for each retired person to receive at least sixty-five per cent of his average wage earned over the most productive fifteen years of his working life. The agrarians, now openly declaring their broader interests by rechristening themselves the centre party, reflected the views of the self-employed by rejecting the idea of compulsory contribution. A voluntary superannuation scheme was offered as an alternative. Yet a third plan, favoured by the liberals and conservatives, rested on agreements to be worked out by the employers' organizations and the unions. Underlying the opposition of the right-wing parties to the social-democrat proposals was the fear that a large state pension-fund could be used to tighten control over the private business sector. It was an objective the government discounted, though it was prepared to admit its intention of raising investment and employment.

With three pension plans on the table and no immediate prospect of a break in the political deadlock, Bertil Ohlin, the liberal leader, suggested that parliament should test the views of the country by holding a referendum. There were advantages to be gained on both sides. The liberals and conservatives hoped for a victory that would reinforce their claim to be considered seriously as the alternative government. For the coalition it was a neat way of separating the partners – both now accepting the inevitable – without the acrimony of a general election. At the same time, the social democrats looked to an overwhelming vote of confidence which would establish them, once and for all, as the natural ruling party. They were to be disappointed. Coming out on top was one thing but it was quite another to do so with sufficient weight to smother all opponents. Forty-six per cent of the electorate favoured the social democrat alternative, compared to fifteen per cent for the centre party and thirty-five per cent for the right-wing alliance. Soon after the declaration of the vote the coalition was formally dissolved and Erlander called an election.

The three opposition parties did not fight a united campaign, but with the referendum as a guide to voting intentions there were expectations that together they might outvote the social democrats. Having been forced to go to the country or abandon the best part of their legislative programme the Erlander team were not at their most confident. And their leading opponents, Ohlin and the conservative, Jarl Hjalmarsson, were formidable talents. In the end there was only one seat in it – the social democrats winning 111 and the communists 5 as against a combined opposition of 115. Apart from the narrowness of the result, the main talking-point of the election was the comeback of the centre, whose gains, chiefly at the expense of the liberals, were a triumphal confirmation of the party's new tactics.

Governing on a tightrope brought out the best in Erlander. Every Riksdag vote was a challenge to his ability as a parliamentary tactician and he survived them all. He was helped, as was every other social-democrat leader in Norden, by the inability of his opponents to work constructively together. But if they were seldom able to agree on what they liked they had less difficulty in deciding what they disliked. None of them, for instance, were keen on the social democrats' pension scheme, although there were a few individual members of the liberal party urging compromise. Erlander waited just long enough for one of the renegades to promise his vote to the government on this single issue. In May 1959 income-related pensions were approved by 115 votes to 114. There were many other close shaves, notably in the finance sector where no reliance could be put on communist support. To introduce purchase-tax in the 1959 budget Erlander had to threaten to resign and let the bourgeois parties take over before the communists came to heel.

Political drama was not limited to the Riksdag votes. There were equally serious – some were saying more serious – conflicts within the social-democrat party. Still smarting from the conservative taunt that socialism was irrelevant to the modern rich industrial state, the ideologists of the left vied with each other to produce a popular and radical programme for the sixties. The retired finance minister Ernst Wigforss reminded his colleagues that the welfare state could not be equated with socialism. Socialism meant equality, and yet Sweden was still a class society with economic power largely based on inherited wealth, educational privileges and knowing the right people. Wigforss called for the state to work more energetically for the egalitarian society. His views were supported by many of the younger party members, for whom the pragmatic consensus style of politics was less attractive than a strong ideology and a programme for radical change.

Erlander was cautious. In response to demands at the 1956 party conference for a reassessment of the aims of social democracy, a policy committee was set up but it did not report until 1960. Meanwhile, the prime minister argued that there was still much to achieve in raising the level of social welfare. The affluent society created its own demand for better housing, more roads and improved medical services and education. He conceded that to accomplish all this, it might be necessary for the state to take a more active responsibility in running the economy, but this was as far as he would go, and as a purely hypothetical prospect it was a long way short of a commitment to doctrinaire socialism. Throughout the sixties events favoured the Erlander interpretation of social democracy. A sharp rise in unemployment, which might have counted against the government, instead discouraged the electors from taking risks and gave the social democrats a slender majority in the 1960 election. By reaffirming his party's commitment to gradual reform – revisionism, as it was called by his critics – Erlander divided and so neutralized the opposition. Two of his opponents – Ohlin and Hedlund – were basically in sympathy with the government's policy on welfare measures and said as much in a joint declaration while the election campaign was in progress. This left the conservatives high and dry as the only party proclaiming outright opposition to social democracy in all its forms.

The conservatives suffered great frustrations in failing to engineer a united front against the left. Consistently held off by the centre and liberals, who co-operated so closely as to invite speculation about a possible merger, they rapidly lost confidence on the far right that their politics would prevail. In a country where front-rank politicians are noted for their professional longevity the conservatives sacrificed two leaders in less than a decade in their unsuccessful efforts to find a winning formula. The social democrats did well in the 1964 election and even better in 1968, when reaction to the Russian invasion of Czechoslovakia brought in a welcome bonus vote from disaffected communists.

For all Erlander's claims to be presiding over a moderate administration, Swedish society registered some important changes in the sixties. The introduction of the nine-year comprehensive school presaged a revolution in which the hierarchical system dedicated to academic excellence for the few was succeeded by a far broader interpretation of education as an instrument of social change. Closer government involvement in shaping the economy was suggested by the setting up of a state investment bank. With the nation's pension fund to draw on, the bank was set fair to become the largest single source of finance in the country – and thus a powerful influence on long-term investment. The old-established bankers took an immediate dislike to the newcomer whom they judged to be a potentially dangerous rival. Their suspicions were confirmed when the government followed up by demanding to be represented on the boards of the private banks.

There was another shock for the establishment in the creation of a state holding company, AB Statsföretag, to co-ordinate the management of the diverse collection of twenty-six businesses owned by the government and to buy other firms as part of its programme to improve the general economic performance of state industry. Though never having made a strong case for nationalization, social-democrat administrations had almost inadvertently gained some important acquisitions in mining, textiles and forestry. It did not take a detailed reading of the balance sheets to realize that AB Statsföretag was in a commanding position, surpassing in size and strength such giant corporations as Volvo, SKF and ASEA. But long practice in calming the sensitive nerves of the business community guided the social democrats in selecting the managing director of their new company. In appointing Gunnar Svärd they opted for a sound capitalist whose political experience included a period as party secretary for the conservatives.

It was a good time for the social democrats. They had just scored their best election result since the war, the economy was booming and with the government's gentle shift to the left there was every expectation of uniting the party on a radical programme which was not so extreme as to rejuvenate the opposition. But then Erlander decided to retire. In choosing a successor the party made a break with the past much as it had done when Erlander had taken over from Hansson twenty-three years earlier. Olof Palme was a youngish left-wing intellectual who was not averse to disturbing the cosy assumption of many of his colleagues that Sweden had long since reached the promised land. New thinking was expected and a more turbulent period predicted for Swedish politics.

Denmark

Having led the pre-war advance towards the welfare state, Denmark in 1945 had to bear with an economy which could scarcely support the existing social legislation, let alone another round of reforms. Yet the vital business of reconstruction had to wait on the purging of the national spirit made necessary by the years of occupation. As in Norway, political leaders depended for their appeal less on programme or ideology than on their war record. But unlike Norway, where there was close accord on priorities between politicians of different colours, Denmark started with a government of diverse personalities who managed, between them, to offer wildly conflicting views on almost every important question. They were led by Vilhelm Buhl who, in his previous experience as prime minister, had distinguished himself by being dismissed by the Germans.

In its short life about the only constructive achievement of the Buhl government was the retrospective legislation setting out the terms of punishment for collaborators. Outside this emotive issue it came in for intense and often unfair criticism for failing to deal with pressing economic problems. After the first excitement of freedom it came as a shock to find that unemployment was returning to pre-1940 levels. A united government might have compensated for the run-down of war industries and the readjustment to traditional export markets, but matters were not helped by the less than satisfactory deal with Britain which allowed for lower prices for Danish agricultural produce than had been squeezed from the Germans. The fact that Britain was also in a bad way, that she at least offered an assured market and that provision was made for price increases as soon as the market could bear them did not weigh heavily with voters impatient for some improvement in their living standards. Unable to agree on any short-term remedies, the government fell apart and an election was called for late October. It was a contest for which the social democrats were singularly unprepared. While, in Hans Hedtoft, they had a respected and popular leader who had been close to the resistance, and a programme of reform much on the lines of that promoted by their colleagues in Sweden, they did not share with the Swedish party the virtue of having tempered their policy to suit the demands of practical politics. Generally the most moderate of all the Nordic social-democrat parties, its turn to the left upset the middle-class voters who had previously rallied to Stauning while failing to bring back to the fold the left-wingers who in the exigencies of war had defected to the communists.

The election deprived the social democrats of eighteen seats, a loss counterbalanced by a sharp increase in communist and liberal strength. Though they were still the largest party and so entitled to first try at forming a government, support from acceptable allies was barely lukewarm. Even the party's old friends, the radicals, were inclined to see the liberals as a safer bet for a stable administration. The liberal leader, Knud Kristensen, went down well with the electorate. Domestically his sensible if unexciting middle-of-the-road policies balanced a measure of social reform with support grants for agriculture, a case of maximum benefit at minimum cost. But on foreign policy he was more adventurous, attracting plaudits for his unashamedly chauvinistic demand that the peace terms for Germany should include a shifting of Denmark's border to take in southern Schleswig. It was an objective from which the other party leaders fought shy, realizing, no doubt, that it promised trouble for the future when the wave of anti-German feeling had receded. But this fear was not strong enough to prevent Kristensen from forming a government with the tacit support of the radicals and conservatives.

Once in office it was agreed with the allies that the Schleswig issue should be settled by a referendum. Kristensen, however, could not resist expressing his own preference for a straightforward frontier revision. It was his apparent inability to compromise that drove the radicals, always the advocates for a moderate line abroad, to show their dissatisfaction by moving a vote of no confidence. The result called for Kristensen's resignation and another appeal to the voters which led to substantial liberal gains. But this time the social democrats came back into their own, winning an extra nine seats, almost exclusively at the expense of the communists. This was a great chance for Hedtoft who, no longer susceptible to pressure from the far left, could stand forward as a moderate, deserving, like Erlander in Sweden, the sympathetic support of the rural interests. In reality the radicals had not much choice, since, having brought down the previous government, they could hardly do otherwise than to turn to the second big party. But Hedtoft was not unmindful of his debt to the radicals. One of his first measures was to set up a state fund to buy land for smallholders.

The Danish version of the red–green alliance survived one

essential difference in policy. The radicals wanted no increase in military expenditure and were resolutely opposed to the social-democrat aim of taking Denmark into NATO. But this was an issue on which the government could rely on votes from the right. The decision to join NATO was taken by a massive majority, with the radicals and communists almost alone in opposition. On the domestic front, the injection of much-needed capital investment provided by Marshall aid allowed for a real start to be made on reconstruction. Denmark entered on a new industrial revolution; by the mid-fifties manufacturing capacity equalled that of agriculture. But in parallel with Swedish and Norwegian experience the race for affluence brought with it short-run economic problems such as a high rate of inflation and a measure of unpopularity for a government needing occasionally to take steam out of an overheated economy by increasing taxes or by restricting imports.

It was disagreement on the need for this second line of economic defence that forced an election in 1950 from which the social democrats emerged with modest gains. But this was not enough to save the government. Early in the new parliamentary session the single-tax party, which was not so light-weight as its simplistic economic views or its strength in the Folketing (twelve seats) might have suggested, called for an end to butter rationing. Hedtoft resisted, fearing a loss of impetus in his campaign to increase exports. A compromise might have been possible, indeed was sought by the main opposition parties, but the prime minister remained adamant, and when he lost the division by a single vote he resigned.

The social democrats were succeeded by the first ever liberal–conservative coalition, which managed to keep the radicals in line by the promise of constitutional reform. In June 1953 the Danish parliament abolished its second chamber, lowered the voting age to twenty-three and followed the Swedish example of appointing an ombudsman. But the election of that year brought the social democrats back into power where they remained, more or less securely, until 1964. Though starting on their own but relying on the benevolence of the radicals, they formed a coalition in 1957 which also brought the single-tax party into government. The union was known as the triangle government, and it turned out to be one of the strongest of recent years. Much of the credit for its success goes to the prime minister, H. C. Hansen, who took over as social-democrat leader when Hedtoft died in 1955. Hansen was a skilled mediator, but he could be rough and tough in the face of economic crisis, an experience he endured with monotonous frequency. Acting on one occasion against the wishes of the unions, when he stopped a series of country-wide strikes by imposing a general settlement, he summed up his philosophy of leadership with the cryptic observation, 'No one is going to piss on me.'

The coalition entered the 1960 general election with confidence, but unfortunately for the junior partners the good marks the voters felt inclined to award the government went entirely to the social democrats who increased their representation from seventy to seventy-six. By contrast, the radicals fell from fourteen to eleven and the single-tax party was wiped out. There were also changes in the balance of the opposition, with a new and lively group called the socialist people's party taking over the far left from the discredited communists, and on the right, with the emergence of the independents, a breakaway section of the liberals, who counted the elderly Knut Kristensen among their founder members. They called for a return to the old rural values which had been crushed in the stampede to urban prosperity.

The failure of the right to prevent a united front was an added bonus for the social democrats, who began to see themselves as the natural ruling party. With radical support they were only one short of an absolute majority, a deficiency which was remedied by a deal with one of the traditionally unaligned members for Greenland who entered the government as minister responsible for his own country. But the two-way protest movement which created the socialist people's party and the independents was a warning and a threat to the social democrats as much as to any of their opponents. The rich welfare society brought resentment both from those who, believing that too many were still missing out, gravitated to the left and, more significantly, from those who were ahead of the game, but who felt threatened by government controls and high taxation and veered off to the right, hoping to find someone there to defend their interests.

The problem for the social democrats was to maintain rapid economic growth, which entailed a further dramatic switch away from agriculture as the first export industry, while at the same time trying to maintain a stable currency. For a minority government it was impossible to keep the balance. Periodic tax increases and wage controls did something to help restrain consumption but these measures were hardly popular. The alternative, to cut public expenditure, was sheer agony for a party committed to improving social welfare. A policy of muddling through, usually with the help of foreign loans, tended to disguise the real economic gains and to concentrate the public's attention on their daily tribulations – higher taxes and prices. By the mid-sixties the ratio of inflation in Denmark was higher than in any comparable industrial country, and among OECD members was only exceeded in Iceland and Turkey.

The voters were deceptively passive in 1964 and signalled no change, but the parties decided otherwise. With the loss of just one seat, the radicals withdrew support from the government. For a time it was hoped that some understanding could be worked out with the liberals, but that party was carried by its right wing towards the conservatives, with whom a joint programme and even the prospect for union were discussed. The only other possibility for the government was a deal with the socialist people's party, whose ten seats added to those of the social democrats would have given the left a narrow but workable majority. It was not simply a question of totting up figures, however. Unlike their colleagues in Sweden and Finland, who were quite used to working alongside the communists, the Danish social democrats were not accustomed to waving the red flag, even half-heartedly. An alliance with the socialist people's party was declared unthinkable. Ironically, the firmness with which the idea was dismissed almost as soon as it was raised made its eventual realization that much more likely. For the time being, the social democrats chose to govern on their own, but with unpopular economic decisions imminent – a reform of the tax system was long overdue – and few, if any, parliamentary friends to count on, the chances of carrying through an election-winning programme or even lasting the full term were minimal. These were precisely the circumstances in which the socialist people's party could hope to pick up votes and seats from disillusioned social democrats – and thus improve their bargaining power.

The government's strongest card was its leader – Jens Otto Krag. Still only in his forties when he took over as prime minister, he combined a fine if arrogant political intelligence with a lifestyle that was more appropriate to a film star than a solemn parliamentarian. He generated excitement at a time when the public needed someone to break them out of their mood of political futility; he attracted the young voters when the youth cult was at its height; and he occupied a place in the party hierarchy which had been left vacant since the early death of Hansen in 1960. It was Krag who, taking a leaf out of Erlander's book, initiated an economic council on the Harpsund model. Unions, employers and agricultural interests came together to advise the government on any aspect of policy it thought fit to discuss. Among its earlier recommendations was a centralized wages policy, which was remarkably successful in achieving a stabilization of incomes, prices and profits in the mid-sixties.

But even Krag was unable to beat the odds against a return to a stable moderate government of the left. Almost any way he turned he risked losing friends. For instance, the government made a brave effort to alleviate the housing shortage by increasing rents on older private property, which had remained fixed for twenty-five years, to encourage renovation and new building. The measure had wide parliamentary support but, in terms of votes for the social democrats, it was a failure. Those who were likely to gain in the long run preferred to wait on results, while those who made the sacrifice of paying more for their homes were inclined to register their protest by switching parties.

There was a better chance of coming out ahead on the question of tax reform. It was not exactly a tax reduction the government was proposing – that was out of the question for an economy already seriously overstretched – but the next best thing was on offer: a less painful way of extracting revenue from the public. A national pay-as-you-earn scheme promised a release from the nerve-breaking experience of dealing directly with the authorities, while the introduction of a value-added tax held out the prospect of shifting part of the tax load from incomes to consumer expenditure – an attractive alternative for those who wanted greater freedom for the individual to decide how he could spend his own money. On the government side

VAT was seen as a handy weapon against inflation, since any increase would have an immediate effect on the nation's purchasing power.

The case for reform was strong; everybody agreed on that. The trouble started when it came to deciding on the details. The right wanted VAT to be set at a level which would allow for an immediate reduction on direct taxation, a move which the left strongly resisted as against the interests of the less well off. With no chance of putting together any sort of tax programme which would satisfy a clear parliamentary majority, Krag had either to abandon his policy and thus admit the impotence of his government or appeal to the country. Neither choice promised well for the social democrats, who had done badly in recent local elections. But even if they lost seats the chances were that the left would come out on top, since dissatisfaction with the government was so far evidenced by a swing to the socialist people's party.

In the event, the social democrats dropped seven seats while the socialist people's party gained ten, so doubling their representation. Together they held a majority, and though there was still no question of a formal alliance it was recognized that without some sort of working arrangement there was a risk of an early election and likely defeat. Axel Larsen, leader of the socialist people's party, was a political realist. He was also near the end of a long political career spent exclusively in opposition. According to Krag, he would have liked nothing better than to have finished his time as a minister in a government of the left. With no chance at all of realizing his ambition, Larsen settled for helping Krag to achieve the social reforms they both wanted.

He allowed the same tax changes which earlier had caused such fierce debate to be given an almost free ride through parliament without demanding return concessions on such pet issues as defence expenditure. This did not stop the other parties from setting the voters' nerves tingling with warnings of a forthcoming red revolution. Some credence was given to their version of events by the antics of the extremists, who were said to be 'raising the banner of socialism so high that their feet did not touch the ground'. But they were not close to the government and were in no position to initiate policy. Whatever influence they had was limited to the threat of withholding their votes on a major issue.

The danger point came after a two-year period in which Krag and Larsen had kept up an amicable relationship. And so they might have continued had it not been for one of those economic emergencies which call for bold action but never seem to get it because no one can agree on what that action should be. In late 1967 a jerk forward in the rate of inflation was accompanied by a run on foreign reserves. To hold down consumption Krag proposed a suspension of the annual cost-of-living adjustment to wages and pensions. Larsen went along with the plan, but if he expected the wholehearted approval of his colleagues, he assumed too much. Six of them stood out against the government, more than enough to bring about its defeat on a vote of confidence. With a general election imminent the dissidents in the socialist people's party now set up their own independent group of left socialists who distinguished themselves by their concern for ideological purity and total lack of interest in practical government.

So it was that the left went to the polls, having first advertised their inability to hold together in a crisis. Predictably, the right claimed that they could do better despite the prospect of sharing power between three parties – the liberals, radicals and conservatives – so far unaccustomed to close co-operation even in opposition. The voters accepted the offer of a change, but with reservations. Feeling against the social democrats was evidenced by a drop from sixty-nine to sixty-two seats (the socialist people's party lost nine seats and the breakaway left socialists won four), but the reversal was made less dramatic by the knowledge that a large share of the corresponding gain went to the radicals, the one-time ally of numerous social democratic governments, and the opposition party closest to mainstream socialist thinking. Altogether the bourgeois alliance picked up sixteen seats, with fourteen of these going to the radicals.

There was no question that an anti-labour coalition could survive – simple counting of heads showed that the potential majority was bigger than for any government since 1935. But before power changed hands there were one or two cross-party matters to be sorted out, not least the frequently quoted conservative view that the radicals were a spent force, destined for extinction. Now, with Hilmar Baunsgaard, the radical leader, as the strongest candidate for the premiership, there was a call for a more charitable view of his party's chances of survival. Another embarrassment, this time working against the radicals, was their lonely crusade against Danish membership of NATO. But in the heady atmosphere of pre-government bargaining, policy differences, along with more personal acrimony, were conveniently set aside. With the division of offices agreed (Hartling, the liberal leader, became foreign minister while the conservatives acquired finance and justice), Krag resigned and Baunsgaard inherited.

The change of government did not signify an early change in strategy. Hopes of lower taxes were soon disappointed, and promises to bring down public expenditure, which might have been considered more realistic and economically desirable, were soon diluted to allow for extensions to social welfare, such as the raising of the school-leaving age and a cost-of-living supplement on pensions.

The new government made its strongest impact on foreign policy with Baunsgaard compensating for the failure of Britain to join the EEC by championing Nordek. After the Finnish veto on a Scandinavian trade agreement, the line of objective for Danish trade diplomacy was once more rerouted to Brussels. Feeling against the EEC, which in Norway lost votes for the social democrats, had the reverse affect in Denmark, where the left was in opposition. An immediate beneficiary of anti-EEC sentiment was the socialist people's party which, having survived its internecine struggles, rallied the support of those who feared the community as an agent of international capitalism. The social democrats gained both ways. Accepting the case for going into Europe as the only means of improving Denmark's trade performance, they were comfortably aware that those who were going over to the socialist people's party would nonetheless give broad backing to a government of the left. When the election came in 1971, the social democrats picked up votes from those who were either disillusioned with the government's general handling of the economy or persuaded that Krag would get the best deal in Europe, or both. A gain of eight seats, together with an increase of six seats for the socialist people's party and the tacit support of the members for Greenland and The Faeroes, gave Krag a narrow lead. And for signing the Brussels Treaty, the most delicate issue facing his government, he could count on the right to give him a massive parliamentary majority.

Norway

Norway's first post-war prime minister had spent the last four years in a concentration camp. Einar Gerhardsen was a quiet man with unobtrusive manners who enjoyed an almost ascetic lifestyle, a politician much in the mould of Tage Erlander with whom he was on very close terms. But also like Erlander he was a committed and determined man who found nothing incongruous in moving from vice-chairman of Oslo city council to become leader of the underground anti-Nazi movement in the early days of the occupation. As recently elected social democrat leader he was the natural choice to head the 1945 caretaker government.

He and his mixed-party group of ministerial colleagues did not come to their jobs totally unprepared. The prestige and authority of the government in exile in London had provided the incentive for a political truce during which the four major parties were able to agree on the basics for an economic plan. The first principle of this concordat was the inviolability of the mixed economy, but in the process of taking over from the German administration, the government assumed wide powers to control wages and prices, direct manpower and investment, regulate imports, and generally enforce its wishes where any economic activity was thought to impinge on the national interests.

That the public went along with the judgement of the politicians suggests a unity of purpose far stronger than could be found in any other Nordic country. But perhaps this was only to be expected in a society operating on such a narrow economic base. The action needed to restore Norway's prosperity was apparent to everyone: to make good the heavy losses in the merchant fleet; to increase the output of hydro-electricity; and to develop new industries. If, in order to achieve these objectives, domestic consumption had to be held down to below pre-war levels, Norwegian labour seemed to be prepared to accept the short-term sacrifice.

All this is said with the wisdom of hindsight. In October 1945 when Gerhardsen had to face an election, the first in Norway since 1936, there was no telling how the voters would react to firm economic management. The conservatives, who had been in quite a strong position in the old parliament, were clearly against further controls, but the liberals, agrarians and the Christian people's party (a breakaway group from the liberals appealing to the fundamentalist vote in the rural west and south-west) were by no means dogmatic on the question. As long as the purpose of the exercise was kept well in view – the achievement of a prosperous economy and the eventual withdrawal of government from its day-to-day administration – the centre parties were prepared for a temporary suspension of their free-market principles. They were also prepared, in varying degrees, to commit themselves to an extension of welfare legislation, a concession to social democracy which was not altogether welcome to the party which had led the way on reform and now wanted to re-establish with the electorate its image as the guardian and promoter of the welfare state.

But the chief worry for the social democrats, as for their counterparts in Denmark, was the likely impact of communists who had gained credit for their leading role in the resistance. Talks on a possible merger of the parties were as unproductive as parallel negotiations in Denmark, but the electoral results of each party's going its own way were markedly different in the two countries. More confident of their purpose, the Norwegian social democrats took the electorate by storm, increasing their share of the popular vote by close on ten per cent and their parliamentary representation from seventy to seventy-six seats. It was an outstanding achievement in a country more accustomed to marginal shifts in the political balance. (For the next dramatic change in party fortunes the Norwegians had to wait until the 1973 election was fought on the issue of joining the European Community.) Their advance gave the social democrats the one prize that eluded their colleagues everywhere else in Norden – an absolute majority and the freedom to govern without always looking over their shoulder. It did not matter to

Gerhardsen that the communists had won eleven seats. The gain was impressive since they had started from nothing, but it was not enough to make any impact on the government, except to confirm it in its determination to maintain a tight grip on the national economy. In this the party was supported whole-heartedly by the trade unions. In return for price controls and food subsidies, which stabilized the cost of living for almost five years, and the guarantee of full employment, the unions accepted compulsory arbitration for all wage disputes and virtually forswore the use of the strike weapon. 'The strike', observed a labour leader in 1946, 'must never be a means for weakening the socialist regime and splitting the working people. It can only be an extreme measure for protecting the govern-ment if it meets with sabotage and threats from reactionary quarters in its work for social and economic reform.'

Returned in 1949 with an increased majority, largely as a result of the collapse in communist fortunes following the Czechoslovakian coup, the social democrats felt no compulsion to modify their tough economic policies. To the growing chorus of protests from the opposition parties the government re-sponded by pointing out the benefits: a rise in productivity and living standards well beyond that achieved by most other West-ern countries, and a stable commercial environment. But it was this very stability that was now under threat from sources which were beyond the power of the Norwegian government to con-trol. The 1949 sterling devaluation brought a corresponding devaluation of the Krone, while the general increase in world prices triggered by the Korean War meant that Norway had to pay much more for her essential imports. The use of subsidies to counteract the adverse movement in the terms of trade reached its limit when they became the largest item in the national budget. In 1950, food prices were allowed to get closer to their own level, the cost of living started on an upward curve, leading to a thirty per cent increase over three years, and industrial investment suffered a sharp cutback.

While the Norwegians were conditioning themselves to the change in the economic climate, Gerhardsen decided that after six years as leader he deserved a rest. His resignation came as a shock to his colleagues, who were not consulted, and to the voters. Like his friend Erlander he was popularly regarded as an institution, the embodiment of the country's essential moderation even when he did happen to be running one of the most tightly centralized administrations in the Western world. The choice of successor fell on Oscar Torp, a long-serving cabinet minister who had spent the war with the Norwegian government in exile. He started from the weak position of always being compared unfavourably with Gerhardsen (who now became speaker of the Storting, a job which his supporters judged to be a good jumping-off point if he should ever wish to make a comeback).

The controversy over state planning took on a new dimension in 1952 with the report of the Sjaastad Committee, whose job was to think long-term about the government role in the economy, particularly in so far as this related to the level of prices and investment. Its proposals were wide-ranging and, looked at from the centre or right of politics, extremely contentious. The power to limit dividends to five per cent, the duty to nationalize firms judged to be performing against the public interest, the right to decide on the viability of new enterprises and thus determine their access to capital investment, all this made excellent sense to the left, who naturally assumed that a sympathetic and strong government would push ahead with the plan just as soon as the parliamentary timetable would allow.

But opposition was not limited to the minority in the Storting. As a consequence of Norway's rapid economic growth, the middle class had been strengthened by the rise of the young technocrats. This was true of all Nordic countries, indeed of all European countries, but in Norway, with its highly centralized economic structure, they had climbed further and faster up the commercial hierarchy. This latest generation of industrial leaders was easily frustrated by an over-conscientious bureaucracy, and it was they who now urged government to loosen up on its relationship with the business community. To the fury of the left Torp responded, but not to an extent that put at risk Norway's reputation as a planned society. If industrialists were given greater freedom to manage and develop their own concerns the government kept its power to regulate prices and to fix dividends, the tax structure continued to favour the lower paid, and full employment remained the first objective of social democracy.

77

In the 1953 elections the government held on to its share of the vote but its parliamentary strength dropped by eight, a not altogether surprising result after the system of proportional representation had been changed to reflect more accurately the appeal of the smaller parties. The social democrats' majority was now down to four, though the three communist members could usually be relied on as a last resort. There was also the consolation of knowing that the opposition parties had not yet worked out a joint alternative programme. But the government had problems nevertheless. What was by now a Nordic preoccupation problem, trying to reconcile full employment with wage restraint, proved in the fifties and sixties to be as intractable in Norway as anywhere. Despite the government's best if often unpopular endeavours to hold back on consumption, price increases crept further ahead of productivity, making Norway a high-cost country whose exports were increasingly uncompetitive. With worries about the economy and another election in the offing, party feeling turned against Torp, who had proved incapable of keeping his government united. A campaign to bring back Gerhardsen, as the only politician with the authority and prestige to pull the social democrats together, was not discouraged by the ex-premier. In the end it was Gerhardsen who told Torp that he had to go. The two men then changed places, with Torp remaining as speaker until his death three years later.

Having survived the 1957 election, which recorded only slight changes to the relative strength of the parties, the government found itself under attack from its left wing, this time on defence policy. Foreign minister Halvard Lange offered himself as a target when he refused to discount the possibility of stockpiling atomic weapons on Norwegian soil. That his bullish commitment to NATO offended the neutralists was nothing new, but this time they gained confidence from the European-wide movement in support of nuclear disarmament. The prime minister tried to tone down the Lange doctrine by rejecting the possibility of Norway's playing host to a nuclear deterrent, while insisting on government freedom to decide what was in the best interests of national security. An equally ambiguous form of words was chosen for a resolution approved by the 1961 party conference, and when a group of left-wingers refused to accept the decision they were expelled. This tough action was obviously expected to weaken the rebels by depriving them of their political base. Instead, they took strength from their isolation, forming a new party – the socialist people's party – which acted as a magnet for left-wing dissidents, whether urban pacifists and neutralists or fishermen and farmworkers in the north who resented the power of the Oslo establishment.

When the SPP managed to pick up two seats in the 1961 election it was an unpleasant surprise for the social democrats, the more so because the newcomers held the balance of power. For the first time since the war, the social-democrat share of the vote fell, if only by one and a half per cent, and while there was still no viable alternative government waiting in the wings, the opposition parties were at least talking about the possibility of coalition. One of the chief obstacles in the way of co-operation, conflicting views on the virtue of Norway's joining the European Community, was temporarily removed when, in 1962, France vetoed the British application to enter the Common Market. There were still big differences in the views of the liberals and agrarians (now called the centre party) on the one hand and the conservatives on the other, but they all detected the beginning of a groundswell against the ruling party. After nearly thirty years of running the country the social democrats shared with their political friends in Sweden and Denmark the challenge of showing that the welfare society was still a developing concept and that lower taxes were not the panacea for public discontent.

Meanwhile, the opposition was quick to move on any issue where the government looked to be remotely vulnerable. The appointment of a prominent trade unionist to be head of the police academy had to be defended against a motion of no confidence, and the department of industry came in for criticism for financial extravagance and bad planning in the construction of coke and iron works at Mo i Rana. Yet these were minor affairs compared to the scandal which broke over a mining disaster in Spitsbergen. That twenty-one died in the explosion was bad enough; but this was just the latest in a series of accidents which had already claimed the lives of forty-three miners. Once again it was the industry minister who took the brunt of the attack. Had his department fully implemented the safety measures recommended almost a decade earlier? The opposition said no and a commission of inquiry, though holding back on an outright condemnation, rebuked management at local and governmental level. The industry minister resigned and the Storting was recalled in the middle of the summer recess to face a no confidence vote. When this was carried with the help of the socialist people's party, Gerhardsen handed in the resignation of the entire government.

The best that can be said about the centre–right coalition which took over the administration was that it at least proved that such a thing was possible. John Lyng, the new prime minister, was a conservative who, avoiding all things controversial in his programme, managed to give the impression that his ministers would make a virtue of inaction. The contrary view of politics was taken by the social democrats, who rushed in with a full bag of controversial policies including a new pension scheme, a statutory four-week annual holiday, a shorter working week and more state involvement in industry. The socialist people's party put out its own policy statement saying that it would not support either of the major contenders for power. So Lyng failed to get his majority, as did Gerhardsen; but because the conservative was defending his claim to lead the country he interpreted his defeat as a vote of no confidence and resigned. Less than a month after the dismissal of the social-democrat government, Gerhardsen and his team returned to office.

Continuing on the radical line they had developed during their brief period of opposition, they immediately pressed ahead with introducing an earnings-based pension scheme on the Swedish model. But with all its efforts to freshen up its image, the government could not escape from its reputation for commercial mismanagement. The arrest of an official of the industry department for misappropriation of state funds was followed by revelations that the development costs at Mo i Rana were escalating to a point where it seemed unlikely that the operation would ever show a profit. Even the long-awaited aluminium plant at Husnes was the object of opposition scrutiny, since it was claimed that the French and Swiss financial stake in the scheme was working against Norwegian interests. Local elections and opinion polls showed votes to be slipping away from the social democrats as the rivals shaped up for the 1965 election. Learning from past errors, the opposition sealed an electoral pact, while the social democrats and socialist people's party made independent appeals to the electorate, so risking a split in the left-wing vote. This time the coalition emphasized its moderation by offering the prospect of a centre party or liberal prime minister, while the social democrats had no choice but to stick to their new-found enthusiasm for radical change. The government prescription failed to attract the marginal vote, which shifted right to a point where the coalition had, for the first time, a working majority over social democrats and SPP together. Per Borten, centre party leader, became prime minister with John Lyng as foreign minister.

It was not a very adventurous government but it suited the mood of the times. By 1969 the social democrats had recovered much of the ground previously lost to an SPP now stricken by internal dissension. But that did not prevent the coalition scraping back. With a majority of two Borten struggled on, until the Common Market issue shook Norwegian politics to its roots.

Finland

Having fought on both sides, or, to give credit to Finnish consistency, having fought for herself first against Russia then against Germany, the country emerged from the war defeated, demoralized and in total political disarray. In these unpromising circumstances a general election was planned for March 1945. The largest party, the social democrats, immediately cut their chances of victory by indulging in an orgy of in-fighting. This started over a move to get rid of the wartime leadership but the central issue was the future relationship of the social democrats with the recently legalized communist party.

Many communists had found a home with the social democrats in the late twenties and thirties when persecution of the left was at its height. Free now to give full voice to their beliefs, they demanded active co-operation between the two party organizations to bring about the socialist millennium. They were supported by some of the more moderate social democrats, who

sought a way of persuading Moscow that they were not intrinsically pro-German. The risk of a takeover by the extreme left was
acknowledged, but it was thought more likely that the communists would be tamed by association with a party dedicated
to free elections. The arguments did not impress those who had
lately worked in the government side by side with the parties of
the centre and the right. For them there could be no alliance
with self-professed revolutionaries. The split ran right the way
through the social democrat and union organizations, and
though the anti-communist forces eventually won the day,
it was at the cost of disillusioning many traditional supporters
and of losing a section of the party which broke away to join a
conglomeration of forces on the far left, the Finnish people's
democratic league (SKDL).

Communist fortunes were riding high in 1945. The peace
treaty with the Soviet Union was still to be agreed, but the
terms of the 1944 armistice – the surrender of one-twelfth of
Finnish territory and reparations to be paid in goods valued at
three hundred million dollars at 1938 prices – suggested that
Russia had no inhibitions about leaning heavily on her weaker
neighbour. The communists returning after years of exile in the
Soviet Union and the die-hards who stayed at home to keep
alive an underground movement could be forgiven for believing
that they were about to come into their political inheritance.

On the face of it, the social democrats threatened the communists with the most serious competition for the working-class
vote. But there was an unknown factor. The agrarians drew
much of their strength from the farming communities in the
north and east where poverty was widespread. In the pre-war
years this party of small farmers and farm workers had stood
out strongly against communism but, ever mindful of its grass
roots, kept to a radical line in social policy which in normal
times made for easy co-operation with the social democrats.
With the communists so long out of the running it was an open
question who would make the biggest gains. Voting predictions
were made more hazardous in the absence of any recent test of
public opinion, the life of parliament having been extended by
emergency legislation for as long as the war lasted. Moreover,
the party stalwarts who had taken an active part in government
in those years were now replaced by party leaders who were

inexperienced and virtually unknown to the voters. The general mood of uncertainty was increased by the fear of what the Soviet Union might do if the election did not produce a result favourable to the Kremlin. This was a strong card for the communists, who were fighting for parliamentary representation for the first time since 1929 and threatening to make up for lost years by quickly taking over the left as a preliminary to taking over the country.

But what hopes remained of Finland surviving as an independent democracy did not centre on the outcome of the elections or on parliament as an institution. If the public looked anywhere for a lead it was to the presidency, and to Field-Marshal Mannerheim, who took over the job in August 1944. Revered as a national hero by the Whites, Mannerheim extended his reputation among Finns of all political colours by bringing his country through the Winter War and by his initial success in the renewed hostilities with Russia in 1941. He was the only possible candidate to take over as head of state when Risto Ryti, who had signed an agreement with Germany promising that Finland would not make a separate peace, was forced to resign in August 1944. Though he was not much loved by the Soviets they acknowledged Mannerheim's unique personal authority.

In circumstances in which Finland had no bargaining strength except the ability of politicians to persuade Russia of their good intentions, the initial selection of ministers was particularly apt. Carl Enckell, a close and trusted associate of Mannerheim for many years, took charge of foreign affairs. Like the president he had been trained as an officer in the Russian army but resigned at the height of the Tsarist oppression and transferred to the Finnish diplomatic corps. He was foreign minister in 1918, representing Finland at Versailles, and twice returned to the foreign office in the early twenties. But his most important qualification for the job was his conviction that if Finland was to survive she had to take account of Russia's interests as a great power.

As a realist in international politics Enckell had nothing to teach the new prime minister, Juho Paasikivi. However at first glance he was a curious choice of politician to lead Finland into the most delicate and dangerous phase of its relationship with the Soviet Union. For a start he was a convinced and well-practised capitalist who had made a fortune in banking. He entered politics in 1905 and advanced rapidly, serving briefly as prime minister before being thrown out of office because he was an ardent supporter of monarchy. Then in 1920 he led the delegation which settled peace terms with the Russians, an appointment which was designed to satisfy the right, who feared a sell-out to the communists. But, proving himself to be a pragmatist as well as a tough negotiator, Paasikivi worked in easy co-operation with his social-democrat colleagues, who favoured a conciliatory approach and ended up scrapping the more extravagant territorial demands favoured by the nationalists. Mannerheim was among those who denounced the peace treaty as a betrayal of all those who had fought against bolshevism. Later, however, Paasikivi gained credit in Finland for achieving a workable compromise and respect in Russia for living up to his promises.

His diplomatic skills were in demand once again on the eve of the Second World War, when he returned to Moscow to negotiate a joint defence plan against threatened German aggression. This time it was the Russians who were extravagant in their demands, and Paasikivi was instructed by his government to reject plans for handing over key areas to satisfy Soviet military strategy, a rebuff which set Finland on course for the Winter War. Given more freedom to act on his own judgement it is likely that Paasikivi would have tried to go some way to meet the Russians, since he made them aware that he did not share the intransigent mood of his masters in Helsinki. What is certain is that his relations with the Soviet leaders remained firm enough for him to be welcomed as envoy to Moscow in the peace period between the Winter War and the Continuation War, and that his return to the premiership in 1944 was at the insistence of the Russians, who overrode Mannerheim's objections.

All this must have made little sense to the Finnish communists, who entered the 1945 elections with high hopes of an outright victory. Nor was there any lack of Soviet encouragement for them to think in such optimistic terms, for, whatever the Kremlin view of Paasikivi and Enckell as men of good will, regard did not run so high as to dissuade the faithful from helping to bring about the dictatorship of the proletariat whenever and wherever opportunity allowed.

Forty-nine communists were elected, which was far short of the number they were expecting but more than enough to worry the agrarians, who also returned forty-nine members, and the social democrats, who won fifty seats. The other parties straggled behind but the conservatives came home with a respectable twenty-eight. Paasikivi and Enckell were reconfined reconfirmed in their jobs and a cabinet was formed giving roughly equal representation to the three largest parties. But while at this early stage the communists showed a willingness to participate in government, even going so far as to drop plans for large-scale nationalization, they were not easy partners, since they behaved as if it was only a matter of time before they monopolized the executive. Their arrogant assumption of revolution to come, combined with a tendency to engage in ideological warfare which few understood or cared about, was ill-suited to the public realization that there was still strong life in the Finnish democracy.

When Mannerheim, who had turned seventy-eight and was ailing fast, was persuaded to stand down in mid-term of his presidency, Paasikivi was the obvious successor. The issue was so clear-cut it was decided to forgo the formality of a popular election and instead invite parliament to authorize Paasikivi's elevation by emergency legislation. He needed no instruction on the working of the Finnish constitution. Power was centred on the presidency – or rather, power was centred on the man who had enough strength of character to use the presidency for all it was worth. As if to signify not only the change in his own standing but in that of the government as well, Paasikivi chose as his successor as prime minister Mauno Pekkala, a social democrat convert to the SKDL who had held various junior ministries in the war years. He was without experience of high office, unless such included the post of director of the board of forestry, the job from which Paasikivi promoted him. Though linked with the communists, Pekkala was in no sense a revolutionary, and he accepted that it was part of his job to restrain the hotheads in the SKDL.

The peace treaty with Russia was signed in February 1947 after protracted but unsuccessful efforts by the Finns to secure a reduction in reparations (this came later, with a twenty-five per cent drop in the amount demanded). Though depressing in their severity the terms did not come as a great surprise, since for the most part they confirmed what had already been provisionally agreed by the 1944 armistice. Finland was to lose twelve per cent of her border territory to the Soviet Union, including the country's second largest city of Viipuri and the port and province of Petsamo on the Arctic coast. With a large part of the province of Karelia taken over by the Russians the frontier was moved back from a distance of only 19 miles from Leningrad to a new line 112 miles from the former Soviet capital. Four hundred thousand people had to be resettled. The Åland Islands were to remain demilitarized and limitations were imposed on the size of the Finnish armed forces and on the weapons they could use.

No sooner had the country absorbed this reminder of the totality of defeat than the Russians raised fears of more far-reaching demands to come with what was euphemistically described as an 'invitation' to negotiate a mutal assistance agreement. With news of the communist coup in Czechoslovakia acting as a further stimulant to already sensitive political nerves, there was a widespread assumption in Finnish government circles (which the communists did their best to foster) that nothing less than an administration directly answerable to Moscow would satisfy the Russians. A delegation led by Paasikivi entered negotiations hoping for the best but half expecting the worst. All that counted in favour of the smaller power (since it was clear that the West could not offer her security) was the knowledge that if Russia was solely and genuinely concerned with protecting herself against the possibility of another German invasion, Finland was of secondary strategic importance to Poland and Czechoslovakia, from which the main thrust of a German attack must come. Added to this was the argument, pursued with much energy by Paasikivi, that the interests of the Soviet Union on her north-western border (the only part of Finland that really mattered to the Russian military) could best be served by a sovereign Finland whose open and sympathetic relations with her eastern neighbour precluded the possibility of her territory being used as a platform for attack.

Starting with the brave assumption that the Russians were in the least interested in living alongside an independent but loyal

Finland and strengthened by the international uproar over events in Czechoslovakia, Paasikivi proposed a series of amendments to the Soviet draft treaty. Skilfully he shifted the emphasis away from Russian ambitions for making Finland an ally (with all that status implied in terms of political commitment) towards the far more attractive prospect (for him) of the two countries' entering into a joint security arrangement which would allow Finland to stand aside from big power politics in all except those clearly specified in the treaty.

In the end it was all a matter of interpretation. Paasikivi sold the grandly named Treaty of Friendship, Co-operation and Mutual Assistance to his own people and to parliament by persuading them that their obligations were no greater than they would have been under less formal circumstances. Finland promised to defend herself against an attack from Germany or an allied state, to confer with Russia in case of war or threat of war and, if necessary, to accept Russian aid. Great play was made of the acknowledgement of Finland's ambition 'to remain outside the conflicting interests of the great powers'. This clause, said Paasikivi, was the keystone of Finland's external relations, but it was noticeable to all that there was no immediate endorsement of his view from the Russians, who were by no means ready to accept a neutral Finland.

The popular view in Norden, as in the rest of Europe, was that Finland had tied herself to the Soviet Union and was as much under the control of Moscow as any of the communist satellites. Paasikivi did his best to counteract this impression and reacted decisively if there was any hint of a threat to his own authority. When in the spring of 1948 there were rumours that a section of the communist party was planning to seize power, he took the initiative by dismissing from the government the powerful SKDL minister of internal affairs, Yrjö Leino. But there were signs also that the president was hyper-sensitive to Moscow's needs for constant reassurances of Finnish good faith. The press was told in no uncertain manner to tone down articles which presumed to criticize the Soviet Union; organizations deemed to have fascist sympathies, like the Aseveliliitto (an old soldiers' union largely drawn from the ranks of the social democrats), were suppressed, and some of the most respected wartime leaders were put on trial to atone for all those who had given aid to the Germans. The Finnish communist leader, Hertta Kuusinen, demanded, but failed to get, death sentences for those like former president Ryti who had not switched sides quickly enough.

The Soviet encouragement of left-wing forces in Finnish politics, which Paasikivi could do little to hinder, whatever his private wishes, did not extend to the social democrats who were associated by the Russians with a pro-German policy before and during the war and therefore could not be trusted on any account. The communists hoped to absorb the social democrats or at least get them into the SKDL where they could be under communist control, but early post-war progress in that direction was halted abruptly when the two parties met each other in government. The social-democrat leader, Karl August Fagerholm, who had initially supported co-operation, was quickly disillusioned, and in the 1948 election made a strong effort to dissociate himself from the communist campaign and to discourage speculation of another government alliance. The suspicion that the communists might anyway have overplayed their hand was confirmed by their loss of eleven seats. Compensatory gains to the social democrats increased their representation to fifty-four while at the same time they managed to rid themselves of a number of colleagues who still hoped for a realignment in politics to allow for a broad power-grouping of the left.

Talks were held with the communists to search for any remaining common ground on which a joint administration could be founded, but when the SKDL insisted on having one of their own number as minister of the interior (a sensitive job bearing in mind that only a few weeks earlier the holder of the office had departed on suspicion of being involved in a projected coup), the effort was abandoned. Relying on the passive good will of the agrarians, Fagerholm formed a minority social-democrat government.

The political climate was unfavourable for any administration, but for the social democrats it was particularly unpromising. The economy was in its first painful stage of recovery. Fortunately, most of the nation's productive capacity had survived the war intact, and the export demand for wood products was strong. But paying off reparations in goods the Russians wanted meant a big transfer of resources to the engineering industry and, initially, the import of expensive machinery. All this had to be achieved without a share in Marshall aid, though US loans totalling 150 million dollars were channelled through in other ways. Skilled labour and consumer goods were both in short supply with the inevitable consequence that wages and prices climbed steeply, each one feeding off the other to send inflation soaring. In 1948 prices were eight times their pre-war level.

The communists were well placed to take advantage of the government's troubles. With the rapid growth in the strength of the trade unions – they had more than quadrupled their membership by the end of the war – many communists found themselves in key positions in the economy. In the summer of 1949 they disrupted industry with a series of strikes which split the trade-union movement, damaged the credibility of the government and aroused fears that another attempted coup was imminent.

But Fagerholm's problems at home were mild compared with what he had to face abroad. From the day he was appointed the Russians chose to see Fagerholm as an agent for Western interests. Even making contact with other social-democrat movements or inviting their representatives to Helsinki was seen as a deliberate effort to sour Finnish–Soviet relations. When Soviet commentators carried the row a stage further by holding the president to blame for his government's backsliding, Paasikivi promptly dismissed Fagerholm and replaced the social-democrat government with one formed by the agrarians under the leadership of Urho Kekkonen.

It was a wise choice. The Russians found it much easier to relate to a party with no pretence to an ideology beyond the protection of purely Finnish interests. The agrarian leaders were essentially pragmatists and, having worked easily with the social democrats (and frequently against the communists) before the war, they had no difficulty in adapting themselves when the ground rules changed dramatically. Kekkonen's own political career was a case in point. As one of just three members of parliament who voted against the peace agreement which brought to an end the Winter War, he became an ardent and outspoken supporter of the Continuation War, urging his countrymen to spare nothing in their struggle against the Soviet enemy. However, when it was clear that only a miracle could save the German army, he was converted to the political realism preached by Paasikivi. In 1944 he joined the government as minister of justice, a job which entailed setting up the prosecution of those held responsible for the association (it was never formally an alliance) with Germany.

Kekkonen lost none of his energy or determination in his new role. At home, where industrial relations were rapidly approaching a state of anarchy, he made good use of Fagerholm as a mediator in the long-running dispute over linking wages to the cost of living. The so-called F agreement of May 1950 awarded the trades union federation (SAK) a general fifteen per cent increase, with a promise of extra to come if the price index jumped more than five per cent. But when this happened faster than anyone had imagined possible the government, fearing an inflationary whirlwind, went back on the deal. The strikes that followed, the worst in Finnish industrial history, were only settled when Kekkonen broadened his government to take in eight social democrats and compromised on a new cost-of-living index which excluded direct taxes and family allowances and was based on the price levels prevailing in October 1951. Wage-indexing remained, but henceforth the government met with greater success in holding down inflation. As a measure of Kekkonen's authority, he was about the only politician capable of forging even a remotely workable alliance between his party and the social democrats, a virtue which in the early fifties always made him first choice as prime minister.

Kekkonen associated himself closely with Paasikivi's foreign policy and worked hard to establish good personal relations with the Russians. But he was not content merely to be an echo of his master's voice. Having decided that the future of his country was dependent on the USSR, he concentrated on evolving a formula to suit both sides. Clearly the 1948 treaty was not the last word on the subject. Differences of interpretation had already emerged, chiefly in the context of Finland's claim to neutrality. The first need was to persuade the Soviets to relax and allow the Finns more international elbow room. In 1952, with Paasikivi's backing, he put up a plan for 'a neutral alliance between the Scandinavian countries', which he saw as of benefit to the USSR – since 'it would remove even the theoretical threat of an attack . . . via Finland's territory' – but of even greater value to Finland (although this was not explicitly stated), because it required the West to endorse her claim to neutrality.

The proposal, contained in what was immediately dubbed the 'pyjama speech' because Kekkonen, being ill, distributed copies to the press from his sick room, caused an uproar throughout Norden. Social democrats jumped to the conclusion that it was all a plot to weaken NATO, since Norway and Denmark would be required to leave the alliance without Russia's having to make any concessions in return. Kekkonen replied that, on the contrary, he was acting positively to strengthen Swedish neutrality, which Finland needed above all else to preserve her own independence. The arguments were thrown back and forth with intense vigour, compensating in passion for what they lacked in reality. Everyone acknowledged that a Scandinavian alliance, neutral or otherwise, was totally impracticable. The projected defence union between Sweden, Denmark and Norway had been lost in 1949 when the two smaller powers had decided that they needed the protection of the United States. There was no way in which Denmark and Norway could now be persuaded to abandon an alliance into which they had so recently entered.

But the gain to Kekkonen in what seemed to be a fruitless exercise lay in a statement of approval from the Soviet Union, in a form which recognized Finland's claims to act on her own initiative. Moscow was delighted by an unsolicited rejection of the Atlantic pact by a north European state and congratulated Finland on pursuing the course of 'strict neutrality'. This was one of the strongest indications so far that Russia was prepared to recognize Finland as a neutral, and though in subsequent references Soviet commentators generally referred to that country as 'striving for neutrality' rather than having achieved the objective, Kekkonen's initiative put relations between the two nations on an entirely new footing.

In 1955, two years after the death of Stalin had brought the first signs of an easing in the cold war, Paasikivi and Kekkonen visited Moscow. The talks led to a twenty-year renewal of the Treaty of Friendship and Mutual Assistance and the return to

Finland of the Porkkala base near Helsinki, which under the terms of the peace treaty had been leased to the Soviet Union for fifty years. This meant the departure of the last Soviet troops on Finnish territory – the most powerful boost to national morale of the early post-war years. The concept of neutrality was beginning to take on real substance. That same year Finland joined the United Nations and the Nordic Council – but stayed out of the latest formation of Soviet defence, the Warsaw Pact.

That Kekkonen was an outstanding political talent was undeniable; that he had set his eyes on the presidency was also evident; but whether he would actually succeed Paasikivi was far less certain. The problem for Kekkonen was that he could not be sure of the support of the social democrats – the largest single party. The Tannerites disliked and distrusted him because of his volte-face in the last stages of the war, but there were others with less bitter personal memories who believed that the prime minister was getting too close to the Russians to recognize their potential for ruthlessness and duplicity. According to these critics, the citizens of Helsinki could expect to see Soviet tanks in their streets any day.

Kekkonen made his opening bid for the presidency in 1950, the year in which he was first appointed prime minister. It was a token effort intended to prepare the way for the next contest six years ahead when Paasikivi, who by then would be eighty-six, could be expected to retire. Support for Kekkonen was limited to his own party, while the SKDL put up Mauno Pekkala. Paasikivi was endorsed by the conservatives, progressives and the Swedish people's party. He won on the first round of voting.

Almost immediately Kekkonen began preparing for his second campaign with speeches up and down the country in the style of an American presidential candidate. His main rival was the social-democrat nominee K. A. Fagerholm, though it could just as easily have been Paasikivi himself. Having been persuaded against his better judgement to stand down, the old man allowed himself to be persuaded by the conservatives to put his name forward in the second round of voting. Kekkonen squeezed in by two votes – 151 to Fagerholm's 149.

Kekkonen's first presidential term started with the attempt to solve crises which he had initiated as prime minister. His last act in that office had been to preside over the demise of his government, a coalition of social democrats and agrarians. A cabinet vote to increase farm prices had triggered the resignation of the social democrats, a protest which was backed by the threat of a general strike if prices were not restored to their previous levels. The farmers countered by refusing to supply produce for as long as the strike lasted. With the presidential elections intervening and the ex-prime minister a leading candidate, there was no opportunity to appoint a new government before the end of February, the deadline for the strike to begin. The job of putting the economy back into order was given to Fagerholm, the closest rival to Kekkonen in the presidential elections but now the leading parliamentary figure and obvious first candidate for prime minister. To succeed, however, he needed a strong government, an unlikely prospect given the relative strength of the parties and their proven inability to disguise their conflict of interests even when sharing power. The only alternative to a minority social-democrat administration – which would almost certainly have fallen within days of taking office – was a broad-based coalition. But as such a government, under Kekkonen, had failed to prevent the general strike, there was next to no prospect of it resolving the conflict.

With the agrarians and social democrats unable to agree on any constructive intervention, the industrial crisis was allowed to run its course. After three weeks the wage increases demanded by SAK to compensate for the rise in food prices were agreed by the employers, the strike was called off, and the government was discredited. Fagerholm's position was further weakened by a split within his own party between those who supported the strike and those who, like the prime minister, wanted a compromise settlement.

Not surprisingly, Fagerholm thought it was time to go. He tried to resign in April 1957 but, lacking a creditable alternative for prime minister, Kekkonen persuaded him to stay on. After another month of party wrangling and cabinet indecision, Fagerholm decided he had been right first time and resubmitted his resignation, this time more forcefully.

If his departure from government in these depressing circumstances could be counted as voluntary, there was no question that his rejection as party leader was a cruel disappointment that he would have given anything to avoid. His downfall was engineered by the supporters of Väinö Tanner, the elder statesman among social democrats whose pro-German associations had put him behind bars after 1945. Released after serving half his sentence, he was elected to parliament in 1951 and quickly re-established himself as leader of the social-democrat right. Fagerholm's inability to solve the economic crisis and the subsequent collapse of the coalition strengthened Tanner's appeal as one of the older and tougher school of politicians who was less likely to submit to employers, farmers or trade unions. In 1957 Tanner was nominated as chairman of the party in opposition to Fagerholm, whom he defeated by a single vote after an acrimonious contest. Now totally disillusioned, a group of left-wingers led by Emil Skog departed to find more congenial fellowship with the SKDL.

After Fagerholm's resignation as prime minister the country was subjected to a succession of government crises, as one politician after another tried to put together a viable administration. Among those approached by Kekkonen was the newly elected leader of the social democrats, but Soviet reaction against Tanner was so hostile that trade negotiations were immediately suspended in protest. Although it was later claimed that the president had made the invitation to Tanner only because he knew Tanner would fail and so lose credibility as the man who could save the country, the experience was a bad one for Kekkonen, who was reminded that Soviet vigilance was as sharp as ever.

A way out of the impasse was sought via the 1958 general election, which brought a revival in communist fortunes, a gain of seven seats making it the largest single party. The badly divided social democrats fell back by six to return forty-eight members, ten of whom refused to acknowledge the leadership. Among the non-socialist parties, there was a swing away from the agrarians and liberals to the conservatives. Overall, the left had a narrow majority, but the antipathy between the communists and Tannerite social democrats precluded a socialist coalition. All other permutations having been tried before the election, Kekkonen returned to first principles, inviting Fagerholm, the moderate most likely to reconcile left and right, to attempt to put together a government representative of all parties. The communists resisted his blandishment but the others, sobered perhaps by the election results, eventually gave way.

In August, Fagerholm took charge of a cabinet consisting of four social democrats, five agrarians, three conservatives, a liberal and a member of the Swedish people's party. Few imagined that mutual tolerance – never a prominent attribute of Finnish politics – had blossomed to a degree that a five-sided government could survive for long. But the probability of failure became a certainty when Kekkonen withdrew his support. Less than enthusiastic from the moment the communists had decided to stay out, he became decidedly cool when the social democrats insisted that of their share of ministerial jobs two should go to members of the Tanner faction. After the row over Tanner's comeback as party leader and candidate for the premiership, it did not take second sight to predict Soviet reaction to the inclusion of any of his supporters in the Fagerholm government. Tanner himself invited retribution by openly voicing his fears that Finnish independence was threatened by Russia, a political indiscretion from which Fagerholm did his best to divert attention by making his own forthright declaration of loyalty to the Paasikivi line.

As seen from Moscow, however, the government of Finland had fallen into the hands of the pro-Western faction at a time when the Berlin crisis made security a sensitive issue. If Kekkonen had spoken out in defence of his prime minister he might have restored a degree of Soviet confidence, but in remaining silent he seemed to justify Russian fears. In what became known as the Nightfrost crisis, Finland had to bear a succession of diplomatic snubs aimed at forcing a change of government. Difficulties were put in the way of Finns travelling to Russia, normal commercial dealings were dragged out or suspended and the Soviet ambassador was recalled.

Fagerholm's only other escape plan – a reshuffling of the government to exclude those distrusted by Moscow – was vetoed by his own party. All he could do was to hang on, anticipating that relations would improve as the Russians came to realize they had overreacted. Kekkonen, however, was less confident that matters would eventually sort themselves out. Though the evidence is sketchy it is almost certain that the president urged his fellow agrarians, who were equal partners in the coalition, to withdraw, and so bring down the government. The key figure in this manœuvre was foreign minister Johannes Virolainen, who disliked being made to appear a sacrificial victim but was brought round to the view that the difficulties with Russia could only be solved by a new administration. Virolainen resigned on 4 December along with the other four agrarian ministers. Fagerholm quickly followed with the resignation of the entire government (the best with which he had worked), blaming the agrarians for an act of wilful destruction.

The Nightfrost crisis brought to an end three decades of friendly co-operation between the centre and the moderate left and initiated eight years of opposition for the social democrats, who had to change policies and leadership before they were welcomed back into government. But of far greater significance for the future of parliamentary politics was the consolidation of power in the office of the president. Having conceded that the composition of a government, though normally purely an internal affair, could bear on foreign relations and was therefore of legitimate interest to the Soviet Union, Kekkonen had strengthened his own position as the essential mediator, the only leader capable of handling the Russians and, by implication, all matters in which the Russians might choose to involve themselves. It was no more than the paternalistic role Paasikivi had claimed, but with a new president Finland's parliamentary politicians had expected more, not fewer, opportunities to influence events. As if to prove how wrong they were, Kekkonen endorsed an agrarian administration to succeed Fagerholm's coalition; in other words, a non-socialist government was put up against a socialist majority. Not surprisingly, it achieved little except to endorse the growing popular contempt for parliamentary rule.

Enjoying his enhanced prestige and authority, Kekkonen was soon back on course with his policy of trying to establish Finland as an independent neutral. Indeed, so forgetful was he of the discomfort of the Nightfrost, or perhaps just confident that it would not recur now that the social democrats were out of the way, he failed to see any warning for him in the Russian protest at the revival of German militarism. At a time when the cement had barely set on the Berlin wall, the disarmament talks at Geneva had collapsed and the Soviet nuclear tests had climaxed with the detonation of a 50-megaton bomb, Kekkonen chose to go off to America where, as evidence of his country's freedom of action, he suggested that recent membership of EFTA was a prelude to a deal with the European Community. The trip ended with a holiday in Hawaii, and it was here that he received the potentially catastrophic news that the Soviet Union was activating article 2 of the 1948 Treaty by demanding consultation on measures to ensure the defence of their frontiers.

The reasons for this precipitate action were set out in a note delivered to the Finnish ambassador in Moscow in October 1961: the growing military strength of West Germany and the suspicion that before long the Germans would have the H-bomb; apprehension at the extension of German military activity in Norway and Denmark; and the presence of the German fleet in the Baltic. What it all amounted to was a Soviet conviction that the German role in NATO had reached proportions where it endangered the Nordic balance and posed a direct threat to Russian security. From the Western point of view it may have seemed like an elaborate piece of fiction; but whether or not NATO believed that the Russians had cause for complaint, or, indeed, whether the Russians themselves believed in the justice of their case, was purely secondary to the indisputable fact that Moscow wanted something to be done and that Finland was expected to fulfil that demand.

The Note crisis represented the most serious challenge yet to Finnish neutrality. It had been said so often – by Finns – that article 2 could be acted upon only when *both* parties agreed that a threat existed, that it came as a shock to realize that the Kremlin had never assented to that interpretation and, on the contrary, assumed that a unilateral declaration of interest by the stronger partner was sufficient to start the process of military consultation. If the Soviet claim went uncontested Finnish independence would be seen as a sham.

Western observers expected the worst; nothing less than military bases on Finnish soil would satisfy Moscow. But Kekkonen remained outwardly placid, warning foreign journalists 'not to sell the bearskin until the beast has been felled'. He refused to cut short his US trip but sent home his foreign minister, Ahti Karjalainen, on a diplomatic sortie.

When the president arrived back in Helsinki he was ready

97

with a compromise strategy which required the Russians to agree to a postponement of military talks in favour of discussions aimed at reassuring the Kremlin that Finland would remain true to her foreign policy. Kekkonen was tacitly acknowledging that he may have overplayed by going to America when the two superpowers were barely on speaking terms. But that was not the only cause of Russian concern. It was made clear in meetings between Karjalainen and Gromyko that Soviet anxieties were focused on the 1962 presidential election, when Kekkonen faced a strong challenge from Olavi Honka, a former minister of justice who was the joint candidate of the social democrats, conservatives, Swedish party and liberals. With the despised Tannerites still in command of the social democrats, Moscow judged that the purpose of defeating Kekkonen was to change Finland's foreign policy – a conclusion challenged by Karjalainen, who told Gromyko that all political groups 'wanted to continue in friendship and confidence with the Soviet Union'.

The president, however, was less inclined to question the Russian view that the preservation of good relations between the two countries was dependent on his own political survival. The Finnish electors were already half persuaded of Kekkonen's indispensability, and there were signs of weakening in the Honka alliance even before Kekkonen decided to make assurance doubly sure by dissolving parliament and by advancing the date of the general election by six months to follow immediately after the presidential vote. He was out to persuade his countrymen that the political guarantees demanded by the Russians as a minimum condition for easing on the pressure for military talks could only come from a strong president (Kekkonen, of course), backed by strong government in sympathy with his foreign policy. The hope was that a great victory for Kekkonen would prepare the way for the defeat of the social democrats or, more particularly, those politicians on Moscow's black list.

Unfortunately, the strategy failed to satisfy the Russians, who felt that they were being asked to take too much on trust. Honka after all was still a threat, or so it must have seemed with so many parties endorsing his candidacy. Yet when the call for military consultation was renewed it came as an unpleasant surprise to the president, who assumed that the Russians, having put their trust in him, would not now undermine his chances of re-election by suggesting he was incapable of preserving the status quo. Evidently there were still those in the higher reaches of the Kremlin who saw the answer to German resurgence and increased NATO activity in Scandinavia and the Baltic purely in strategic terms, without regard for the wider political consequences of any action that might follow military consultations. The only chance of persuading them to take the broader view was to appeal directly to Khrushchev. This Kekkonen did, requesting an urgent and personal meeting with the Soviet premier. Khrushchev, who was on his travels inspecting farms in Siberia, agreed to break his tour, and the two leaders sat down together at Novosibirsk.

Kekkonen was at his best as the sympathetic but tough negotiator who was capable of arguing his case on the principles of sound common sense. He had nothing to give except the sure knowledge that if military consultations went ahead there would be a war scare in Scandinavia, possibly leading to counter-measures by the West. Why take the risk of creating another international trouble spot when all that was needed to guarantee the northern frontiers was a reaffirmation of the Finnish commitment to the 1948 treaty? Kekkonen was only too happy to provide this – assuming, of course, that he was re-elected president.

It is not known how much persuasion Khrushchev needed – whether or not he was initially sympathetic to the Finnish view. In 1962 the question was irrelevant, because the sense of relief in Helsinki when Khrushchev agreed to postpone military talks was so great that nothing could detract from Kekkonen's prestige as the country's saviour. Even before he arrived home the Honka alliance was toppling, as many of his one-time supporters concluded that to press ahead with their plan to unseat Kekkonen was to invite a rekindling of Soviet anger and a savage retribution at the polls. Anticipating mass desertion Honka withdrew from the contest, leaving his rival to be elected for a second six-year term by an overwhelming majority on the first round of voting.

But as a twist to the end of this chapter in Finnish politics, the humiliation of the social democrats and their allies in the presidential election was not repeated in the parliamentary election. The agrarians came through as the largest party, overtaking the SKDL, but the social democrats also improved their position, if only marginally, and, though Tanner himself did not stand, his leading followers had no trouble in holding their own. It was almost as if the voters had decided to show Khrushchev that he could not get it all his own way.

Kekkonen was unruffled. The division of forces in parliament excluded the possibility of any party leader's attracting enough support to challenge presidential authority. At the same time the agrarians, all president's men, had first claim to the key positions – prime minister, foreign secretary, speaker – and with the balance of power having shifted away from the left it was reasonable to construct a government from the parties of the centre and right. It was well known that the social democrats had to be kept out to reassure Moscow, and the communists to reassure everybody else. But an effort was made to keep open the lines of communication to the proletariat by appointing three trade-union leaders to the cabinet. The tactic failed to strengthen the government. When hard economic decisions were needed it proved impossible to reconcile the interests of farmers and urban workers.

The weakness in the political structure stimulated the ambition of the social democrats to regain office. From 1958–66, when government was either in the hands of the agrarians acting alone or of centre–right coalitions, the social democrats gradually – and often painfully – adapted themselves to the Kekkonen relationship with the Soviet Union.

The breakthrough came in June 1963, when Tanner retired as party chairman at the age of eighty-two. A candidate sympathetic to the Tannerite tradition was put up to replace him but was beaten decisively by Rafael Paasio, a social democrat of the new image. His victory was reinforced when Väinö Leskinen, Tanner's closest lieutenant and architect of his election to the leadership in 1957, was removed from the party's executive committee, an event which encouraged Emil Skog and his friends – who had broken away in protest against Tanner – to return to the fold. The process of change was helped along by a growing mood of self-assertion among the voters. With rapid economic growth came the popular demand for reforms which would put Finland on the same level of social welfare as that enjoyed by the central Scandinavian countries. The social democrats seemed to offer the best chance of achieving that objective, though important innovations such as comprehensive health insurance were made in the early sixties.

But before satisfying the aspirations of the people it was necessary to re-establish links with the man who saw himself as the personification of all their interests. After the critical changes in the party leadership, the reconciliation with president Kekkonen and, indirectly, with the Russians took the form of a campaign to prove the social-democrat allegiance to the principles of Finnish neutrality. This consisted largely of speeches in favour of general disarmament, spiced with unfavourable references to American military strategy, particularly in Vietnam. At home, the social democrats withdrew objections to collaborating in government with the SKDL and the communists, while at the same time reviving with the agrarians, or, as they called themselves after 1965, the centre party, the prospect of a red-green coalition, an approach which led to social-democrat support for Kekkonen in his bid for a third term in 1968.

An indication of the new strategy came in the 1966 election when the social democrats raised their share of the vote to twenty-seven per cent, a record in post-war politics, and gained seventeen seats. Offered the first chance to put together a government, Paasio followed the Kekkonen line in attempting a broad-based coalition with ministerial places going to the centre and the communists. Critical to his efforts was the exclusion of those social democrats who were too closely associated with the old party regime. These included Leskinen, who had tried to make amends by disavowing his former policies, and even Fagerholm, whose temporizing in the interests of party unity was now seen by many as having contributed to the descent of the social democrats into the political wilderness.

The new administration was not without its internal conflicts but, in bringing some sort of order to the economy without losing sight of growth targets or of the need to improve the standard of social welfare, it must be counted as a greater success than most of its predecessors. And despite the defection of the communists, who had their own split to contend with, the government had what was for Finland the unusual quality of staying-power. The social democrats remained in charge for the rest of the decade and on into the seventies.

Iceland

Iceland decided on 1944 as the year of unilateral declaration of independence. The news was not well received in occupied Denmark, even though the termination of the act of union was little more than a formality. Home rule had been conceded in 1918 as part of a constitutional package which allowed either country to cut loose entirely after another twenty-five years. It was an option the Icelanders made no secret of wanting to take up; and, even if they could be accused of anticipating events by four years, it was also a fact that the German invasion of Denmark in 1940 had effectively ended that country's responsibility for Iceland's foreign relations. The only governmental innovation of any note after June 1944 was the election of a president to carry out the ceremonial duties previously assumed by the monarch.

Yet in one sense the birth of the republic did have real political significance. It meant that the Icelanders were on their own when it came to dealing with the Americans. The country was occupied peacefully by Britain in 1940, but with Icelandic approval US troops took over a year later. They poured money into the economy, improved roads and docks, built an airport and employed a large number of local people at high wages. Now, the first important question for the free state to consider was an American request for a long-term lease on three military bases.

The ruling coalition of independents and progressives was sympathetic. It realized that Iceland could no longer rely on distance for her security – the latest aircraft and submarines put paid to that – and with no means of defending herself, another world conflict would put her at the mercy of whichever power could get to her first. But the continuing presence of American forces at the strength envisaged by Washington somehow gave the lie to the act of independence so recently celebrated. The Althing temporized with an offer to hand over the Keflavík airport for a limited period while at the same time calling for American troops to be evacuated within six months.

It was not a happy solution for the United States, whose strategists felt that a country so conveniently placed half-way in the Atlantic between the two superpowers should be bound more closely to the interests of the West. The answer was to recruit Iceland to NATO. A delegation of White House officials set out for Reykjavík to explain the benefits of participation. Their task was made easier by warnings from Norway and Denmark that even if a Scandinavian defence union got off the ground there could be no guarantee of security from that quarter. It was then only a matter of assuring Iceland that she would not be expected to finance a military establishment for her to accept that the NATO option had everything to be said for it.

There remained the question of the American involvement. On one hand it was mutually agreed that the stationing of foreign troops in Iceland in peacetime was undesirable. Yet military installations were essential, and there were no Iceland-ers qualified to run them. Objection to the Americans' operating the Keflavík airbase were gradually withdrawn and in 1951, when it was feared that the Korean War could lead to a general conflagration, a separate defence agreement with the United States allowed for an increase in the number of troops brought in 'to defend Iceland and ... to ensure the security of the seas around the country'.

As the danger of another world war receded the Americans stayed on to maintain the latest sophisticated military equip-ment and to provide the focal point for the longest-running dispute in Icelandic politics. Even while doing their best to keep themselves to themselves, a force 45,000 strong could not help but make its social impact on a population of barely 125,000. At various times and with various governments there have been proposals that some of the Americans should leave, that all of them should leave, that they should leave in stages and that they should remain but pay for the lease of the bases at the going market rate. The balance of political forces in Iceland is such that calls for an end to foreign intervention are seldom unequivocal. It does not escape the notice of the electorate that the NATO base contributes up to three per cent of the gross national product, that it allows Iceland a modern airport which might otherwise be too expensive to maintain and that over two thousand Icelanders are indebted to the military for their employment. To cap all this the United States is one of Iceland's best markets, taking over thirty per cent of total exports. It is then hardly to be wondered that even the left-wing coalition that came to power in 1971, pledged to rid the island of the defence force within the parliamentary term, nevertheless managed to postpone the moment of decision until new elections brought in a government more favourably disposed to the Americans.

When Icelandic politicians are not concerned with the affairs of their Atlantic ally, conversation invariably turns to the state of the fishing industry. Fish is central to the economy, until recently accounting for ninety per cent of the export trade. But over-dependence on a single product has led to sensitive political nerves, since no one has felt safe in predicting how long the good times will continue. Soon after the war there was concern that other nations were taking too large a share of the Icelandic catch (foreign vessels had kept away while the sea lanes were potential deathtraps, but they were back in force after 1945), and that more efficient trawling techniques would cause a dangerous depletion in fish stocks.

In 1948 the coalition, by then joined by the social democrats, brought in a law authorizing the demarcation of new fishing zones to be subject exclusively to Icelandic jurisdiction. Two years later one mile was added to the three-mile offshore zone which Iceland had administered since 1901. This was just acceptable to other fishing nations but when, in 1958, the limit was extended to twelve miles, Britain made her feelings clear by sending in naval vessels to protect trawlers from harrassment and arrest. This was the first Cod War, a cat-and-mouse game between the British navy and coastguard patrols which continued up to 1961. At that point Britain and West Germany, the other major fishing nation involved in the dispute, accepted the twelve-mile zone on condition that if Iceland intended to widen her jurisdiction still further she had to give six months' notice of her intention and, if challenged, refer her claims to the International Court at The Hague. The agreement caused resentment in Iceland, where it was felt that concessions had been gained from her under duress. The terms were not therefore an inhibiting factor when, in the late sixties, action was needed to compensate for a drastic fall in earnings from the herring catch. The left coalition of 1971, which drew back from challenging the Americans, fulfilled its promise to do something about over-fishing by unilaterally extending the offshore zone to fifty miles.

A second Cod War was made inevitable when Iceland refused to participate in the subsequent proceedings at The Hague; but despite her clear contravention of treaty commitment she gained sympathy as the tiny nation fighting the giants, and understanding for her natural preoccupation with an issue which meant life or death for the Icelandic economy. There was something else working in her favour. Other countries including Britain and members of the European Community were giving serious thought to revising the scope of national jurisdiction over the continental shelf. When figures were mentioned, a limit of two hundred miles seemed to gain most favour, a claim which put the Icelandic declaration into a rather more modest perspective.

In fact, such was the speed at which international opinion changed on the question that in 1975 a new government of independents and progressives felt strong enough to make real what others were still speculating about. In announcing a two hundred mile limit, prime minister Geir Hallgrímsson used emotive language: 'Our livelihood is at stake and our cause is so strong and just that victory will be won.' It was a safe prediction. Britain again intervened but only to fight the third Cod War as ineffectually as the first two. A six-month moratorium was supposed to give time for a settlement to be agreed, but when the talks reached stalemate in December 1976 British vessels were nevertheless banned from Icelandic waters.

To discuss Icelandic politics in terms of party ideology can be dangerously misleading. On the first big issue, the presence of American forces, there was a broad agreement between the independents, progressives and social democrats on support for NATO with only the people's alliance and other far-left groups wanting a total, if gradual, withdrawal. On fishing limits, all parties favoured an extension. The only real difference between them was how far they could go in offending the nations who traditionally shared the Icelandic catch. Judged in the context of big-power politics, the parties in Iceland indulged in some remarkable alliances. For instance, between 1959 and 1971 the country was governed by the independents and social democrats in tandem. In any other Nordic country such a combination of right and left would have led to uninspired legislation, if not to a seizure of the economy. But in the close, family-like environment of Iceland the pooling of diverse ideas, talents and personalities achieved a liberalization of trade and a much-needed expansion of manufacturing that was not tied exclusively to fishing or agriculture. It is all the more remarkable, then, that Iceland was unable to avoid the political upheavals that characterized Norden in the seventies. But by that time Icelanders were complete Scandinavians, with all the problems and frustrations of living in an advanced welfare state. Nor were they immune to the effects of a long-term international recession. The besetting problems of inflation struck Iceland more forcefully than any country in Europe.

The short story of post-war Nordic politics up to the end of the sixties is the achievement of an advanced welfare society based on rapid economic growth. Though taxes were frequently a bone of contention, and were certainly high by European or American standards, this was as much a result of inflation (usually between three and eight per cent) lifting incomes into the higher tax brackets as to any deliberate intent by government to 'soak the rich'. Nordic social democracy remained essentially moderate even in Norway, where the left enjoyed a period of majority rule at a critical time in the country's development, and in Finland, where class divisions were sharper and more deep-rooted.

To ask why moderation was a ruling principle is to risk making dubious or at least unproven claims about national characters; but it is fair to say that a policy of gradualist reform must stand its best chance of success in small homogeneous societies where late industrial development has put social conflicts into a manageable context.

In terms of everyday politics, stability of voting behaviour allowed for continuity in government, a factor which may have restrained the social democrats from going too far too fast. The social-democrat share of the vote remained steady at forty per cent in Norway and Denmark and at forty-five per cent in Sweden. The party did less well in Finland, scoring about twenty-five per cent, but by the mid-sixties its popular rating rose to a point where no government could be formed without a social-democrat presence.

The post-war continuation of the red–green coalition in Sweden and Denmark and intermittently in Finland was another force for moderation. Even when the social democrats were the dominant partner or eventually able to rule alone, no one in government forgot the strength of the radical farming interest or underestimated the traditional hostility to Marxism among rural voters.

Though the three central Scandinavian states show remarkable similarity in the central features of their political development, the extent to which parallel advances in social welfare were the result of positive efforts to co-ordinate policies is difficult to gauge. The Nordic Council did not really get under way until the late sixties, at the end of the period under discussion. Politicians of similar persuasion and civil servants conferred regularly, but it was a long way from the exchange of information at conferences or seminars to any conscious attempt to define a Nordic reformist ethic. Consultation was always closest when the topic under discussion was either uncontroversial or of low political priority. Tage Erlander has said that the only time all the Nordic premiers found themselves together in an atmosphere where they could talk informally about general principles was when they were summoned to a royal funeral. At the same time Sweden was generally the standard-bearer of reform. Given the close cultural ties between the Nordic states, it was the most natural thing in the world for them to follow Sweden's lead as they had followed Denmark's in the inter-war years.

A reaction against social democracy showed itself in the sixties, when the conservatives led the way in proclaiming the creative virtues of the free-market economy against the torpidity of wet-nurse socialism. But with no prospect of gaining power independently, the conservatives had to reconcile themselves to an accommodation with the liberals or agrarians. This presented a serious obstacle. As a declining force everywhere except Sweden, the liberals were sensitive to overtures for an alliance which could easily lead to their obliteration. On the other hand the agrarians, or centre parties as they were now calling themselves, were trying to compensate for the declining rural vote by competing against other opposition parties for support in the towns. There was the additional problem for the conservatives that liberal, radical and centre parties were by no means sold on a return to classical economics. In championing the underdog they accepted the basic principles of state welfare, and in some cases were even in favour of its extension.

It soon came to be realized that there was a better chance of an agreement if, instead of trying to come to terms on a positive formula for social economics, emphasis was put on rectifying what appeared to many to be excesses of social democracy. With the virtual completion of the welfare society there was a tendency for the far left to become more vocal in its demands for purely socialist measures. The growing power of centralized bureaucracy, for example, gave warning of what could be expected in the future and offered a target on which centre and right-wing parties could co-ordinate their attack. But notwithstanding the occasional breakthrough, such as that achieved by the Baunsgaard government in Denmark, it remained to be seen if botched chances by the social democrats, or their failure to elaborate policies which appealed to the moderate vote, would make the basis for lasting centre–right coalitions.

4
Not quite economic union

The high point for the supporters of Nordic economic unity came in 1968, after Britain's second unsuccessful effort to make a place for herself and, by association of interests, for Norway and Denmark, in the European Community. Seeking compensation for this latest rebuff, the Danes revived proposals for a Nordic common market, and pursued their initiative with such determination that recommendations covering most aspects of economic co-operation were prepared and submitted to the Nordic prime ministers in a little over seven months. The plan, known as Nordek, was for a tariff union, excluding agriculture which carried its own special problems, to come into force at the beginning of 1971. This was to be the first push towards full co-ordination of the four economies – Iceland was not immediately involved – and the joint exploitation of natural resources and technological skills. It was an exciting time for unionists, whose single-minded enthusiasm made them lose sight of the weakest point in the agreement – the conflict of interests which threatened any long-term dealings with the EEC.

In Denmark there was no backtracking on the commitment to keep trying for entry to the Community. Nordek was promoted as a bridge-building exercise which would eventually make it easier for all the Nordic countries to enjoy the advantages of a wider European market. There was even a suspicion that the Danes wanted to delay the tariff charges to give the Common Market a chance to make an alternative offer. This was precisely the opposite of what was intended by the Finns. They warned that any attempt to pull them closer to the EEC – and so to the western defence system – would put at risk their special relationship with the Soviet Union.

But with the approach of the eighteenth session of the Nordic Council, set for February 1970, the abundance of reassuring words on the adaptability of the treaty and the good will of the participants made it seem as if there really was some way of accommodating irreconcilable interests. The delegates to the Nordic Council duly gathered in Reykjavík to urge their governments to submit Nordek for parliamentary approval, a proposal endorsed by the four prime ministers. The idea was to complete this formality, for that is how many regarded it, in the first days of April. But then, on 24 March, the Finns, probably acting under Soviet pressure, revived all their fears of creeping European integration and refused to endorse the treaty. Deprived of one quarter of its strength, Nordek died within hours.

In retrospect, it is clear that Sweden and Norway also had their reservations – Sweden because she had her neutrality to think about, Norway because she could not rid herself of the nagging fear that she might be swallowed up by her economically more powerful neighbour. Supporting nationalist sentiment was the argument that each country was best able to look after its own trade interests. Membership of Nordek was supposed to increase their negotiating strength, but members would have remained vulnerable to outside pressures. The Scandinavian market was just too small either to produce most of what it needed or to absorb most of what it produced. No politician could afford to forget that well over half the region's exports went to European countries outside Norden.

In this respect nothing had changed since the 1940s, when for the first time the idea of a trade association was seriously considered. This was the period when, after two cataclysmic wars in little more than thirty years, European leaders thought of organizing their political systems so that they were best able to work with instead of against each other. Encouraged by the Americans, whose purpose in mounting an economic rescue for their allies was partly inspired by the need for a continental bulwark against communism, they talked of superseding nationalism with interdependence and the pursuit of European union. But where to start? There was an immediate difference in emphasis and style between the federalists, led by France, who wanted a blueprint for integration complete with a constitution identifying centres for legislature and executive power, and the functionalists, represented by Britain, who thought that practical experience in selected areas of co-operation should precede the creation of new supranational institutions. The Nordic countries were inclined to the second view. They tended to think of mainland Europe as the breeding ground for political instability, a contagious disease best kept at a distance. Before attaching themselves to a grand scheme for international government, they wanted firm evidence that the big powers really intended to act in the common interest and not simply try to impose their opinions on their weaker neighbours.

Suspicion of federalist motives increased with the realization that those pushing hardest for the European idea – Schuman of France, de Casperi of Italy and Adenauer of Germany – envisaged a predominantly Catholic union dedicated to holding back the advance of socialism. This had no appeal to the Protestant north where social democracy was in the ascendant. But the old man's vision of Europe – the triumvirate was pre-First-World-War vintage in age as in much of their philosophy – bore little relationship to practical politics, and the Scandinavians, not to mention the British, should have realized this. In fact, the European movement was so loosely conceived as to be capable of adapting to almost any ideology short of outright communism. Among those who were quick to recognize the possibilities were the Belgian socialist Paul Henri Spaak and the French socialist leader Guy Mollet, who, at a series of meetings in which Dutch and Italian social democrats figured prominently, prepared the ground for the creation, in 1947, of the Socialist Movement for the United States of Europe.

Early efforts at working together seemed to confirm the Nordic view that the major European powers were unreliable partners. To take one central issue, the setting up of NATO, to which Denmark, Norway and Iceland were signatories, was followed by an American-supported plan to unify control of European forces. This was intended to reassure those who were nervous about German rearmament while at the same time strengthening the defence system to compensate for the US preoccupation with the Korean War. For the Nordic countries involved, it was a big step from participating in the Atlantic Alliance, where they had the right of veto on decisions deemed to count against their interests, to delegating wide-ranging powers to a European Defence Community on which they might have difficulty making their voices heard. Intense suspicion of supranational authorities had to be balanced against the risk that refusal to take part might damage relations with the United States. After much agonizing the Norwegians concluded that the Atlantic Alliance, the cornerstone of their defence strategy, had to take priority, and foreign minister Halvard Lange moved for a constitutional change which would have allowed his country to transfer powers to a European command. But Lange acted prematurely. Having championed the defence community as a guarantee against possible German aggression, France now rejected the plan, a dramatic turnabout explained by one of the frequent changes in the composition of the government, this time from centre to right. That the issue should have been decided in this cavalier way only seemed to confirm the Scandinavian view that the continental powers were not dependable.

The experience of the trade liberalization programme initiated by the Organization for European Economic Co-operation was scarcely more encouraging. The OEEC was an inter-governmental body set up in 1948 at American behest to ensure the fair and effective distribution of Marshall aid. It was also charged with the responsibility of trying to prevent a recurrence of the protectionist movement which held back economic revival after the First World War. Unfortunately for the Scandinavians, OEEC only concerned itself with the removal of import quotas, the much more complex and longer-term process of bringing down import duties being left to those working with the General Agreement on Tariffs and Trade. Inevitably there were accusations of unfair treatment. It was not just that leading participants were inclined to counterbalance quota increases with a corresponding rise in import duties. Of more immediate concern was the imbalance between the low tariff and high tariff areas. As part of the first group, the Scandinavians justifiably complained that when they abolished quotas they were left with virtually no protection at all, while high tariff countries were able to cushion themselves very comfortably against foreign competition. This was particularly hard on countries dependent for a living on a narrow range of exports. Denmark and Iceland were among those who pointed out that while they were doing their best to take in more industrial goods, no one was too concerned to open the European market to their fishing and agricultural produce.

About the only aspect of European integration which gained unreserved Nordic approval was the Council of Europe. Though federalist in design – the Council was intended as the first step to a freely elected European parliament – it was denied legislative or executive powers by virtue of the British reluctance to get too far embroiled in continental matters at the expense of its commonwealth and American connections. As a forum for debate, the Council had its uses but, since it lacked the authority to follow up on its conclusions, the Nordic members had no fear of being pushed into action against their will.

Where European co-operation was genuinely productive was when it concerned just two or three immediate neighbours or when it was aimed at securing a clear and limited objective. Nordic interest focused on the Benelux customs union which provided for the scale-down and eventual abolition of tariffs between Belgium, the Netherlands and Luxemburg. Equally acclaimed (except by the UK), and just as speedily implemented, was French foreign minister Robert Schuman's proposal to place French and German coal and steel under a common authority. The anticipation of removing national rivalries from this strategic sector of industry appealed also to the Benelux countries and to Italy, who partnered France and Germany in the European Coal and Steel Community. What the Nordic countries did not immediately realize, and later chose to ignore, was these agreements – not the European Army or the Council of Europe or OEEC – were the real forerunners for the Rome Treaty and the European Community. Failing to see any benefit for themselves in the wider European movement they turned away from the continent to concentrate their efforts on strengthening the concept of Norden as a political and economic entity.

A not very promising start was made with an attempt to co-ordinate defence policies. The impetus was provided by the communist takeover of Czechoslovakia in 1948, a timely reminder of the vulnerability of the smaller democracies to the predatory tendencies of a powerful neighbour. Sweden took the initiative. 'It was', prime minister Erlander later recalled, 'my only serious attempt to do something significant for Nordic co-operation.' His enthusiasm for a defence agreement was to be expected. That Sweden emerged from the war without suffering

a German occupation was the result of good fortune supplemented by skilful manœuvring in the twilight world of Nazi
diplomacy. But there was a limit to ingenuity and luck which
few were prepared to test against the new power structure in
Europe. With the growing threat of east–west confrontation
Sweden felt the need for others to join her in proclaiming the
virtues of neutrality. Naturally she looked first to Norway and
Denmark. Both countries had kept out of international power
politics before the war and their ruling social-democrat parties
had strong neutralist sympathies. Talks on the possible shape of
a defence treaty started in the spring of 1948.

Early on it was made clear that Norway had serious reservations. The traumatic experience of five years' enemy occupation
argued strongly against a return to isolationism. Moreover, the
Norwegians had developed close political and personal contacts
with the West through their government in exile in London.
Frequent discussions on the question of post-war security had
produced a consensus in favour of an alliance with the US, a
solution first mooted as early as 1940.

The preference for staying outside the two main power blocs
was far stronger in Denmark. Though sharing with Norway the
humiliation of a German occupation, leading politicians had
not had the chance to escape and were consequently less influenced by military thinking in the West. But there was a noticeable shift in opinion towards a wider measure of security than
could be provided by a Nordic grouping after the communist
coup in Czechoslovakia seemed to prove that a small country
protesting neutrality was no safer now than when Germany was
on the march.

While these various points of view were being considered by
a joint defence commission, interest focused on events in Finland, another small power apparently destined to fall victim to
Russian colonization, and one for which sympathy was all the
stronger because it was part of the Scandinavian family. Finland
had ended the war a defeated country. The 1947 peace treaty
with Russia which confirmed the annexation of one-eighth of
her territory and the payment of heavy reparations was quickly
followed by a pact of Friendship, Co-operation and Mutual
Assistance which required Finland to confer with her neighbour
if war threatened and to accept Russian aid. It is easy in retro-

spect to interpret this agreement as a great victory for moderation and for Paasikivi's negotiating skills, a first step in Finland's progression towards genuine neutrality. But at the time it seemed far more likely that the treaty would pull Finland deeper into the Soviet sphere of influence.

It was against this background that the defence commission came out publicly with the admission that aggression against Scandinavia by a major power could only be repulsed with outside help. Even in the unlikely event of the mainland surviving the brunt of an attack, protection of the outlying parts of Norden – Iceland, Greenland, The Faeroes, the Norwegian island of Jan Mayen and the Svalbard archipelago, all of which occupied strategic positions in the Atlantic – was well beyond the bounds of practical logistics. Doubt too was cast on Sweden's capacity to supply the necessary military hardware for a Scandinavian defence union.

America was the other possible source of cheap weapons, but she was prepared to help only if the recipients agreed to cooperate in a wider European defence plan. Sweden resisted, claiming that non-alignment was the first requirement of a Nordic union. The argument did not impress the Norwegians, whose instinctive preference for an understanding with the United States was reinforced by the views of the military advisers, who held that Scandinavia could not protect itself unaided. The Soviet pressure on Finland could easily be imposed on other north European countries; indeed, *was* already being imposed, since Stalin had let it be known that Norway could soon expect an invitation to sign a mutual assistance pact.

Still inhibited by her neutralist tradition, Denmark was slower to commit herself. Russia appeared not to be interested in Danish territory, though it was conceded that her attitude could change if Norway sought protection from the West. Another consideration favouring an Atlantic agreement was the status of Greenland. In 1941 the Danish ambassador to Washington, Henrik Kauffman, authorized the US to build two air bases on the island, an initiative later to prove invaluable when America was ferrying supplies to Europe and the sea lanes were threatened by German U-boats. With technological advances in air transport the strategic importance of Greenland actually increased, since it did not escape notice that the shortest air route between the industrial heartlands of the US and the Soviet Union crossed directly over the island. Hence America's interest in renewing the agreement after the war – a request which Denmark could hardly refuse if she valued Washington's good will and wanted a share in economic aid. But to comply was to invite Soviet anger, and that might also be difficult to resist. 'It would be unrealistic to believe', warned Kauffman, 'that the American people would be so grateful for a new Greenland agreement that this would prompt the USA to go to war if Russia demanded bases in Denmark. ...' The only realistic choice, he believed, was for his country to guarantee its defence by joining an Atlantic pact.

While the talks with Sweden neared deadlock, progress was being made elsewhere on a defence structure for the rest of Europe. What had started as the Western European Union, bringing together Britain, France, Belgium, the Netherlands and Luxemburg, ostensibly to protect themselves against a re-surgent Germany, had now, with a strong injection of support from America, expanded to become the North Atlantic Treaty Organization. Norway and Denmark both knew that if the Scandinavian union came to nothing, membership of NATO was an open offer.

First to accept was Norway, though not before she had run the gauntlet of Russian protests. The Soviets expected NATO membership to lead to foreign air and naval bases on Norwegian territory, allowing the West to control access to the Baltic. In the north Russia was vulnerable along its narrow border with Norway, while naval vessels from Murmansk (where latterly a large proportion of the Soviet fleet is based) had to pass through the Barents Sea and the Norwegian Sea to reach the outside world. An attempt was made to nullify Soviet complaints with an unequivocal declaration forbidding foreign bases on Nor-wegian soil as long as the country was not attacked or exposed to threats of attack. The condition was not greatly disturbing to other NATO members but served in helping to win support at home from those who wanted to preserve some links with their neutralist past. The formula worked again a few years later when a ban was put on the storage of nuclear weapons on Norwegian territory.

The rumbling of Soviet anger continued to be heard in Oslo,

its volume rising whenever Norwegian troops took part in NATO exercises or when allied forces visited the country. Mostly it was diplomatic play-acting, since it did not take a logistics expert to realize that, whatever restrictions there were on the stationing of NATO units, Norway had more than adequate drawing rights on American forces based in Germany and Iceland. Likewise the nuclear guarantees made less of an impression as the destructive power of the opposing blocs increased in quantity, range and accuracy.

After Norway joined the Atlantic pact it was only a matter of time before Denmark followed suit. There were thoughts of a bilateral defence treaty between Sweden and Denmark but, lacking the third obvious partner, the plan failed to serve either basic defence needs or the cause of active neutrality. In line with the Norwegian example, Danish membership was made contingent on the exclusion of foreign bases (except in Greenland) and nuclear stockpiles on any of her territory including Greenland so that, it was said, military security could be balanced with the freedom to conduct an independent foreign policy leaning towards *détente* and conciliation with the East.

Iceland too joined NATO. In fact, of the Nordic group she was first in, notwithstanding that she did not have any armed forces of her own and that by agreement with Denmark she was pledged to 'eternal neutrality'. But Iceland was not invited, nor did she expect to participate in the negotiations for a Nordic defence treaty. It would have been a pointless exercise. In any case, with an American force already established on the island it was natural that she should look to the United States for her first line of defence. Domestic discord centring on the continuation of what some regarded as an American occupation was settled, for the time being, by the 1946 agreement which allowed the US military to share control of Keflavík Airport.

Sweden was left alone, but her faith in neutrality was, if anything, strengthened by the experience of failing to sponsor a Nordic alliance. The relationship between Finland and Russia was so delicately balanced that if, by some amazing volte-face, Sweden had decided to throw in her lot with the West, the temptation for Moscow to take tighter hold of the only part of Scandinavia outside American influence would have been overwhelming. Quite apart from any feelings of loyalty between members of the Nordic family, a satellite Finland on the model of Hungary or Romania could not possibly have served the interests of either Sweden or the NATO powers. Events thus compelled Sweden to take the line of least resistance, something she had wanted to do all along, anyway.

There remained the problem of financing the military back-up needed to make neutrality a credible policy. It was essential that no other country, including the superpowers, should assume as part of their grand strategy that Sweden was an easy victim. Fortunately post-war Sweden was in better economic shape than the rest of Europe and she already had the techno-logical base for a modern armaments industry, including the capacity, if she ever cared to use it, to produce nuclear weapons. It was a heavy burden for a small country – by 1960 she was the world's fourth biggest defence spender per capita – but with no alternative on offer, the taxpayers could take consolation in knowing that they were buying for themselves a place in world affairs enjoyed by no other country of comparable size.

There were better prospects for a trade agreement – or so it must have seemed in 1950 – when the Bramsnæs Committee, led by the chairman of the Danish National Bank, reported favourably on the advantages of a customs union taking in Sweden, Iceland, Norway and Denmark. But against the argument that joint investment and economies of scale would improve Scandinavian competitiveness, the Norwegians (ironi-cally it was they who had suggested the enquiry) set doubts that their infant industries could survive in the open Nordic market. While achieving one of the highest national investment rates in Europe, Norway felt the need for more time to recover from the war. As Norway was protected by higher tariffs than Sweden or Denmark, a commitment to free trade called not just for faith in industry to thrive on its merits but trust in her partners not to be too aggressive in their commercial dealings. It was asking a lot. Thought was given to breaking the deadlock by completing a Danish–Swedish agreement which the Norwegians could feel free to join whenever they judged their economy to be ready, but it was quickly realized that, far from allowing Norway a breathing space, a one-sided deal would force her to look to an expansion of her trade beyond Scandinavia, thus further reduc-ing the chances of Nordic economic union.

In the end, Norway suggested and the others accepted a delaying tactic whereby the Bramsnæs Committee was instructed to examine specific areas where tariffs could be abolished without harming any national interests. Denmark made the way easier by agreeing to exclude agriculture, still her first industry and one in which she was so far ahead of her Scandinavian competitors that, given a free market, she was quite capable of putting Norwegian and Swedish farmers out of business. Recommendations for a customs agreement covering more than twenty industries were duly made; Norway rejected them. Sweden and Denmark now suggested making a start with no more than eight products: furniture, dyes, porcelain, leather and shoes, agricultural machinery and machine tools, textiles, chemicals and radio sets. If successful the project could be extended to take in other goods. A Norwegian counter-proposal ignored the tariff issue altogether, urging co-operation in specific areas of economic development and industrial research. One idea, already explored in a different context, was for Danish and Swedish capital to be used to increase Norwegian hydro-electric capacity on behalf of all Scandinavia. A compromise merging both lines of thought was put on the agenda of a meeting of senior ministers held at Harpsund, the summer residence of the Swedish prime minister, in November 1954. The result was another committee, briefed to put together a programme of economic co-operation. Three years later it produced a five-volume report which included a plan for a customs union covering eighty per cent of Scandinavian trade. Norway turned it down. Prime minister Gerhardsen, who was personally in favour of closer trade co-operation, as were many of his social-democrat supporters, possibly surprised some of his Nordic colleagues when he declared that the door was still open for a commercial agreement.

That Norway had genuine difficulties in sorting out her trade policy was undeniable. As the smallest of the three Scandinavian economies, her fear of domination by Swedish enterprise was accentuated by her relatively brief experience of independence and recent memories of German occupation. It was also a matter for concern that seventy per cent of her business was outside Norden. To join a Scandinavian customs union was therefore to risk offending some of her best customers, who might be tempted to retaliate. From a strictly nationalistic point of view, which was put most forcefully by the non-socialist parties, it was in Norway's interests to prolong the negotiations until she had secured her industrial base and could meet competition with greater confidence. She did not want to lose the Nordic connection but, at this stage, neither did she want to bind herself too closely.

Norway's prevarication on international trade might have proved more irritating for her neighbours if she had been equally obstructive in other areas of co-operation. But along with the other Scandinavian states she responded constructively, if cautiously, to a plan for setting up a permanent institution, where affairs of common Nordic interest and suggestions for joint action could be debated. The initiative came from Danish prime minister Hans Hedtoft, who had taken a leading part in the defence negotiations and was a keen supporter of closer ties between the Nordic countries. Speaking at a gathering of the Nordic Interparliamentary Union, a discussion club for senior politicians, Hedtoft called for a Nordic Council, to be composed of representatives of the national parliaments.

The idea appealed on several levels. Though intended as an innovatory body, the Council was to be purely advisory; no country had to worry about surrendering any part of its sovereignty. Though occasionally a pooling of resources might be suggested to achieve a particular objective, each case could be decided on its merits. The Council had another virtue which appealed to the Nordic sense of economy. It was a means of salvaging part of the effort expended on the abortive defence treaty, not to mention the customs union, though at the time there was still slight hope of saving the latter.

Hedtoft was an ideal promoter for the scheme. As a leading social democrat he was listened to with respect by his party colleagues abroad; and he had time to give to the project. In 1950 his party lost power to a liberal–conservative coalition. As opposition spokesman, Hedtoft devoted much of his energy to persuading the social-democrat prime ministers of Norway and Sweden to go along with his plan. He was supported by an Interparliamentary Union committee representing all five Nordic countries. Apart from Hedtoft, the committee consisted of two social democrats – Oscar Torp (Norway) and Karl-

August Fagerholm (Finland) – and two conservatives – Sigurd-ur Bjarnason (Iceland) and Nils Herlitz (Sweden). It was Herlitz who produced the first draft constitution for the Council, an honour which he could genuinely describe as unexpected, since he had imagined that Hedtoft had taken on the responsi-bility. When he found that this was not so he put forward the proposals he had set out in the course of a single morning.

Bringing in Finland was a brave move, which raised the whole question of how best to accommodate this member of the Nordic family without upsetting her domineering and fre-quently touchy eastern neighbour. No one doubted that what had happened in Czechoslovakia in 1948 could just as easily recur in Scandinavia. All it needed was for the Soviet Union to sense provocation in Finland's attempts to run her own affairs. Her spokesman on the Interparliamentary committee, Karl-August Fagerholm, was a master tactician who had learned his trade in the hard school of Finnish presidential government. He put a high value on Nordic co-operation but, as a social demo-crat who was not trusted by the Russians, he was aware of his own and his country's limitations. While helping to give much to the Council by successfully advocating that governments should be required to report back on recommendations made to them, he let it be known that for Finland to continue playing an active role, foreign and defence policy had to be excluded from Nordic Council deliberations. Even so, Russia declared the infant body to be 'a creature of NATO aggression', and when the Council was set up in 1952 there were only four members – Denmark, Iceland, Norway and Sweden. It was three years before the Soviet attitude softened and Finland felt able to join the Nordic club.

Fears that the Norwegians would follow precedent by pur-suing an exhaustive search for real or imagined difficulties turned out to be unjustified. There was a moment of panic when Torp failed to appear at the critical meeting of the Interparlia-mentary Union committee in October 1951, but his message of personal support for the Nordic Council was interpreted as an assurance that rumblings of opposition at home would be con-tained. When it came to identifying specific Norwegian causes of complaint, the only serious objection came from the conser-vatives, who disapproved of government members of the

proposed council being allowed to vote. The question was discussed at a special conference of the Interparliamentary Union
and at a meeting of the Nordic foreign ministers in Copenhagen
in March, but it was not until the last moment that Norwegian
wishes were acknowledged by a suitable amendment to the
Council's draft statutes. In June the proposals for setting up a
Nordic Council came before the Scandinavian parliaments. The
Norwegian Storting voted in favour by seventy-four to thirty-
nine, a resounding success for the internationalists but one
which paled in comparison to the achievement of their colleagues in the Danish and Swedish assemblies, where approval
was unanimous.

Despite warnings against an immediate preoccupation with
economic matters voiced by, among others, Norwegian foreign
minister Halvard Lange, one of the first acts of the Nordic
Council was to support yet another inquiry aimed at calming
Norway's fears of a customs union. The collapse, or rather the
fading, of this initiative after the 1954 Harpsund conference in
no way deterred the Council from trying other means to adapt
the economic pattern. An early success which seemed to show
that unity was to be won not by a full-length jump but by a
gradual step-by-step progression was the introduction of a free
labour market. In 1954 the system of work permits controlling
the cross-border flow of labour in Scandinavia was abolished.
The agreement was conditional on the four governments' holding to a policy of full employment and keeping each other in
touch with work development plans. A year later Denmark,
Norway, Iceland and Sweden agreed to the transfer of social
security benefits for people moving from one country to another.
The labour reform did not extend to civil servants or the professions for which nationality determined qualifications and conditions of service varied greatly. To bring these groups into line
was one of the tasks of the Nordic Labour Market Committee;
but with old-established restrictive practices to overcome, de-
lays were inevitable. It was not until 1965 that doctors and
dentists were granted the same rights as less skilled citizens, and
today teachers are still waiting to be given their Nordic status.

Even so, to have pushed through the labour market and
social-security conventions was a remarkable achievement for
a young international organization. Once Finland had joined

the Council and accepted the principle of free labour movement, a Nordic citizen could go looking for a job in any of the
five countries without even bothering to carry a passport. Moreover he was entitled to all the social benefits of the country in
which he settled, a bonus welcomed especially by the growing
number of itinerant Finns attracted by the high industrial wages
in southern Sweden. At first solicited by an economy hungry for
workers, they were later to be the centre of an immigration crisis
– but that was a problem for another decade.

While the Nordic Council was testing its authority, continental Europe was preparing to set up its own body for consultation
and co-operation, with expectations that were pitched much
higher than those set by the northern countries. Six nations –
France, Germany, Italy, the Netherlands, Belgium and Luxemburg – gathered at Messina in June 1955 to talk about
European unity. With economic co-operation dominating the
agenda, the idea for a customs union was generally welcomed.
The alternative of a simple tariff reduction was ruled out by the
General Agreement on Tariffs and Trade, which pledged the
twenty-three member states not to lower duties to each other
without extending the same concessions to the rest of the world.
But GATT did allow for the abolition of duties between two or
more countries where the intention was to set up a common
external tariff. This was how the Benelux customs union came
to be formed; and more and more it seemed to be the best
opportunity for the bigger powers – France, Germany and Italy
– to achieve the economic co-operation they all desired. Any
fears that the supranational institutions needed for such an
enterprise could not be made to work were stilled by the entirely
beneficial experience of the Coal and Steel Community. It was
thus an easy decision at Messina to appoint an inter-governmental committee, chaired by the Belgian foreign minister
Paul-Henri Spaak, to explore ways of creating a European
customs union. Spaak was urged to make speed. The German
elections were due, and while the European economies were
booming no one could be sure how long the mood of confidence
would last.

Spaak broke diplomatic records by taking less than a year to
produce a report which was, in effect, a draft treaty for the
European Economic Community and the European Atomic

Energy Commission (Euratom). The Six were to commit themselves to the eventual free movement of goods, capital and labour across their internal borders while erecting a tariff wall against outsiders. But there was more to the Community than the harmonization of economic policies: this was seen as simply the first move towards the great objective – political integration. Ratified by the member states in just a few months, the Treaty of Rome came into force on 1 January 1958.

The Nordic countries kept well away from the Community negotiations. Finland was automatically excluded by her association with Russia, Sweden would do nothing to impinge her neutrality and Denmark, Norway and Sweden together were unable to shake off their distrust of mainstream European politics. Even so, an attempt to reach an understanding with the EEC might have been made if the economic indicators had pointed that way. But from a strictly commercial view there was a lot to be said for procrastination, at least until Britain, the leading trade partner of Scandinavia, had made up her mind about her relationship with Europe. Britain shared most of the Nordic reservations but had a few on her own account. Her chief problem was in deciding whether or not she was still a world power. The Second World War had deprived her of the best of her foreign investments and, with huge loans to the United States to pay off and costly welfare programmes to implement, she lacked the resources to regenerate industry and exports. Yet Britain behaved as if she had emerged from the 1940s with limitless wealth at her disposal and her international authority undiminished. Throwing troops into this or that crisis and promising to defend those, including some close neighbours, who might just as well have defended themselves, Britain deluded herself into believing that Europe needed her more than she needed Europe. Support for this view was to be found in the comforting reassurances from across the Atlantic that whatever else happened the special relationship between Britain and the United States promised access to the latest military technology. A sense of power came too from association with other English-speaking countries. Loyalty to what was left of the Empire was fostered by the hope that the Commonwealth could soon shape itself into a major power bloc.

In the early post-war period Britain joined in only those

efforts at co-operation which did not require her to surrender any part of her sovereignty. With Labour in power a greater stress on the virtues of internationalism might have been expected, but the last thing the government wanted was European interference in its plans for creating a socialist economy. When the Conservatives came back in 1951 the case against Europe was strengthened by growing national confidence and a return to traditional values: as Harold Macmillan rather loftily observed in the parliamentary debate on the Coal and Steel Community, 'One thing is certain, and we may as well face it. Our people will not hand over to a supranational authority the right to close our pits or our steelworks.' Further implied and sometimes openly stated was the conviction that whatever Britain's view on an issue like this, the other Europeans would soon fall into line. To many, therefore, it came as a genuine surprise that the Coal and Steel Community was able to work effectively without UK participation. But at most the ECSC was seen as a mildly interesting experiment which if successful might help rationalize continental industry. The only threat to British commercial interests was in the guarantee of sharper competition. The Rome Treaty was quite another matter. The prospect of an EEC external tariff high enough to restrain imports from non-members raised the fear of a trade war between Britain and her closest neighbours. It was bad enough contemplating virtual exclusion from one of the richest and most accessible export markets, but there was also the nightmare of becoming the dumping ground for the Community's surplus produce. The concern was shared by the Nordic countries, particularly Denmark, whose second best market for agricultural exports was West Germany.

Britain was quickly converted to the idea of broadening the scope of the Common Market to allow for the associate membership of those countries who were prepared to remove obstacles to European trade but who fought shy of other commitments, including the common external tariff. It was a middle way which appealed to the Scandinavians, as to Austria and Switzerland, who also wanted a trade agreement without political strings. Since there was no objection in principle from the Six to a formula already commended by the Spaak Report, the two sides agreed to a OECD working party to 'study the

possible forms and methods of association'. Meanwhile, however, the programme for ratifying the Treaty of Rome went
ahead as planned, a warning to Britain and her friends that the
Six were not to be diverted from their course.

While negotiations were left to the officials the chances of an
agreement were thought to be good. It was quickly acknowledged, for instance, that the main issue, reconciling the
British support system for agriculture with the continental preference for allowing retail food prices to find their natural level,
was open to compromise. But when the politicians started talking, practical economic considerations took second place to the
long-standing antagonism between Britain and France. France
was the least enthusiastic participant in the European Community. Protectionist by tradition, politically unstable, nervous
of a revival of German ambitions for continental hegemony, she
was carried along by the willingness of her EEC partners to meet
nearly all her demands for special treatment. The few sacrifices
France was called upon to make were more than compensated
by the deeply satisfying knowledge that Britain was to be left
out in the cold. The conflict between the two countries was born
of a sense of national superiority which each found irritating
and faintly ludicrous when claimed by the other. In the 1930s
and '40s Anglo-French co-operation was secured by mutual fear
of German expansionism; but by the mid-fifties when anti-German feeling was almost burned out, the old sense of rivalry
reasserted itself. Britain's efforts to liberalize the Community
constitution were thus destined for failure from the moment
that France signed the Treaty of Rome. This became obvious
when, in mid-negotiation, the frail Fourth Republic collapsed
and Charles de Gaulle came to power. Chauvinism personified,
the general turned president saw himself as the natural leader
of the Six, who were expected to support him in what he believed
to be his first duty – to free Europe from the Anglo-Saxon
tutelage. In November 1958, after eighteen months of talks, the
French government declared that the European Community
would not be extended to provide a half-way house for reluctant
members. It was all or nothing – and in Britain's case, it was
implied, preferably nothing. Negotiations were broken off.

Reactions in Norden pointed up the differences which were
to bedevil trade relations in that area over the next decade. In

Norway the failure of the British initiative was greeted with relief. She had felt bound to follow the lead of her largest export market but was frankly distrustful of even a limited involvement in European affairs. Denmark had taken a more positive line, calculating that EEC association would yield great benefits for her farmers. Sweden too was disappointed, though she expected as a result of the setback to gather more support for a Nordic customs union which could then bargain effectively with the Community. In this she was mistaken, finding that Denmark, previously the strongest advocate of a Nordic trade arrangement, was now less than excited by the local option, preferring instead to keep alive the hope of achieving a free-trade convention extending well beyond Scandinavia. They were all agreed, however, on the need to preserve the sense of common interest with European countries outside the Community. Some time before the French had put up their diplomatic blockades, the industrial and employers' organizations of Sweden, Norway, Denmark, Austria, Switzerland, Portugal and the UK put together a programme for tariff reductions which was in no way dependent on EEC approval. Was not now the moment to apply it? To act together was to prove that a free-trade association could be made to work, and at the same time to show France that she had created a formidable opposition.

Everything depended on how Britain as the major trade partner viewed the future. In the anger of the moment various retaliatory moves against the EEC were debated but dismissed as impracticable. A transatlantic trade pact was a popular alternative until it was realized that the benefits were negligible. Even the grand imperial concept of a free trade area encompassing the entire Commonwealth was revived briefly only to be put back to rest when it was recalled that young countries eager to industrialize were sensitive about opening up their markets. In the end, the only counter-grouping to make any sense was one which brought together those who had favoured associate membership of the EEC – Norway, Sweden, Denmark, Britain, Austria, Switzerland and Portugal, or the Outer Seven, as they were soon to be called.

Between Britain and the Scandinavians there was already a strong basis for co-operation. The pattern of trade which made Britain the single most important customer of Nordic exporters was long enough established to be counted almost as a permanency of life. Since the setting up of Uniscan in 1949 there had been regular economic consultations between the four countries, whose representatives kept friendly contact throughout the negotiations with the EEC.

The idea of an exchange of trade privileges between the Seven was especially attractive to Sweden, the second largest commercial power among the European outsiders. Here was an opportunity to secure easier access to the heavily protected British market without giving much in return, since Swedish tariffs were relatively low. But more than that, if Britain and Sweden and Denmark together led the way to a free-trade area, Norway was bound to follow to avoid isolation. In other words it was a means, and possibly the only means, of overcoming Norwegian resistance to the prime objective of a Nordic common market, the dismantling of trade barriers between the Scandinavian countries. This development in Swedish thinking explains her sudden coolness when the Nordic common market proposal was revived for a meeting of Scandinavian prime ministers in January 1959. Like Denmark she had decided that if she had to belong to an economic club then Britain had better be a member. Moreover, she was now convinced that the best chance of achieving a Nordic trade pact was to make it part of a wider European agreement.

But for Britain the attractions of a partnership on the outskirts of Europe were by no means clear-cut. On a population count the Seven offered a combined market of ninety million; but of that total, Britain accounted for well over half. The comparative figure for the European Community was 230 million, an imbalance which suggested that the EEC was not to be easily coerced. Then again, if the main objective was to put pressure on France, it had to be acknowledged that her links with the Seven were of minor significance. Only fourteen per cent of her trade was with the Outer Seven, as against twenty-six per cent with Germany. If anything, Britain's prospects for a new round of EEC negotiations were weakened by the projected trade alliance, since she was planning to get involved with three neutrals – Sweden, Switzerland and Austria – who were irretrievably at odds with the political clauses of the Rome Treaty. But, lacking an alternative counter-policy to the EEC, Britain's pride would not allow her to reject the European Free Trade Association. She could not pass up the opportunity of showing that the principles by which she had stood in her dealings with the Community really did have practical application.

After preliminary talks between the trade ministers of Britain and the Nordic group, the Swiss took the initiative in calling a meeting of the Seven at Geneva in December 1958. Agreement in principle was secured without difficulty – much of the groundwork had been covered in the OEEC negotiations – and officials of the participating governments were brought together first in Oslo and a little later in Stockholm to work on the details. With Britain not wanting to take a leading role in what might have been seen by the Community as an act of vindictiveness, it fell to Sweden in the person of Hubert de Besche, secretary general of the foreign office, to produce a draft convention. This was approved at a ministerial meeting in Stockholm in July 1959 and signed the following January.

The Stockholm Convention adopted the same timetable for the reduction of tariffs as that set by the EEC. The target year for the abolition of duties was 1970. The elimination of quantitative import restrictions, a form of protectionism favoured by some countries with serious balance-of-payments problems like Denmark and Norway but virtually unknown in Britain and Sweden, required sensitive handling. Sacrifices and benefits had to be seen to be shared equally. But after the tough negotiations with the Community, whose leaders meanwhile reasserted their determination that the removal of trade barriers against the Seven could only be achieved within the framework of the Rome Treaty, the mood of the EFTA partners was conducive to friendly understanding and mutual concessions. If the feeling of *camaraderie* stopped short at trying to open the markets for agriculture and fishing, both of which were excluded from the EFTA agreement, Britain lifted a ten per cent duty on bacon to please Danish farmers and helped the sale of Norwegian frozen fish by the expedient of counting it as an industrial product.

A special problem for the Nordic contingent in EFTA was the status of Finland. Obviously there was enthusiasm for her participation, but experience had shown that Russia was less than understanding about any agreement which could possibly be interpreted as political in nature. EFTA was frequently proclaimed as a purely business arrangement, but there were members who made no secret of their desire to get closer to the EEC, and no one could doubt the political elements in that organization. Finland herself was attracted to any proposal which allowed her to diversify her trade and made her less dependent on the Soviet Union. This was to continue a trend started in the fifties, soon after the completion of reparation payments when Russia accounted for twenty per cent of Finnish exports. By 1960 the proportion had dropped to fifteen per cent, with the difference being made up by the expansion of sales to Western Europe. Imports too showed an increasingly western bias as tariff reductions secured by GATT (Finland joined in 1949) began to take effect. Now, with two trade associations carving up the European market between them, a reverse movement was threatened.

Moscow was unequivocally opposed to any Finnish deal with the EEC; but the circumstances in which EFTA was formed and the declared intention of its members to restrict themselves to matters of commerce made the prospects of Finnish participation not unattractive. It was in the Soviet interest that Finland, a rich export market with easy access to western technology, should continue to develop her economy, yet her leaders were suggesting that unless EFTA rules could be adapted to suit Finland's special needs, prosperity was at risk. With the tacit approval of the Soviet Union and in the knowledge that EFTA understood the Finnish dilemma, the negotiating teams started work. From the beginning it was made clear that Finland was not so much seeking to join EFTA as to secure an entirely new free-trade association, with the Seven as one party to the agreement and Finland as the other. This subtle distinction was not lost on the Russians, who felt reassured by the changes required in the EFTA administrative structure to permit the Council, the highest body representing the Seven, to become the Joint Council when it was dealing with purely Finnish affairs. It was a reminder to all that Finland was different.

Access to Finland for Soviet exporters was protected by the 1947 commercial treaty, though trade between the two countries was by no means free. Here then was the opportunity to give Russia a positive gain from the negotiations by extending to her the tariff reductions introduced under the FINEFTA agreement. Interestingly, Finland did not feel compelled to grant most favoured nation status to the socialist states of Eastern Europe. Consequently business with those countries declined steadily after 1961, when Finland became an associate member of EFTA.

Iceland took longer to prepare herself for the challenges of free trade. In the 1950s the country was still dependent on fishing for nearly all overseas earnings, the level of which fluctuated wildly according to the state of the harvest and the buoyancy of the international market. In an effort to bring a semblance of order to the national revenues, agreements were sought with countries willing to offer long-term guarantees on the purchase of fish products. But these customers, which included six Eastern European states with Spain, Israel and Finland, in turn wanted an assurance that Iceland would put business their way. This required a complex system of licences and multiple exchange rates to ensure that selected imports were ordered from her fish-buying partners. A change of policy favouring trade liberalization came at about the same time as the EFTA states were signalling accord on the abolition of import restrictions. But what was on offer from the Seven was almost totally irrelevant to Iceland's immediate needs. Until she had diversified her economy, all she had to sell was fish; and that product was specifically omitted from the EFTA negotiating brief. That it would long continue to be so was suggested by the unresolved and bitter dispute between Iceland and Britain over the twelve-mile fishery limits.

The creation of new export opportunities was unexpectedly protracted, and Iceland continued to suffer economically from the vagaries of the fishing industry. In 1967–8 the failure of the herring harvest, caused mainly by over-fishing and the collapse of export prices, brought about the worst crisis the country had experienced since the 1930s. But even as real income was cut by sixteen per cent, it was possible to find an encouraging trend in the returns on the latest industrial investment – the aluminium and diatomite plants, for example, as well as the smaller manufacturing enterprises based on Icelandic raw materials such as wood, fur and skins. With the future of the country's staple commodity at best uncertain, it

was time to encourage alternative exports by gaining easier
access to European markets. In late 1968 Iceland asked to join
EFTA but on terms that were favourable to the expansion of her
infant industries. She wanted immediate duty-free access to
EFTA markets for all products covered by the Stockholm Convention but offered in return only a gradual reduction of her
import duties. A sympathetic hearing was guaranteed from her
Nordic friends who backed their judgement of Iceland as a
special case by linking membership of EFTA with the provision
of interest-free development loans via a Nordic Industrialization
Fund. Eventually the EFTA partners settled for an immediate
thirty per cent cut in Iceland's domestic tariffs with further
gradual reductions leading to abolition in ten years. The Seven
became Eight plus Finland in March 1970.

The Stockholm Convention lived up to the determination of
its signatories to be pragmatic in all things; not to be hidebound
by general principles or constitutional niceties. But the absence
of a permanent arbitration body made for difficulties in inter-
preting a code of behaviour that eschewed precise definitions.
It was one thing to prohibit policies which 'frustrate the benefits
expected from the removal or absence of duties and quantitative
restrictions on trade between member states', but what means
was there of assessing 'benefits' or of judging what constituted
'frustration'? The hours of discussion devoted to procedural
matters by the Council or its delegations deterred any immediate thoughts of extending the area of co-operation. It was only
when hopes of closing the gap between the EEC and EFTA were
frustrated that attempts were made to strengthen the rules and
to make the organization a more effective pressure group in
international affairs.

In its early years, EFTA's sole reason for existence was the
expansion of trade within the partnership. This it achieved,
even if the rewards were shared disproportionately. As generally
anticipated, Britain gained little. The market was too diffuse for
her to pitch her energies into an export drive. In any case, for
reasons only marginally to do with the European trade war, five
of Britain's founder partners (Portugal was the exception) were
heading for a period of rapid growth and consumer sophistica-
tion which put them beyond the range of much of British mass
manufacturing. The UK industrialist was schooled in the belief

that selling abroad depended on keeping prices down, even at the expense of quality. His German counterpart, who took the opposite view, had an easier ride into the rich markets of Europe.

Those who did best out of EFTA were the Nordic countries: it was their success story. In the first decade trade between the EFTA members increased by 186 per cent; but between Norway, Sweden, Denmark, Finland and Iceland the gain was 284 per cent. The most remarkable advance was the proportion of Finnish trade with EFTA, which rose to over 50 per cent by the end of the sixties, even though in that period trade with the UK actually declined. The surprising explanation was that business with Sweden had thrived – a development no one had anticipated because traditionally the two countries were trying to sell the same products. But Finland had taken advantage of her new-found commercial freedom to extend the range of her exports to take in machinery and metal goods, textiles, furniture and glassware; often distinctively designed and expensive items that had their strongest appeal in the other Scandinavian markets. The Nordic achievement with EFTA was only partly the result of commercial acumen: politics came into it as well. The fact of British involvement made Norway more relaxed about the possible effects of Swedish competition. But when it was shown that Sweden had neither the will nor the capacity to overwhelm her neighbours, irrespective of any part Britain had to play, the way was open for other forms of co-operation. These in turn created an environment which was conducive to good business.

Expansion was healthiest in consumer products. The general rise in economic activity bringing full employment and higher living standards, combined with the cut in what overall had been the highest rates of duty, stimulated manufacturers to look beyond the home market. Once over the border, they soon realized their advantages over exporters from outside the Nordic area. There were no serious language problems, consumer tastes were similar and business legislation followed the same pattern. A director of the Federation of Swedish Industries maintained that the gain from using one's own language in export sales was equivalent to a five to seven per cent tariff preference. There was encouragement too from government trade departments, whose officials were instructed to think Nordic and to shower firms with offers of help and advice. The lead was followed by the commercial and professional organizations, so that companies who did well in the Nordic market were lauded by their peers, an experience ever calculated to spur on the recipients to further efforts. Nor was it only big business which benefited. As a leader of the Federation of Swedish Industries advised, 'Even a small manufacturer can take his car, his samples and his catalogues and cross the frontier with no more difficulty than he would have going to some out of the way part of his own country.'

Finally, there was the considerable influence of the Nordic Council, keen to act as a co-ordinating body in trade as in other areas of Scandinavian co-operation. Though meeting for only a week once a year, the Council had built a network of permanent committees for economics, communications and social policy and had set up special inquiries into such matters as employment policy. Best progress was made where the civil servants were allowed to beaver away without too much interference from their elected masters – customs control, railway freight tariffs, vehicle insurance. But on the bigger problems – those which were categorized as politically sensitive, like regional development, the harmonization of external tariffs and the extension of free trade to agricultural products – movement was barely perceptible. Co-operation was a long way short of integration.

The preoccupation of the Nordic countries with their own trade may have diverted attention from important changes in the British attitude to EFTA and to the rest of Europe. In any event it came as a surprise when, in 1961, Britain declared her conversion to the Treaty of Rome and her wish to reopen negotiations with the Community. That much of the conventional political wisdom of the fifties could be rejected so decisively was less a sign of brave new thinking as a belated admission that the old ideas were leading nowhere. The Suez débâcle of 1956, followed by the abandonment of a costly nuclear arms programme and with it any pretence of possessing an independent nuclear deterrent, brought home the fact that Britain was no longer capable of deciding her own destiny. It was the same with the economy. It only needed a run on sterling, a not infrequent occurrence, to prove that as a trading nation Britain was dangerously vulnerable to outside pressures. The old fallback, the special relationship with the United States, declined in value as the Americans acknowledged a shift of power in Europe away from Britain and redirected their attentions accordingly. Even the Commonwealth was a disappointment. With its growing proportion of newly independent black nations it was more often than not a source of opposition to British policy. The long-awaited expansion of trade had failed to materialize; more was exported to Western Europe than to all the Commonwealth countries put together. Hopes of building a world power bloc on the old imperial foundations were almost forgotten.

It seemed as if Britain could not do without Europe. One by one government members acknowledged that they had underestimated their neighbours; and yes, perhaps they should try to be more flexible in their dealings with the EEC. An admission from a senior minister that Britain had made a serious error in not joining the Schuman Plan negotiations was followed in mid-1960 by an announcement that Britain now wanted to be part of the Coal and Steel Community and Euratom. It became fashionable for politicians of the right to talk admiringly of the economic progress made by the Six and to suggest that open competition from that quarter might be just what was needed to mount a second industrial revolution at home. A dramatic reshaping of the government which brought forward pro-marketeers like Edward Heath, who was given special responsibility for relations with Europe, preceded a formal application in July 1961 for Britain to join the Community.

The response from her Nordic partners in EFTA revealed the wide differences that remained in attitudes towards European integration. Taking a severely practical view Denmark gave unqualified approval to a move which promised to secure freer access to her two best markets, Britain and West Germany. Her own request to be admitted to the EEC was snapped in to arrive in Brussels at the same time as that from Britain. Norway was more reserved. The business sector had gained sufficient confidence to see exciting possibilities in being part of a wider Europe but the farmers and fishermen felt threatened by EEC policies which affected their interests, and the opinion polls showed barely twenty-five per cent of the electorate positively in favour of EEC membership. In the Storting, however, a majority wanted to follow Britain. A split in EFTA was regrettable, especially if Sweden, a growing market for Norwegian exports, was left outside the Community, but in trade terms Britain was more important, and the similarity of views between the two countries on the need to preserve national freedom of action offered an insurance against the ambitions of supranational institutions. The other vital consideration, maintaining the strength of the Atlantic Alliance, was guaranteed by American support for an enlarged Community. In March 1962 Parliament approved a constitutional reform, first mooted in the early fifties in the debate on European defence, permitting the transfer to an international organization of powers normally vested in Norwegian authorities. In deference to popular opinion, the government promised that the final verdict on EEC membership would be subject to a referendum. In April 1962, nine months after Britain declared her commitment to Europe, Norway too announced that she wanted to be part of the Community.

Expectations that Sweden and possibly even Finland might follow her example soon faded. Both refused to compromise their neutrality, though Sweden asked for associate status under article 238 of the Rome Treaty, which would have allowed her certain trade concessions without a corresponding political involvement. But before serious thought could be given to the proposal there was a crisis in Anglo-French relations which put into doubt the whole future of an enlarged European Community. France complained that in acting on behalf of Commonwealth or EFTA friends by insisting that this or the other commodity should have special status, Britain was attempting to change the rules by which the Common Market was run, and so renege on her commitment to abide by the spirit of the Rome Treaty. This presumptuous behaviour, not entirely unexpected in view of Britain's wider responsibilities, might have been endured by the French had not the candidate given further and more damaging evidence of her contempt for Community principles by dealing with the Americans behind the backs of her European colleagues. The point at issue was prime minister Macmillan's effort to compensate for his government's inability to continue financing an independent nuclear deterrent by accepting an American offer of Polaris warheads to be installed in British-built submarines. De Gaulle took the news as a personal insult (even though a similar offer was made to France), since Macmillan had previously rejected his proposal to combine the resources of their two countries to produce an Anglo-French atomic force. Strictly in terms of creating an efficient defence system the British premier undoubtedly made the right decision, but it was at the cost of losing the initiative in the EEC. De Gaulle was now able to assert that by acting alone Britain had proved her unreliability as a prospective European partner. It was the breaking-point in the negotiations.

As a final dismissive gesture de Gaulle took on one side the Danish prime minister Jens Otto Krag, and told him that exclusion of the British did not mean that Denmark also had to leave. She was welcome to join the club. The offer was politely refused.

While the chances of the British application succeeding were still thought to be good, the Scandinavians tried to minimize any division in their ranks which might be caused by Denmark and Norway's joining the EEC by strengthening their links on the Nordic Council. The original agreement setting up the Council was loosely formulated to overcome any suspicions that here was a supranational authority in the making. There was not even a joint commitment to work together; just five declarations, one from each of the participating governments, accepting the principles of co-operation as itemized in the Council statutes. But after nearly a decade's experience of wholly beneficial deliberation on joint problems, there was a growing feeling that more should be done to promote to outsiders the idea of Nordic identity which, in its way, was as strong as the association of interests forged by the signatories to the Rome Treaty.

The 1961 session of the Nordic Council approved a resolution urging the governments to enter into a formal agreement of co-operation. For Finland, the transmitter of Soviet anxieties and therefore the country most likely to raise difficulties, the resolution was timed perfectly for securing Russia's endorsement. The completion of the FINEFTA arrangements promised well and, though soon afterwards relations with the Soviet Union entered a critical phase – Finland was about to suffer the agonies of the Note crisis whereby Moscow demanded consultation on joint defence measures in reaction to German rearmament and NATO activity in Norden (see page 96) – it was in these circumstances that Russia could see a positive advantage in Finland's having a closer attachment to her Scandinavian neighbours. Her influence might then be brought to bear on reducing the NATO presence in Denmark and Norway.

A draft convention agreed between the Council presidium and the Nordic premiers meeting at Hanko in Finland in late 1961 was presented to the full Nordic Council at its session in Helsinki the following March and ratified by the five governments by the end of the month. Much of the Helsinki Treaty was a restatement of what was already accepted practice. The recognition of the Council's right to be consulted on all questions of Nordic co-operation was seen as an important innovation, but the national governments could escape this obligation whenever urgency was the first consideration. No concessions were therefore made to supranational power. As a statement of intent, however, the treaty served its purpose in showing Europe that there was a Nordic voice to be heard and that it was not to be weakened by accessions to the Community.

The unexpected interlude in the negotiations for a wider Common Market refocused Nordic interest on EFTA as the only practical economic counter-force. In May 1963 at a meeting in Lisbon, the member states welcomed the acceleration of the date for achieving a completely free trade area. Industrial tariffs were to be abolished by the end of 1966. With the revival of interest in EFTA as something more than a half-way house for Community applicants, thought was given to increasing its range of influence by taking in the unattached members of the OECD, namely Iceland, Ireland, Spain and even Japan. But the mood of self-confidence disappeared abruptly when in October 1964 Britain tried to solve one of her periodic balance-of-payments crises by imposing an across-the-board fifteen per cent import surcharge. The action was known to be in breach of the Stockholm Convention but was taken without warning to Britain's EFTA partners. Their anger was all the greater because there was nothing they could do; the Association simply had no procedure for dealing with such cases.

The Danish reaction was a Folketing resolution authorizing the government to 'seek new ways of realizing the goal of Danish market policy; a comprehensive European Community'. This was taken to mean that British entry was no longer a precondition of Danish membership of the EEC. But there were other loyalties which deterred Denmark from making an independent bid for Community recognition. That the EEC ignored EFTA requests in 1966 and 1967 for a conference to 'facilitate the removal of trade barriers' suggested that Denmark's friends, including those in the Nordic sector, might not benefit at all from any initiative she might take. Indeed the prospects for any sort of breakthrough at this time were not hopeful, as was shown by the unsuccessful attempt by Austria to achieve an association agreement.

The prospects for trade liberalization were little brighter on the wider international scene, though as a side advantage of the long-drawn-out negotiations within GATT there were opportunities for Nordic co-operation which did not go to waste. In the mid-sixties there was an attempt to shift from the slow, painstaking product-by-product approach to freer trade, towards a bolder concept of across-the-board reductions. The Kennedy Round attracted only a dozen participants willing to negotiate on this basis, but these included the EEC acting as one unit. To put up a united front also made sense to the Nordic states, who soon noticed that the list of exceptions to any agreement favoured by the big four – USA, Japan, UK and the EEC – generally included products which figured high on the Nordic table of exports. Negotiating as a bloc, Denmark, Norway, Sweden and Finland could back up their argument for a more equitable trade pact – a straight fifty per cent tariff reduction across the board was their ideal – by pointing out that with total imports from the EEC of nearly 3.5 billion dollars, they ranked as the Community's best customer. Since far less was sold back to the EEC, the bargaining strength was with the Nordic countries, if they cared to use it.

There was at least one precedent for a Norden trade spokesman. At the 1956 GATT conference, Norway, Sweden and Finland used a joint negotiator to argue the case for lower tariffs on paper and pulp, a tactic which the other delegates had not previously encountered at their meetings and one which met with moderate success. Subsequently, at other negotiating tables, where each Nordic country had its own place, there were invariably prior consultations to try to work out a common approach. With the post-war rash of international organizations, those on the world conference circuit came to accept that the Nordic representatives generally spoke in unison.

Meetings between the heads of the trade departments of the Nordic foreign ministries started in the early 1950s and were soon established on a regular three-monthly basis. When the European free-trade movement and the attempts to join up with the Community widened the range of questions needing discussion, contacts between foreign ministers and ministers of commerce took on an added significance. Every high-level EFTA meeting was preceded by a purely Nordic session. Inevitably, topics of mutual interest ranged outside the European context. Policy co-ordination on international shipping – of vital importance to Norden, which registered the largest merchant tonnage in the world – and an understanding on how best to handle trade relations with the developing countries were among the achievements of this period. When the Helsinki Agreement on Nordic co-operation was signed in 1962, it was no more than a confirmation of what already existed to note that 'in issues of international commercial practice', every effort should be made '... to promote the interest of Nordic countries and with this purpose in view, to consult one another'.

But the Kennedy Round was something else again. Since it was impossible to win prior agreement on a policy for all aspects of international trade the proposal was to map out a framework of negotiation within which the Nordic frontman could have maximum room for manœuvre. But the individual economic interests of the four countries were sufficiently diverse as to create problems on the construction of the broadest rules of procedure. There was no counterpart for the role of agriculture in Danish exports, for example, or for the place of precision engineering as a foreign-currency earner for Sweden. There had to be some kind of check that the joint negotiator was labouring to achieve the best possible Nordic deal and not, perhaps unintentionally, serving the interests of one country at the expense of another. Concern was strongest in Denmark, and it was on a visit there that the Swedish premier, Tage Erlander, finally won approval for a formula which appeared to answer all objections. The chief negotiator was to work to a political briefing from the four capitals and to receive advice – though not necessarily assent – from four national deputy negotiators. Signatures were put to the agreement on 21 November 1966.

Because the Kennedy Round talks were held in Geneva, it was the Nordic ambassadors to Switzerland who qualified as deputies. Heading the team was a Swede, Nils Montàn, who had led the Norwegian–Swedish–Finnish delegation at the 1956 session of GATT. In so far as it was proved that a combined assault in a highly technical area of negotiation could be achieved without first building the sort of institutional pyramid much favoured by the European Community, the experiment was a great success. The Nordic group was accepted as an equal with the other key economic powers, and so gained access to the informal but decisive bargaining which took place outside the main conference.

The results were good for Nordic manufacturing industry. An average reduction on tariffs of thirty-five per cent, including a cut of nearly fifty per cent on duties on machinery, machine tools and chemicals was greeted as an impressive achievement. There was far less satisfaction for those seeking concessions on agricultural produce. In this sector the EEC led the forces of protection, which were strong enough to resist any pressure from the Nordic group on behalf of the Danes. The sole credits were a relaxation on the rules for the sale of live cattle abroad and a marginal lowering of duties on certain categories of cheese. It was like throwing a rubber bone to a hungry dog. Even with the shift to a mixed economy, agriculture was still pre-eminent in Denmark, accounting for forty per cent of the country's exports as against six per cent in Finland, four per cent in Norway and three per cent in Sweden. Despite the decrease in the number of farms and in the proportion of the population earning their living from agriculture – for Denmark the second figure was as low as twelve per cent – productivity continued to rise, and with it the pressure on government to find a way through the maze of tariffs, quotas and controls which held back sales in Europe. The job was made more difficult by wage inflation, which reduced Danish competitiveness, particularly in those markets also benefiting from gains in agricultural productivity.

Experience in EFTA had taught Denmark not to expect concessions to be easily won. Agriculture was excluded from the free-trade convention because Britain refused to abandon her price-support system which kept down the cost of food in the shops, and the other member states feared that open competition could ruin their own farming industries. As if to acknowledge the intractability of the problem, article 23 broke with the first principle of EFTA by sanctioning bilateral agreements aimed at expanding trade in agricultural produce. This was the only immediate possibility for Denmark to gain some advantage from her Nordic friends, who were sympathetic to her problems if limited in their power to do much to solve them. The very goods which Denmark wanted to sell – dairy products, beef, pigmeat and poultry – were precisely those which her neighbours produced in abundance. It was hardly surprising that only about six per cent of Denmark's total agricultural exports went to other parts of Scandinavia. However, in 1963 Sweden declared she was no longer aiming to increase agricultural production, so that Denmark could at least hope to maintain her share of that market. There was no question then of Sweden's lowering her import levies on foodstuffs, but she made protectionism just bearable by paying compensation of twenty million Swedish Kronor a year to Danish farmers (strictly speaking a contravention of GATT rules). Four years later the duty on imported beef within the yearly quota (three thousand tons in 1968) was reduced by fifteen per cent.

A bilateral agreement with Norway led to a few minor concessions in the horticultural sector while Finland granted import quotas on selected products including bacon and pork. There were particular reasons why Finland had to act cautiously. Of all the Nordic countries she had the highest proportion of population in agricultural work – twenty-six per cent, as against Norway who was next in line with sixteen per cent – but her rate of industrial growth was such that she could not easily reabsorb the surplus labour from the rural areas. Farm rationalization was creating its own social problems without adding to them by opening up the market to Danish competition. So the help Norden was able to give Denmark came nowhere near solving the problems of her leading industry. Quite simply, she needed wider export opportunities. Hence her rush of enthusiasm when, in 1967, Britain was once again ready to storm the French barricades and attempt a grand entry into Europe.

Britain now had a socialist government led by Harold Wilson, a politician whose record was anti-Common Market and who, in the election campaign a year earlier, had sneered at Heath for 'fawning like a spaniel before de Gaulle'. Once in office, however, he reversed his view. The influence of George Brown, the party's deputy leader, who was in charge of relations with Europe, was critical here. His forceful advocacy on behalf of the Community helped to swing opinion among Labour stalwarts. What they thought was on offer was the only likely means of escape from economic problems at home, harrassment abroad and that growing feeling of political isolation which afflicted the country. Even spirited pleas on behalf of the Commonwealth were lost and forgotten in the wake of the Rhodesian crisis, which lined up African, Asian and Caribbean states against British policy.

Early in 1967, Wilson and Brown toured the Common Market capitals canvassing support for a second attempt to broaden the Community membership. The response was encouraging – so much so that by the time they arrived in Paris they were in euphoric mood. Perhaps for this reason they misinterpreted the president's cordial welcome or, less charitably, de Gaulle may have deliberately misled his guests. A general election was not far off and he knew that the 1963 veto had been unpopular with French voters. In any event, the British government felt sufficiently encouraged to request that negotiations on entry to the Community should be resumed.

Denmark immediately followed the British lead, though on this occasion, in contrast to 1961, more value was put on assurances that the Nordic connection would not suffer. Sweden's position had also undergone a subtle change. Her previous application had been for association to the Community. Now she was prepared to negotiate 'to ensure participation in the enlarging of the EEC in a manner consistent with the policy of neutrality'. Thus the form of membership was left open, suggesting that the social-democrat government felt less inhibited than hitherto by the political clauses of the Rome Treaty. For all its heavy bureaucratic apparatus the Community was essentially a trade organization, and would remain so, it was reasoned, just as long as the French held to their rigid concept of national sovereignty. But there was also a feeling, shared by the Norwegians, that Britain was unreasonably optimistic about her chances of avoiding another French veto. The risks associated with a bold approach to the Brussels negotiations did not therefore seem so serious as in 1962 when the prospects for reaching an understanding with the EEC were viewed with far greater confidence.

The negative factor was important to the Norwegians, who were just getting used to the experience of being governed by a non-socialist coalition which happened to be split between pro- and anti-marketeers. It took nearly six months for the centre and Christian party opponents of the Community to reconcile themselves to a loosely framed government recommendation that Norway should renew her application 'as the best means of clarifying the basis of Norway's relations with the EEC'. But when a conservative and pro-market foreign minister took this to mean that full membership was intended objectors in the coalition decided to keep silent, calculating that the issue would soon die a natural death. As in 1961, entry was made conditional on British membership and on safeguards for agriculture and fishing. Once again, a consultative referendum was promised before parliament made its final decision.

As expected, having won a vote of confidence in his parliamentary elections de Gaulle quickly returned to form with an announcement to the world press that Britain had to undergo a 'profound transformation' before there was any question of even resuming negotiations. It was a gesture of defiance by a master of political drama. But at least one spectator thought that the performance had gone on far too long. With an uncharacteristic but understandable show of impatience Denmark turned to her Nordic friends and suggested that if, as then seemed likely, the European Community was to remain inward-looking, they had best think of other ways to protect and to further their economic interests. After the productive experience of their joint efforts in EFTA and the Kennedy Round, further co-operation had to be worth considering.

The 1968 session of the Nordic Council welcomed the idea. In April the same year the prime ministers, senior members of their governments and representatives of the Nordic Council meeting in Copenhagen decided to follow up on the Danish initiative, and at a subsequent gathering in October, the Nordic

Council's committee of government officials dealing with economic matters was instructed to present draft proposals for a Scandinavian common market by early new year. These were discussed and amended by the prime ministers in February 1969 when the officials were given the go-ahead to complete their work. Their final report was submitted in July.

Nordek, an abbreviation of the Scandinavian equivalent of 'Nordic Economic', was so called in deference to the Norwegians and Finns, for whom the word 'union' had unfavourable connotations. But the fact remained that the 1969 four-power negotiations were almost entirely concerned with the question of union: how far and how fast were the Scandinavian partners prepared to move towards that goal? The Danes were for going almost the whole way. They wanted, in addition to a common external tariff, a common agricultural policy, though not necessarily a replica of that practised by the EEC, and a political and administrative organization capable of exercising supranational authority. But even the Danes were not so strongly attached to the idea of union as to risk losing out on a possible reconciliation with the EEC. Pro-marketeers in all the Nordic countries agreed that 'co-operation must have the objectives and forms which will facilitate the achievement of wider European economic integration'. With this in mind the common external tariff levels were to be set as close to those of the EEC as GATT rules would permit.

Least enthusiastic were the Norwegians, who were openly hostile to any aspect of the proposal treaty which could be interpreted as supranational. Above all they feared that closer attachment to two neutrals would put at risk their defence policy. Assurances on this point, that Nordic unity was not to impinge on questions of national security, were written into the preamble to the treaty. It was a principle heartily endorsed by Sweden and Finland who, for their part, were equally concerned that co-operation should not be seen as an invitation to NATO forces to extend their area of influence. Norway also led the opposition to free trade in farm commodities, eventually compromising on a long-term stage-by-stage progression towards a common agricultural policy. Under protest, Denmark accepted an arrangement whereby a selection of food products would be considered for customs union treatment at three-yearly intervals. Meanwhile mutual preferences were to be agreed to ensure that goods presently imported from outside the Nordic area could be supplied by home producers, and an agricultural fund was to be established to nationalize production and contribute to price stabilization. The terms were too vague for Denmark 'to assess whether co-operation in the agricultural sector will be of a scope and a nature that are equivalent to the co-operation in other fields'. Her delegation held out to the last for a major concession, such as the inclusion in the customs union of industrially processed food products, but was disappointed. Even the threat to boycott the introduction of the common external tariff failed to swing opinion in Denmark's favour.

The co-ordination of fishery policies was a less intractable problem. Sweden and Finland wanted to retain some form of protection for their Baltic herring industries but otherwise restrictions on intra-Nordic trade were to be lifted, including the prohibition on direct landings by those other than home-registered fishing fleets. Price stabilization was to be achieved by grants from a jointly financed fishery fund. The advantage to Norway of these arrangements was considerable and helped to reconcile her to other less attractive provisions of the Nordek treaty. But her fear of Swedish economic domination remained and, paradoxically, was even strengthened by her neighbour's willingness to take the lion's share in financing Nordek. Sweden was to subscribe forty-two per cent of the agricultural and fishery funds, as well as the general fund set up to capitalize projects of Nordic interest which could not expect to achieve adequate backing from the commercial banks. The contribution was calculated on relative gross national products which, in 1969, suggested that Denmark would be paying twenty-four per cent, Finland fourteen per cent and Norway sixteen per cent. A Nordic Investment Bank, operating on normal banking terms, was planned on the same principle. The initial capital was to come from member states in proportion to their gross national products.

The return for Sweden from these outlays was in the achievement of a full industrial customs union with a uniform external tariff. Though many claims for special treatment for particular commodities were made by the other Nordic countries, the

Swedish hard line permitted few exceptions. The main argument was about raw materials, such as iron and steel, plastics and certain chemical products which were allowed into Denmark duty-free and into Norway and Finland on very low tariffs. Sweden, however, was less generous to importers of these goods and was disinclined to change her policy to meet the full demands of her partners. Common tariffs there had to be, even at the risk of increasing manufacturers' costs. Denmark, Finland and Norway concurred, though they were permitted the right to suspend certain duties for a limited period if economic conditions called for radical action.

This and other provisions for member states to act independently in times of economic crisis suggested the need for some sort of governing body to determine whether national governments were behaving reasonably. The responsibility was delegated to the council of ministers, the senior institution created by Nordek, members of which (one from each of the Nordic governments) were to take the lead in developing broad areas of co-operation, from labour market and social policies to education and energy. But neither in its role as arbitrator nor as innovator was the council empowered to instruct the national governments. The unanimity rule implied that any member could reject a council recommendation by the simple procedure of not voting for it. Even where a council decision was unanimous, thus acquiring status under international law, it still required parliamentary endorsement before it could be said to be binding on an individual country. This was in direct contrast to practice in the European Community, where regulations approved by the council or commission had immediate applicability in all member states.

Though leaving a number of questions unanswered, the Nordek treaty as set out in draft form in the July report was approved by the prime ministers and the presidium of the Nordic Council when they met in Stockholm in early November 1969. The next step was for the full Nordic Council to give its blessing and then for the governments to submit proposals to the respective parliaments. This was to happen in April 1970. As the deadline approached, some of those who had taken a leading part in creating Nordek spoke as if the treaty was as good as signed. But increasingly, events in wider Europe were making it less, not more, likely that another customs union would be formed.

In April 1969 de Gaulle unexpectedly resigned. His successor, Georges Pompidou, made it clear that if Britain cared to resume her efforts to join the Common Market, France would not stand in her way. Six months later Willy Brandt, a declared supporter of Britain in Europe, came to power as West German chancellor. At a Community summit at The Hague in early December the two leaders agreed that negotiations with Britain and other applicants for EEC membership could begin 'in the course of the year'. As the prospects for an enlarged Community improved so Denmark's enthusiasm for Nordek declined. The change was noted with interest more than consternation in Norway and Sweden. The pro-market lobbies in those countries accepted what was assumed to be the Danish line – that a deal between EFTA and the EEC would make Nordek superfluous – but there was no virtue in spelling this out until the Community had given more evidence of its good will. The wait-and-see policy also made sense to the anti-marketeers who had long since learned not to take Community statements of intent on trust.

But in Finland, the Soviet connection required politicians always to react to hints that their country might somehow be drawn more closely into the Western sphere of influence. A Nordek meeting in Turku planned for December was called off, and shortly afterwards the Finnish government warned that if any of its prospective partners entered negotiations with the Community, Finland's participation in Nordek would be at risk. Observers identified foreign minister Ahti Karjalainen as the restraining influence, while the prime minister Mauno Koivisto, who had led the social democrats to a sweeping victory in the 1966 elections, put greater store on drawing together Nordic relationships. As a noted economist he appreciated the benefits Nordek could bring to his country, not least a widening of financial channels via the Investment Bank for Swedish resources to be pumped into Finland's developing industries. Nordek might also serve as a means of securing trade concessions from the EEC without necessarily committing Finland to a policy of wider European integration.

Denmark and Norway made no secret of their hope that with Nordek behind them they could negotiate with the Community in the interests of the wider Scandinavia. If either or both decided on full membership of the EEC then Nordek could be revised to accommodate all points of view without compromising Finnish neutrality. In retrospect it may have been naive to expect to play both games simultaneously; but those who were involved genuinely believed that the Finns were reassured, and were as surprised as anybody when after approving the final draft of the Nordek treaty the government announced, on 24 March, that it could not after all sign the treaty. Though no official explanation has ever come from the Finns it is generally assumed that Soviet pressure forced the decision. But why did the Russians leave it so late in the day to make their feelings known? Part of the answer can almost certainly be found in the results of the March parliamentary elections, which produced a sharp swing to the right. It was unsettling enough that the conservatives increased their representation from twenty-six to thirty-six seats, but even more disturbing was the dramatic advance of the populist rural party, which jumped from one to eighteen seats. Its leader, Veikko Vennamo, in his blunt attacks on Soviet policy, helped to revive ill-feeling over the loss of Finnish territory to Russia after the war.

The decline in the popularity of the centre–left coalition and uncertainty about the political complexion of the next government came just at the time when the Swedish prime minister, Olof Palme, set off on a tour of the European capitals to assess the chances of an accommodation between his country and the Community or alternatively a Nordek deal with the EEC. While there was no question of his attempting a merger between the two associations, it might have seemed to the Russians as if Finland was about to delegate negotiating rights, possibly at the expense of Soviet interests. It was enough to tip the scales against Nordek.

Finland's withdrawal provided a not unwelcome excuse for Denmark and Norway to concentrate their diplomatic efforts on securing the best possible agreement with the Community. Denmark's application was straightforward, the centre–right coalition having far fewer reservations about Common Market membership than the government of similar complexion in Norway. As in 1967, the approach was made dependent on British accession to the Rome Treaty and on 'the expectation that the other Nordic countries would be helped towards a satisfactory working relationship with the Community'. Otherwise, no special considerations were asked for and the obligations of membership, including closer political co-operation, were accepted wholeheartedly.

Away from Brussels, however, the Danes were less sure of themselves. Anti-Common Market feeling, which was largely associated with Marxist ideology, was evidenced in the mounting support for the socialist people's party. Though incapable on its own of taking on the Community supporters in the Folketing, the far left threatened to make further inroads into the social democrats' popular vote and so damage that party's chances of winning power in the September 1971 elections. The remedy, it was argued, was to take the heat out of the Common Market debate by submitting a parliamentary recommendation to join the Community to a vote by referendum. The party was contemplating the wisdom of this tactic when Per Hækkerup, the former foreign minister, unexpectedly forced the issue in a May Day speech in support of a referendum. The parliamentary group and the national executive now hurried in with their contribution, which was to make the popular vote binding instead of advisory. Since the social democrats had enough seats in the Folketing to enforce their wishes (according to the 1953 constitution an appeal to the people rested on the approval of just one-third of the members), the other parties, not wishing to be labelled anti-democrats, soon fell into line. The strategy was successful in so far as it helped the social democrats to gain a slight edge in the September 1971 elections. But the socialist people's party also did well, leaving Krag no option but to take them into partnership to secure a one-seat majority over the bourgeois parties.

Norway's approach to the EEC was more circumspect. Storting approval for the resumption of negotiations was firm enough; only seventeen members dissented. But the vote indicated not strength of purpose as much as a reluctance by the anti-Europeans within the frail right-wing coalition to threaten the survival of the government before they knew how far the Community would go in meeting their objections. Talks started on a low key. Foreign minister Svenn Stray made an opening address which left no room for doubt that Norway expected strong safeguards for her agricultural and fishing industries. Passing reference to the aim of achieving closer political ties between the European countries was made only to emphasize the Norwegian view that political co-operation was not part of the current negotiations.

Possibly because they realized that Stray was in the difficult position of not being able to express his own opinions, which were strongly in favour of European unity, the Community representatives remained surprisingly amenable, promising to take account of Norway's problems and hinting at exceptional measures to satisfy fishing interests. But at home the anti-European factions were getting more, not less, agitated as they realized that this time the EEC was genuinely prepared to open the door to new members. To add to their concern the European Commission now proceeded to give its blessing to the Werner plan for establishing economic and monetary union by the end of the decade and to the D'Avignon Report which detailed 'the best way of achieving progress in the matter of the political unification of Europe'. This post-de Gaulle enthusiasm for breaking down national barriers suggested that the Norwegians could not count on special treatment for more than a brief transitional period. As if to confirm the worst fears of the anti-marketeers, guidelines for the development of an EEC fishing policy – non-discriminatory access to fishing grounds within the Community limits except for some narrow coastal belts reserved up to five years for local industry – were provisionally approved at almost the same time as assurances were being made to Norway, the leading European fishing nation, that her vital interests would not be ignored. Pro-Europeans argued that once in, Norway would be in a position to help shape Community policy to take account of her economic needs; but there was nothing certain about it, and the opposition played on fears that a small country would just as likely be bullied into submission.

Tensions within the coalition came to the surface in November 1970, when centre-party members challenged the government to say whether European union as envisaged by the Werner and D'Avignon Reports could be reconciled with the Norwegian constitution. Prime minister Per Borten, who was also from the centre party, avoided a direct answer but later suggested that the question of closer economic and political ties with Europe was one which the voters had to consider while negotiations were in progress. Borten's failure to give a strong lead (his conservative foreign minister was more forthright in his assertion that failure to heal the split in Europe would be calamitous) angered pro- and anti-marketeers alike. But what was he to do? If the first objective was to keep alive the coalition, taking sides on such an emotive issue was the last thing Borten could contemplate. His only chance was to steer a middle course, hoping all the way that political self-interest would lead his colleagues towards compromise.

Few observers expected him to succeed. Watching for signs of dissension among the ruling parties, political observers were certain that a crisis would come, and they disagreed only on when it would happen. In the event, everyone was taken by surprise. On 19 February, *Dagbladet* revealed the contents of a confidential report from Norway's ambassador in Brussels, Jan Halvorsen, in which he recorded the opinion of a French EEC commissioner that Norway could not expect a successful outcome of the negotiations if she continued to insist on permanent special arrangements for agriculture. Follow-up stories hinted that it was the prime minister himself who was responsible for the leak. Borten strenuously denied he was in any way involved but then, within forty-eight hours, issued another statement in which he admitted that he had shown the report to Arne Haugstad, leader of the grass-roots campaign against Norwegian membership of the EEC.

There was nothing inherently wrong in this. The document was not classified as secret, both Haugstad and Borten insisted that they had not spoken to *Dagbladet* and the circumstances in which the information was shared – a flight from Copenhagen to Oslo when the two men happened to be seated together – hardly suggested a devious political manœuvre. But the event deprived Borten of what little confidence the pro-marketeers had in his ability to represent their view and alienated other ministers, who felt cheated when they heard that the prime minister had made his public admission only after an unsuccessful attempt to persuade *Dagbladet* not to reveal his indiscretion.

Borten resigned on 2 March. His departure signalled an

intensive but futile effort to reconstruct the coalition under a new leader, after which the social democrats were invited to form a minority government. The prime minister, Trygve Bratteli, was a strong believer in European unity as the only guarantee of lasting peace, and his party immediately adopted a more positive line in the EEC negotiations. There was no backtracking on the request for a special arrangement for agriculture and fisheries, but far greater emphasis was put on Norway's willingness to play a full part in the political development of the community. In this Bratteli was distancing himself from the popular view, which showed signs of swinging against involvement in European affairs. Opinion polls showed less than fifteen per cent of voters who were ready to declare themselves in favour of EEC membership. Official opinion in Oslo that the fifty per cent or so who were still undecided would eventually follow the government's lead sounded less convincing as three of the opposition parties – liberal, centre and Christian – responded to grass-roots pressure by hardening their criticism of Common Market policies.

Since negotiations with the EEC had barely started when the social democrats took over, it fell to them to make the first serious bid for concessions to satisfy the farming and fishing industries. Full protection was obviously not in prospect (though this is what the farmers wanted), but the government asked for the system of price subsidies to be retained, knowing that this too contravened EEC rules. After three months of talks the European council of ministers conceded the need to compensate for all the fall in incomes that would follow accession to the common agricultural policy but rejected the idea of price subsidies, except for milk. Instead, after a transitional period, supplementary payments varying according to area and type of producer would be made direct to farmers. Given Norway's exceptional communication problems, transport subsidies were to be retained. The Norwegians wanted a permanent settlement but the EEC refused. The best that could be achieved was an admission that the problems were not likely to go away, which implied that Norway would always remain an exception to the common agricultural rules.

At first glance the fishery question offered fewer chances of compromise. EEC policy of non-discriminatory access to all community waters was totally unacceptable to the Norwegians, who wanted protection for their coastal fishermen and recognition for the powerful producer organizations which virtually controlled the domestic market. It was a battle they had to fight on their own. The first concern of fellow applicants Britain and Denmark was to protect the rights of their trawler fleets, which mostly operated well outside coastal waters. Denmark was happy to adopt the EEC principle of free access, but Britain wanted a continuation of that part of the 1964 London Convention to which all European fishing nations except Norway were signatories, which allowed for a six-mile coastal belt to be fished exclusively by nationals. This was acceptable to the EEC for a transitional period of ten years, as was another provision not sought by Britain, reserving an outer six-mile band for those with traditional fishing rights in the areas. Although Norway had rejected the six-by-six formula in 1964, it was more attractive a decade later, by which time other nations' fishing rights along the Norwegian coast had been reduced to vanishing point. But more was wanted, notably an acknowledgement that the peculiar geography of Norway made coastal fishing an essential industry deserving an open-ended commitment to special treatment.

The council of ministers was left in no doubt as to the importance of the issue to the future of Norway's relations with the EEC and to the future of that country's social-democrat government, which had a strong electoral interest in meeting the demands of the fishing lobby. But as with agriculture the EEC could not bring itself to accept permanent deviations from the norm. Norway's problems would be given proper consideration when it came to reviewing fishery policies, and it was thought likely that exclusive national rights in certain coastal areas would be extended beyond 1982. Thereafter it was all a matter of trust, and though it did seem unlikely that on such a vital matter the EEC would act in defiance of a member's wishes, it was asking a lot of the doggedly independent Norwegian fishermen that they should put their confidence in the Brussels establishment.

Neither the agriculture nor the fisheries agreement with the EEC found favour with those who were directly affected by the proposed changes. The farmers heartily disliked the substitution of what looked like a form of social security for the less personalized system of price supports; the fishermen resented the transfer of economic decision-making, including pricing, from their producer organizations to the community civil servants. But above all, farmers and fishermen were angered by the refusal of the EEC to declare in plain words that the special arrangements negotiated for their industries were to be regarded as permanent. Efforts to reassure those who failed to appreciate the subtleties of community diplomacy served only to gain sympathy for the diehard anti-marketeers. EEC insistence on holding open its options was taken as evidence that the more powerful member states intended acting against Norway's interests at the earliest chance.

Any doubt the government had as to the strength of feeling aroused by its apparent failure to secure a lasting settlement was removed when Knut Hoem, the fisheries minister, resigned in January 1972. Hoem was a loyal social democrat, but he was also a former director of the fishing industry's national sales organization and a popular spokesman for fishing interests. The government had hoped that his endorsement of the settlement would swing opinion in favour of the EEC. With his departure, however, it was the anti-marketeers who gained most from his brief period in office.

The leaders of manufacturing industry and the trade unions were still strongly in favour of joining Europe, together with a majority of members of the Storting. But there were signs that the roots of opposition were beginning to spread beyond those groups with special privileges to protect. In the early part of 1972 the liberals and Christian people's party recorded national conference majorities against Community membership. The previous year both parties had settled their internal differences by postponing a firm policy declaration until it was seen where the negotiations were leading. The centre party too shifted away from the 'membership with safeguards' policy it had promoted whilst in office towards a free-trade agreement without any political strings.

Even loyal social democrats were beginning to have doubts. Their leaders did not feel strong enough to discipline opponents of the EEC. With their own propaganda organization within the party they set out to persuade traditional supporters that on this issue they could, with a clear conscience, declare against the

government. The opportunity for them to do so was provided
by the referendum, to which all parties were committed. It was
the government, however, who decided the date. It was fixed
for 24–5 September 1972, three months later than originally
expected, a delay calculated to give the pro-marketeers time to
rally their supporters. It was also a follow-up to the Danish
referendum, which was confidently predicted to give a favourable vote to the EEC and which might consequently set an
example for the Norwegians to emulate. But the Danes had
second thoughts. Officially they wanted to give the Swedes a
chance to complete their negotiations for a free-trade agreement
with the EEC; but it was more in order to pre-empt a cry of foul
play from the anti-marketeers, who looked to a Norwegian 'no'
vote to help their cause, that the government fixed to go to the
polls a week after their northern colleagues.

This blatant manœuvring for position was an early indication
of just how tough the two campaigns were likely to be. In one
sense the political contours were clearly defined. Instead of
having to choose between a multitude of parties as in a general
election, the voters of both countries were faced with something
approaching a straight yes or no decision. It was either full
Community membership or, since no one could imagine total
isolation from the wider Europe, a limited economic association
on the lines of the free-trade agreement negotiated by Sweden
and her five EFTA partners. The problem for the electorate was
to try to make sense of the barrage of conflicting arguments
without, in many cases, any clearcut guidance from their
political leaders.

The social democrats, the largest party in both Storting and
Folketing, were in varying degrees of disarray. In Norway,
where the infighting was particularly bitter, even some leading
political families were divided, so that the former prime minister
and pro-marketeer Einar Gerhardsen found himself in opposition to his son who, as chairman of the youth organization, was
against membership. Small wonder that it was difficult to trace
an official policy. In his efforts to hold the party together Bratteli
allowed national conference resolutions to mean anything and
everything, and despite his own clear commitment fought shy
of accusing social-democrat no voters of disloyalty. He was well
into the campaign before he even suggested that the government

might resign if the referendum went against him. This was a strong card to play, since the conservatives, who were strongly in favour of joining the EEC, were hardly likely to join a coalition dedicated to keeping Norway out. Only the smaller parties would be left to put together a frail minority government. For a country accustomed to stability it was not an appealing prospect.

That Bratteli left it so long before raising the spectre of a parliamentary crisis was evidence of his conviction that the Norwegian people would eventually follow his lead. For the same reason he kept his distance from the conservatives, choosing to avoid the embarrassment of working alongside his old enemies instead of frankly recognizing that their help was essential for a European victory. Not suffering these inhibitions, the opposition, a motley but determined collection of urban left-wing idealists and rural traditionalists, stole the initiative from the prime minister and held on to it until the last stretch of the run-up to voting day. By then it was too late for the government to recover its lost ground.

Danish social democracy could boast a long record of support for Community membership, but during its brief period of opposition the party had taken the line of warning the government not to be too eager to accept whatever terms the EEC was inclined to offer. Perhaps for this reason, but also because social democrats had championed Nordek to such good effect, doubts set in as to the wisdom of either going into Europe alone or in the company of Norway at the possible cost of weakening Scandinavian links.

Social-democrat leaders got early warning that something was wrong when in mid-1971 the opinion polls registered a sharp increase in anti-Community feeling, from around ten per cent where it had remained throughout the previous decade to about thirty per cent. At the same time support for membership dropped to below the forty per cent level. Those who changed their minds were for the most part from the left. For much of 1972, opponents of the official line who gathered under the banner organization of 'Social Democrats against the EEC' had a majority following in the party. But in comparison with Norway, the party managed to give a better impression of holding together, with the leadership playing down the political

commitment to Community institutions (the most sensitive point
for anti-marketeers), whilst emphasizing that in plain economic
terms neither extended Nordic co-operation nor a free-trade
agreement could be a viable substitute for membership.

Where the Danish government was at its strongest was in
knowing that, whatever the feeling of disillusionment with the
EEC as the cure all for the country's economic problems, there
was no indication that the majority wanted anything else but to
join on the best possible terms. The recent shift in public opinion
was worrying but thought to be ephemeral. Mostly it reflected
concern among urban industrial workers, whose social-democrat allegiance was never in doubt and who could be expected
to respond to government reassurances that their jobs were not
at risk. The trade union federation favoured membership, if
only marginally, and this was an important factor in this calculation.

It was quite different in Norway. Throughout the campaign
the polls showed that most people would prefer to stay out of
Europe. That nearly all the newspapers and other opinion
leaders took the opposite view tended to obscure the strength of
the opposition. Moreover, feeling against the EEC gathered impetus the further one travelled out of Oslo, climaxing in the
provinces along the western and northern coast. These were the
areas where social-democrat leaders had to be very optimistic
to anticipate a natural rallying to the government on voting
day. A sharper contrast to Denmark, where the rural community, with its dependence on exports to Europe, was among the
most passionate advocates of EEC membership, was difficult to
imagine.

Both campaigns were energetic and emotional by Scandinavian standards, with the Norwegians attracting international comment on the unexpected ferocity of their debates.
Young people on the left, who saw Europe as a capitalist ogre
ready to devour whatever parts of Scandinavia it could get
within reach of, were highly active in the anti-EEC lobbies, and
provided the enthusiasm for a cause so often lacking in ordinary
elections. Their arguments for staying apart from Europe were
reinforced in Norway by the emotional appeals to nationalist
sentiment from the traditionalist right. The two sides, though
having nothing in common in any other respect, could join in

dreadful warnings of what would happen if, for example, the EEC got control of Norwegian oil.

As the time for decision approached, the upsurge in EEC support in Denmark came, as promised. In Norway it did not. The turnout in Denmark was one of the highest ever recorded, 90.1 per cent. In Norway, it was one of the lowest, 79 per cent. In Copenhagen, prime minister Krag celebrated: in Oslo, prime minister Bratteli contemplated resignation.

One explanation for the contrasting results was the degree of cohesion in the two political structures. While in Denmark the social democrats and the radicals had their internal differences, their leaders took a firm European line. The conservatives and liberals (the latter representing the farmers) were even more strongly in favour of membership, leaving only the socialist people's party to declare outright opposition. In Norway, the picture was more complex, with splits of varying width opening up in the social-democrat, liberal and Christian people's parties. The centre party was opposed but had only recently changed its mind. There remained the far left, in the form of the socialist people's party and the communists (anti) and the conservatives (pro), who alone seemed to know what they wanted.

It is likely that many Norwegians, faced with the political disarray in Oslo and the collapse of traditional party loyalties, felt unable to make a sensible choice and simply stayed at home. But whatever the reason, the poor turnout gave the advantage to the anti-marketeers, who scraped home with 53.5 per cent of the votes. Guttorm Hansen, president of the Storting, called the result 'an earthquake that has savaged the Norwegian political landscape'.

The Norwegian rejection of Europe led to great uncertainty among political forecasters in Denmark but had no observable effect on what was left of the campaign. Another week of intense electioneering produced a decisive 63.3 per cent in support of entering the EEC.

The progress of negotiations between the remaining EFTA countries, led by Sweden, and the EEC was a big talking point throughout the referenda. That they sought a free-trade agreement without political strings and, what was more, by the end of 1971 looked likely to get what they wanted, made a profound impact on the anti-market forces in Norway and Denmark. A similar plan put forward by Britain in 1958 had received unanimous Scandinavian endorsement. What had changed in the meantime – except the strengthening of the Nordic connection? If anything, this seemed to give less cause for getting embroiled in purely European affairs. The pro-marketeers argued the advantage of participating in European decision-making, though this hardly accorded with the strategy of playing down the political commitment.

The real problem of course was that free trade with the EFTA rump was dependent on the successful outcome of the applications for full Community membership. It was only with the accession of Britain, Denmark, Norway and Ireland that the EEC felt able or inclined to accommodate EFTA. These four countries acted as the front team of negotiators, advancing their own case for membership but at the same time pressing for the best possible terms for those of their friends who were not candidates. It was a responsibility they performed with such diligence that, at one stage, Sweden asked them to relax the pressure so that talks could advance beyond the preliminaries.

Following prime minister Palme's tour of the European capitals in the spring of 1970 Sweden renewed the application which in 1967 had never got beyond the stage of formal submission. It called for 'participation in the enlargement of the European Economic Community in a form that allows fulfilment of Swedish neutrality'. While none of the admission procedures allowed for by the Rome Treaty was immediately discounted, Sweden soon followed up by rejecting full membership or an association leading to future membership as impracticable. This did not mean that she wanted to minimize her relationship with the Community. On the contrary, she appealed for the widest possible free-trade agreement, expressing willingness to accept the common external tariff and to co-operate in eliminating non-tariff barriers.

It was to Sweden's advantage to act boldly. She wanted a simple, straightforward free-trade arrangement covering all products. The alternative was a long process of item-by-item haggling, leading inevitably to the imposition of special terms on Sweden's strongest exports, together with a complicated system of certificates of origin, proving, for example, that goods were not being re-exported via Denmark or Norway..

The Community, however, was not to be rushed. To begin with, the Commission, the powerful administrative wing of the EEC, was strongly against putting agriculture on the agenda, arguing that it was only possible for full members to participate in the common agricultural policy. Sweden conceded and asked instead for a system of mutual preferences. More serious difficulties arose over the so-called 'sensitive products' – steel, pulp and paper. Here the Community wanted to minimize the impact of competition by imposing a three-year freeze on tariff reductions to be followed by a long transitional period to free trade. Concessions eventually won included the abandonment of the freeze, but for Sweden the terms were less than satisfactory. As late as 1977, the year when free trade for most products was to be established between Sweden and the EEC, a quota was still imposed on paper exports which carried an eight per cent duty on entry into Europe. Some restrictions were to last until 1984.

Throughout the negotiations Sweden kept close contact with her Nordic colleagues and, together with Finland, entered talks with Britain – their major purchaser of pulp and paper – on the level of tariffs to be temporarily reimposed following the breakup of EFTA. But this was less than Sweden had hoped for. On his European travels Palme had asked for Sweden's submission to be considered at the same time as those of Denmark and Norway. The intention was to establish a working partnership and to present a united front on shared problems. This was ruled out by the Six, who recognized a flanking move when they saw one and, anyway, took the view that the confusion of dealing simultaneously with two sorts of application would serve only to delay the entry of those who sought full membership.

Finland's dealings with the EEC were naturally more wary than those of Sweden, but president Kekkonen was quick to acknowledge that the entry of Britain, Denmark and possibly Norway into Europe was potentially a serious blow to his country's economy. In calling for a free-trade arrangement with the Community he was warmly supported by industrial and banking interests, who looked beyond marketing opportunities to prospects of attracting much-needed investment from the prosperous European powers. Noticing that commercial enthusiasm for the EEC was apparently greater than for the recently lamented Nordek, some observers concluded that the business lobbies had opted for Europe even while Nordek was being negotiated, and for that reason had turned against the local team. The Russians may not have been solely responsible for the collapse of the Scandinavian trade pact.

Approval from the right was a sure guarantee of communist and far-left opposition to any dealings with the EEC, but the centre party was reconciled once it was agreed to exclude agriculture, and for the moment anyway the other parties were concerned only to get favourable terms.

The next step was to gain Soviet approval for talks to begin. After the failure of Nordek this might have seemed to be a near impossible task, but by dealing directly with the EEC, it was argued, Finland was less likely to get politically involved (the sticking point for the Russians) than by associating with Scandinavian partners committed to gaining full membership of the Community, as would have happened had Nordek succeeded. Intense diplomatic activity, and four visits by Kekkonen to Moscow in 1971-2 to explain the Finnish position, led to a package of measures designed to attract Soviet good will. First, in direct response to a Russian initiative, the Treaty of Friendship and Co-operation between the two countries was renewed five years before its expiry date. This was sufficient to allow negotiations with the EEC to start in November 1971. A month later, when it was already clear that matters were proceeding smoothly on the Western side, Finland concluded terms for closer economic, technological and industrial links with Russia, a policy later extended to the Comecon states, who also gained some important tariff concessions.

None of this disturbed Community members, who had little to lose or gain whichever way Finland decided to handle her economy. In fact the absence of a strictly commercial motive in relations between Finland and the EEC must have aroused Soviet suspicions (if not commercial, where was the political angle?); but in treating her as part of the Nordic family the Community could not exclude Finland once she had declared a wish to be associated.

The terms she eventually secured were broadly the same as those gained by Sweden – a progressive reduction of duties over a four-year period ending in July 1977 on all items of trade, with the exception of some paper products, on which the transitional period was to be eleven years. Moreover, Finland was free to extend most favoured nation treatment to other trading partners, thus protecting her bilateral arrangements with the Soviet Union.

But this was not to guarantee Moscow's approval. The assurance Moscow needed that Finland was not about to embark on a dramatic reorientation of foreign policy centred on Kekkonen's political future. The president had already said that he would not seek another term. Yet now the Russians were suggesting that he stay on beyond 1974 to oversee the early stages of his country's involvement with the EEC. Kekkonen accepted the task in principle, but after the experience of the 1968 elections in which his reappointment was secured against the forceful showing of two rival candidates, and the more recent fallback in the support of all the pro-Kekkonen parties, he was not prepared to submit to the test of public opinion. Something more than personal vanity was at stake, since a narrow victory or, worse, a defeat, would undermine Soviet confidence and probably wreck the EEC convention.

The problem was resolved in typically Finnish pragmatic style. In February 1972 the leader of the centre party and a close associate of the president suggested that all parties should agree to an exceptional prolongation of Kekkonen's term of office. To effect this, a constitutional amendment was approved by the Diet with the necessary five-sixths majority.

Even then, Kekkonen's difficulties were not over. In late 1972 the social democrats decided to link the ratification of the EEC agreement to parliamentary approval for new governmental powers to control the economy. This was an attempt to force the right-wing parties, all eager supporters of Europe and free trade, to concede the need for a radical approach to domestic economic issues. The year it took to work out a compromise came close to the time limit set for the initial round of tariff reductions. But with their unfailing sense of political drama, the Finns made it just in time, with a signature in Brussels in October 1973 and an overwhelming vote of approval in the Diet the following month.

Iceland's position was complicated by her quarrel with Britain and West Germany over coastal fishing. Fearing the rapid depletion of fish stocks by the ever-increasing number of factory trawlers appearing off her shores, Iceland unilaterally extended her fishing limits from twelve to fifty miles. Though weighty expert evidence, not to mention the majority view of numerous law-of-the-sea conferences convened by the United Nations, supported the Icelandic view, her action was in strict contra-vention of international law. It was also badly timed. Negotia-tions with the EEC gaining her duty-free access to European markets for processed fish and significant tariff reductions on fresh fish were all but completed when Iceland embarked on another round in the Cod War.

With fifty per cent of her exports going to EFTA or EEC coun-tries, the need for a trade agreement was generally accepted in Iceland. Hopes of broadening the export base to allow for a higher proportion of light industrial goods also rested largely on favourable treatment by her European partners. But Iceland too had her bargaining strengths. As a focal point of the Atlantic security system she was capable, if so inclined, of extracting a high price for continuing to accommodate a NATO force. How-ever, when it came to prising concessions from the community, Iceland's greatest asset was her size. As a tiny country almost exclusively dependent on a single product for her overseas earn-ings, she was well placed to argue for special treatment. How could the EEC ignore her appeals? The friendly giant did not want to be seen stamping on Tom Thumb. What then of Ice-land's provocative disregard for the rights of two leading mem-bers of the Community? In the end she had to make do with a delayed-action settlement. Implementing the tariff charges on fish was made conditional on a satisfactory resolution of the dispute with Britain and Germany.

Post-referendum Norway was a country stunned by her own political daring. She was the only EFTA member without a trade agreement with the EEC. No one doubted that she would get one eventually, but exporters feared losing their competitive edge if, as seemed likely, they were to be left behind in the first round of tariff charges. The immediate difficulty was the lack of a government willing to negotiate with the Community. Bratteli and his colleagues flatly refused to renege on their cherished principles, promising only to stay in office until another admin-istration could be formed. The preferred alternative, a grand centre–right coalition, was out of the question because the conservatives were also unable to compromise on their commitment to Europe. This left the liberals, who were split on the issue, and the Christian people's party, whose leaders feared a partnership with the liberals, while the pro- and anti-market factions were at each other's throats and the centre party said no to governing alone. The deadlock was broken when the liberal pro-marketeers broke away to form a new party. The way was then open for the liberal rump to reorganize into a united team able to participate in a coalition along with the centre and the CPP, whose chairman, Lars Korvald, became prime minister.

The new government had the firm support of only 38 of the 150 members of the Storting, but there was no threat to its authority while talks with the EEC were in progress. On that front, events moved remarkably smoothly. The terms sought were basically those already secured by Sweden, thus simplifying the negotiations. And after the traumatic impact of the referendum there were special efforts on both sides to create an atmosphere of good will, so that, for example, there was no difficulty in protecting Norway's free-trade rights in Denmark and Britain until the formal treaty came into force. This was approved by the Storting in May 1973 and implemented in July, a mere three months after a start had been made on dismantling trade barriers between EFTA and the EEC.

Given Norway's declared lack of enthusiasm for the EEC and her modest bargaining position (these events took place a full year before the oil price war transformed her international status), the terms of the agreement were better than might have been expected, even if they did not quite measure up to expectations. Thirty four per cent of Norway's exports were categorized as sensitive as against twenty-four per cent for Sweden. These included paper (an eleven-year transitional period), aluminium and ferro-alloys (seven years), which were also subject to quota limitations.

After the favourable treatment given to Iceland's fishing industry, great hopes were pinned on securing free trade in this leading primary export. But at this point mutual good will was found to have its limits. The Norwegian fishermen's chauvinistic regard for their own interests, combined with the fact that the country, unlike Iceland, was not exclusively dependent on the prosperity of this single industry, weighed heavily against the EEC's permitting unrestricted imports. Still, the tariff imposed on most fish products was low enough to be accepted as a tolerable burden, and Norway was still free to develop her fishing policy, if necessary, in defiance of EEC regulations.

On 1 July 1977 the relationship between the EEC and the remaining seven EFTA countries – Austria, Finland, Iceland, Norway, Portugal, Sweden and Switzerland – took on a new significance. It was on that date that the remaining duties on most industrial products traded between the two blocs were finally removed, so creating the largest free-trade area in the world. Bruno Kreisky, Austria's federal chancellor, greeted the realization of 'an objective to which the best minds of our continent have devoted so much effort in the decades since the war'.

Outside Denmark, Nordic leaders were more reserved in their acknowledgement of an economic milestone. It was mildly re-sented that while non-tariff restrictions on sensitive products such as pulp and paper had up to seven years to run, free trade should be described as complete. Nonetheless, the quota system had rarely impinged on commercial dealings. Even when in 1975 limits were put on paper imports, they had a barely perceptible effect on Nordic trade figures. The curbs on steel imposed two years later caused more of a jolt to Sweden, but they were short-lived and were no more than could be expected at a time when the steel industry as a whole was under pressure. Really, the only Nordic business to suffer major damage from the decision to stay on the sidelines of Europe was Norway's hard-fat industry, whose exports were duty-free to EFTA coun-tries. Its two biggest customers, Britain and Denmark, were lost when hard fat was awarded EEC status as an agricultural prod-uct carrying a seventeen per cent tariff.

A more convincing reason for the subdued Nordic reaction to the Common Market was the knowledge that had it developed as its founders intended towards full economic and political integration, relationships with the Scandinavian states might have come under heavier strain. If, for example, the EEC had, as originally expected, set its will against the distortion of trade by subsidy or other forms of government help, would Norway and Sweden have enjoyed the same freedom to combat recessional unemployment? That continental Europe was not in any real sense a united force was in many ways advantageous to the Scandinavians. But there was always the chance that one day the EEC would find cohesion, and hence the capacity, within its sphere of influence, to push the smaller powers in whatever direction it chose.

The expectation that policies decided in Brussels to serve the interests of the Nine would at some time impinge on the sovereignty of neighbouring states, led Sweden to seek the widest possible framework of consultation. All the EFTA arguments, except Finland's, included an evolutionary clause by which both sides declared their willingness to extend co-operation beyond matters purely concerned with trade. In Sweden's case this clause was open-ended, and her negotiators made it clear that they were prepared to consider any area of collaboration where neutrality was not at issue. A strong representation at Brussels was soon complemented by an elaborate network of bureaucratic contacts, which brought Sweden in on almost every new development programme from telecommunications and computer techniques to environment protection and food technology.

Yet Sweden must still be counted as an outsider. A reminder of this came recently when Sweden wanted to ban the use of cadmium, a metal commonly found in plastics and red paint. Against arguments for protecting environment and health were ranged the protests of European manufacturers, who claimed that phasing out cadmium would lose them valuable exports. The Swedish authorities backed down. In putting their case it is unlikely that anyone from the EEC even mentioned, let alone threatened, retaliation, but the possibility certainly figured in the Swedish decision to concede. A recession is no time to expect economic favours.

The evolutionary clauses for Norway and Iceland (like those for Austria and Switzerland) were restricted to economic matters. Norway in particular was keen to keep a distance between herself and the Community. An understandable aversion to starting another debate on sovereignty stacked the odds against any agreement which could be interpreted as a means for bringing Norway into the EEC via the back door. For this reason, having participated in the 1974 negotiations to set up an oil-sharing scheme to operate in the event of another embargo,

Norway disappointed her European friends by rejecting membership of the International Energy Agency.

But as the seventies advanced there was less concern in Norway about the risks of getting involved with the EEC and more about the dangers of being left out. The immense wealth from North Sea oil raised national self-confidence and at the same time revealed weaknesses in the country's economic base which could only be corrected by attracting technological expertise from the big industrial powers. Sweden was well placed to help, and the spirit of Nordic co-operation counted in her favour, but the contribution expected from Germany, and possibly even France and Britain, argued for a closer understanding with the EEC.

Another powerful motive for the Norwegians' taking a less myopic view of Europe was the common interest in the well-being of the shipping and fishing industries, the first a victim of recession, the second of commercial greed. There may have been those who believed that the troubles of the fishing industry were solved once and for all when Norway declared a two hundred-mile 'exclusive economic zone', but until a means was found to persuade the fish to acknowledge territorial demarcations, reasoned opinion held that the intelligent exploitation of maritime resources required concerted action from the fishing nations. The Community's own two hundred-mile limit, confirmed in 1977, the abundance of new technology and further worries about the conservation of stocks prompted Norway to rate more highly the possible benefits of EEC collaboration. Diplomatic feelers tentatively extended in the mid-seventies to secure talks on shipping questions were put out again, this time in early 1979. Declaring Norway's intention 'to avoid becoming a passive recipient of EEC decisions', foreign minister Knut Frydenlund asked for 'increased co-operation which would extend beyond the boundaries of the existing trade agreement'.

In arguing the case for a change of heart towards the Community, the Nordli government could claim that it was doing no more than following the lead of Norway's partners in EFTA. Two years earlier, chancellor Kreisky had appealed for joint action with the EEC on bringing down non-tariff barriers to trade. The response from Brussels was encouraging, an indication that despite the defection of Britain and Denmark, EFTA was still a force to be reckoned with. Talks started on simplifying rules of origin, stimulating trade in agricultural products, exchanging information on state purchasing and other related topics. In these, Norway and Sweden were both active participants, the former using the experience to overcome the inhibitions of dealing directly with the EEC.

What of Denmark, the insider? The highly favourable provisions of the Common Market agricultural policy made Denmark a beneficiary on current account. By the late seventies her net annual gain from the Community budget was in the region of seven hundred million pounds, better than any other member. But the oil recession and recurring economic crises linked to the country's heavy borrowing overseas led the Danes to *feel* less well off. With the contrast of a relatively stable Sweden and a booming Norway just next door, the first instinct was to fasten on the EEC as the source of their troubles. Laws made in Brussels were said to encroach on basic freedoms and to pull Denmark more securely into the Franco-German sphere of influence. Both were damaging charges. Even pro-market voters liked to think of their politicians as the independents of Europe who stood out for Scandinavian values. For the most part this was precisely what they tried to do. Offering themselves as the essential link between Norden and the EEC, they took every opportunity to establish their credentials as good Scandinavians. It was for this reason as much as to compensate for the failure of Nordek that the Danes threw their weight behind efforts to strengthen the formal structure of Nordic co-operation.

To supplement the work of the Nordic Council, essentially a parliamentary pressure group without formal powers to legislate, the Nordic Council of Ministers was created. It was to be made up of one member from each of the five governments, but the composition of the council of ministers could change according to the subject under discussion. Thus one meeting could be of ministers of education, another of finance, yet another of transport and so on. There was nothing in the rules to suggest that several meetings of the council, representing various specialist interests, should not take place at the same time.

Disagreement on the precise nature of the powers of ministerial delegates was avoided by the expedient of playing safe. For some time after its inception in 1971, the issues taken up by the council were generally those with a good track record of Nordic co-operation, such as the co-ordination of aid to developing countries. At this stage, the importance of the council of ministers was in introducing questions of Nordic interest into the highest level of government. As it gained experience, so the council was able to establish, by precedent, its competency to make decisions without citing approval for its action from previously enacted legislation.

Critical to this progression was the relationship between the council of ministers and the Nordic Council. The clauses of the Helsinki Treaty setting up the council of ministers also promoted it as the main body of co-operation. But quite clearly the two institutions had to be in agreement for any major initiative to succeed. The problems of working in tandem were eased by the broad sweep of Nordic Council membership which included several senior politicians who were also active in the Council of ministers. Another link was provided by the minister of Nordic affairs, originally a Danish government post but one which the Helsinki Treaty made mandatory on the other Scandinavian countries.

Central to the 1971 package of reforms on Nordic co-operation, but now only mentioned in passing since it more naturally forms part of the theme of Chapter 7, was the Cultural Treaty. It came at a time when traditional ideas of élitist and popular culture were under attack, and gave the opportunity to the Nordic states to make their own distinctive contribution to the debate on cultural democracy.

Raising the political status of the Nordic connection did not act as an immediate antidote to a general sense of disenchantment with formal co-operation. The very success of the individual Scandinavian countries in coming to terms with the EEC made them look more critically at the achievements and aspirations of Nordic institutions. Sweden complained that too often she was required to meet the cost of joint projects, that others were prepared to give support only as long as it did not cost them anything. This charge triggered off the reaction that Sweden put only her second-rank politicians into Nordic affairs while her neighbours gave their political best to solving common problems. Nordic relations were further impaired by Iceland's arbitrary extension of her coastal limits and by the fear among Swedish and Danish fishermen that Norway would follow her example. The radical Swedish law on marriage and divorce came into force in early 1974, to a chorus of protests from Norway and Finland, where opinion on this issue was more conservative. What had happened, they asked, to the unwritten rule that Nordic countries should attempt to harmonize their legislation? Most damaging of all, the partial breakup of EFTA and the varying agreements of the Nordic countries with the EEC seemed to count against a repeat performance of the trade co-operation achieved, for instance, in the Kennedy Round.

But fears of a dramatic breakdown in Nordic co-operation had to be set against the longer-running complaint that the Nordic Council and its offshoots were so caught up in the minutiae of inter-governmental transactions that they lost sight of the really big issues. This preoccupation with detail was seen as a deliberate strategy to blot out the memory of Nordek, the failure of which deterred politicians from ever again expecting co-operation to yield dramatic results.

Both lines of criticism failed to take account of the true purpose and value of the Nordic institutions. They have not and never have been in business to make grand gestures. As a forum for Nordic debate they touch on affairs which make the headlines – currently energy and recession are the predominant themes – but the serious business, the co-ordination of policy and legislation to bring closer the idea of Nordic citizenship, is essentially low-key work requiring painstaking attention to the small print. The reward for this effort encompasses the gradual harmonization of commercial, criminal and civil law and the pooling of much scientific and technical research. An agreement on rules and standards for environmental protection – the first of its kind in the world – includes an obligation to equate Nordic and national interests. A citizen of Sweden, Finland, Denmark or Norway now has the right to legal redress if pollution from any of the other three countries has a deleterious effect on his local environment. In transport and communications, joint solutions are sought for traffic problems; freight rates are coming into line; and many postal and telegraph rates are applicable throughout the Nordic region. Aid to developing countries is a joint exercise, and it is rare now for there not to be a Nordic view on matters raised by third-world organizations.

The work of the Investment Bank and the Investment Fund

has led to numerous industrial developments involving two or more Nordic countries, and has strengthened Nordel – the project for co-ordinating the production and distribution of electricity – and Nordtest, which governs the standardization of materials testing. The Nordic Investment Bank was the more adventurous and potentially more powerful of the two financial institutions. It was set up in 1976 after a long gestation period, during which the established banks argued that anything needing to be done could best be done by them, and governments agonized over the size of their contributions to the capital stock. Eventually Sweden accepted the lion's share of the responsibility for the joint finance, balancing her forty-five per cent with twenty-two per cent from Denmark, sixteen per cent from Norway and Finland and one per cent from Iceland. The instruction to the Bank was to provide support for Nordic investment and export projects 'in accordance with regular banking practice and in line with general economic considerations'. Up to 1979, investment loans totalling over 330 million dollars had been granted to support projects as diverse as the expansion of a plant producing glue for the chipboard industry in eastern Finland, and the restructuring of a sector of the aluminium industry in Norway and Sweden.

So far, of the six hundred or more Nordic Council recommendations, over sixty per cent have had positive results, while only twenty per cent have been lost and another twenty per cent are still under consideration. A run-through of the volume of topics on which the Council has recently pronounced with some effect includes everything from the use of seat belts in motor cars and the abatement of traffic noise to the protection of Lappish culture, the banning of restrictive commercial practices and the development of tourism. Some of the outstanding successes of Nordic co-operation, such as the free labour market introduced in 1954, have been subsequently adopted by the European Community; but the full list of achievements on the Scandinavian side must sometimes cause the European commissioners to wonder where they are going wrong. A possible answer to this question is to give more attention to cultural policy as a basis for other forms of co-operation, a theme which will be taken up in the final chapter when the work of the Nordic cultural secretariat will be examined.

It is at its full annual session that the failings of the Nordic Council show up most obviously. Differences which have been contained within high-level ministerial meetings can burst out into spectacular rows, as for instance in 1977, when Finland and Norway clashed on the presence of West German troops in NATO exercises in northern Norway. On a more general note there are always criticisms of the painfully slow progress on some aspects of co-operation. A Norwegian delegate to the 1979 session of the Council pointed out that some sixty items on the agenda had been coming up for discussion in one context or another and without apparent results for more than fifty years.

One long-standing issue is the construction of a bridge linking Denmark (Copenhagen) and Sweden (Malmö) across the Sound. In the early sixties, when commercial centralization was still a respectable concept, there was talk of making the Öresund region the leader for economic growth in northern Europe. Then, it was not just a bridge that was visualized, but a new international airport, motorway connections with other great business centres and ring communications linking Copenhagen, Malmö, Helsingborg and Helsingør. In the more environmentally conscious mood of the seventies such ambitions were quietly downgraded, but there were still strong social and economic arguments in favour of a bridge. Crossings by ferry totalled 24.2 million in 1976, and this number was expected to increase to about 40 million by the end of the century. But the latest feasibility study, published in 1978, estimates the cost of a four-lane road link at 450 million dollars, with at least as much again needed for a two-track rail connection. At a time when Denmark is still considering the practicalities of joining its two major islands, Zealand and Funen, the prospect for an agreement of the diversion of expenditure for a bridge across the Sound looks as remote as ever.

5
Norden in the seventies

The standard assumption of the Nordic political scene, that it was stable and predictable, was shattered in the early seventies by the rise of populism. The widespread disillusionment with established government showed itself in the dramatic gains made by the rural party in Finland, the progressive party and the centre democrats in Denmark and the Anders Lange party in Norway. Icelandic voters gave unexpectedly strong support to a new left-wing grouping. Only Sweden failed to produce a party of dissidents, but such might well have occurred had not the centre party broadened its appeal to attract a strong populist element. The mainline opposition parties in Sweden were also distinguished by not having had any recent experience of participating in government. Untarnished, therefore, by sins of commission, they were well placed to pick up protest votes which might otherwise have gone to a new party.

Is it possible, then, to identify a Nordic protest movement? The overall voting pattern showed a swing away from the social democrats, a movement no doubt accentuated by an international recession which governments, let alone individuals, seemed ill equipped to combat. But each country had its own special reasons for bucking the trend, and it might be as well to consider these before trying to detect any common features.

Finland

The cracks in the Nordic party system first appeared in Finland where, in the 1970 election, Veikko Vennamo, previously the sole parliamentary representative of the smallholders or rural party, stormed back at the head of a contingent of eighteen members, who together collected 10.5 per cent of the popular vote. Vennamo was a charismatic performer who appealed to the emotions of the 'forgotten people', the small farmers of the north and east whose meagre livelihood was threatened by lack of investment, their inability to achieve economies of scale and the disappearance of the young people to the towns. Even starting from a narrow political base Vennamo was in a good position to attract dissidents. With almost every other party leader tied to the coat-tails of the social-democrat-led coalition, he was virtually alone in protesting the inadequacies of government.

It was not so easy to keep up the performance after the 1972 election, when he was joined in opposition by the communists, who had their own claims on the protest vote. Also, by this time the government had taken some of the steam out of Vennamo's campaign by supporting agricultural prices and promising more aid for regional development. A short-lived but nevertheless welcome recovery in Finland's exports, notably timber products, gave another boost to the rural economy. But of all the problems of trying to sustain a populist movement, Vennamo himself presented the greatest obstacle to success. As a natural loner he was incapable of acknowledging his fellow party members, except as appendages to his own ambitions. When they disagreed, as for example over Vennamo's single-handed effort to come to a deal with the social democrats, he tried to win submission by the most outrageous bullying tactics. In the end two-thirds of the party abandoned Vennamo to set up their own Finnish people's unity party. They soon found that they could not make it on their own. When next the voters were asked to record their judgement the breakaway group was reduced to a single representative, just one less than the number of members returned by the rural party.

In the context of Finnish government, which was never stable at the best of times, Vennamo's return to the political backwoods was only a minor bonus to the politicians who were trying to run the country. After the first big rise in oil prices it was not long before Finland was back in recession. Having achieved one of the highest growth rates recorded by OECD in 1974, output remained static for the two following years while inflation roared ahead at eighteen per cent and the trade deficit widened to an incredible eight per cent of gross domestic product. Unable to agree on measures to deal with the crisis, the coalition broke up so that the parties could put their individual cases to the electorate. But the electorate was just as indecisive.

What little movement there was in the voting pattern for the 1975 election gave the edge to the centre, and it was a seasoned politician from that party who was presented with the unenviable task of forming the next administration. Martti Miettunen spent two months trying to find the right permutation, but without success. At this point president Kekkonen decided to take a hand. In doing so he was putting his prestige at stake, but he had never been in a stronger position to dictate his wishes to the Eduskunta. Having almost stood down in 1972, when the opinion polls showed that he faced a real challenge for the presidency from the former social-democrat prime minister Mauno Koivisto, he was persuaded against retirement by a Soviet threat to veto the proposed Finnish free-trade deal with the European Community. The prospect of greater dependence on trade with the east, a sure consequence of virtual exclusion from European markets, so electrified the politicians that they abandoned the presidential election altogether and instead mustered the necessary five-sixths parliamentary majority for an emergency law arbitrarily extending the presidential term of office by four years.

Now Kekkonen put the full force of his office behind a demand that the parties should behave responsibly and, in the national interest, lose no time in composing a 'national emergency government'. He got what he wanted; but almost as soon as ministers had been appointed, they fell out on what precisely needed to be done. The centre and social democrats favoured strong action such as a price freeze, which they achieved, and a modest wages settlement, which they did not, but they were inhibited by the presence of the communists who were disinclined to share responsibility for unpopular measures. Kekkonen insisted on their being in government on the principle that this would deter them from making trouble in the unions. What he did not anticipate was that, in trying to outmanœuvre their colleagues by appearing to be more sympathetic to the workers' cause, the communists put a stop on nearly all government initiative. The crunch came when the communists broke government ranks to vote against a two per cent increase in sales tax needed to finance measures to reduce unemployment. On the president's insistence the coalition remained intact; but Miettunen knew when he was beaten, and four months later, when social democrats and communists were once again falling out, this time over housing grants, the prime minister finally persuaded Kekkonen that the government could not go on.

Then followed an eight-month interregnum when power centred on the president's office (not in itself an unusual occurrence) and, if newspapers and television reports were to be believed, on the Bank of Finland. This institution had at its head the former social-democrat prime minister and presidential aspirant Mauno Koivisto. Believing in a tight monetary policy, Koivisto used his own authority to restrict borrowing, while berating the politicians for failing to cut spending, the employers for encouraging wage drift and the unions for allowing their members to make excessive demands. The Finns seemed to take to Koivisto much as they had taken to Kekkonen, as a strong man capable of the sort of action that was quite beyond the parliamentary leaders. The point was emphasized when another grand coalition, led by the social democrat Kalevi Sorsa, lasted less than a year, departing in February 1978 with little more than two currency devaluations to its credit. It was the sixtieth government in Finland's sixty years of independence.

Public interest in Koivisto was stimulated by the need to find a successor to Kekkonen. Not that this was an immediate problem. At seventy-seven the president was in buoyant health and made no secret of his wish to remain for a fifth term. Few were prepared to deny him the burden of soldiering on. For the 1978 election he was supported by the six largest parties, including the social democrats, an alliance which cleared the field of all save four right-wing challengers. The only surprise of the campaign was the lower than normal turnout, a reflection not of Kekkonen's unpopularity but more the voters' inability to get excited about a one-horse race. Of the 300-strong electoral college, 260 members were returned on the Kekkonen ticket, a result described by the victor as 'quite tolerable'. His closest rival, Raino Westerholm, chairman of the Christian league who campaigned for a return to 'basic values' and was rewarded with almost nine per cent of the popular vote, went on television to thank the Lord for his success.

Political observers saw more interest in the breakdown of the votes obtained by candidates for the electoral college. The highest number went to Koivisto, with other notables like prime minister Sorsa trailing well to the rear. It was Koivisto also who gained most credit when, in late 1978, signs of economic recovery were detected, though the biggest single reason was a rallying of the US market for timber products, which diverted Canadian supplies from Europe and opened up the way for an expansion of Finnish exports. In any effort to put together a viable administration, Koivisto had to be first in line as the man most likely to succeed. But some note had to be taken of the balance of power in the Eduskunta. In the election of March 1979 the voters recorded their dissatisfaction with the leading parties by giving a boost to conservative fortunes and by restoring credibility to the rural party, which gained six seats. As an exercise in protest politics it was, in one important respect, more effective than the 1970 election. By promoting to second place in the Eduskunta hierarchy a party which had not participated in government for over a dozen years, the voters were consciously ignoring the advice freely given by Finnish and Russian commentators that increased support for the conservatives could damage relations with the Soviet Union.

But the conservatives were still out on a limb, and Kekkonen was not risking much when he invited the party leader Harri Holkeri to try his hand at forming a government. When, as expected, he failed to attract allies the president turned to Koivisto. The result of his bargaining was a mixture as before – 'something old, something new, something pink and something blue', as a television commentator put it. The only major change from earlier coalitions was the entry of the Swedish people's party to replace the liberals, who had been all but obliterated at the polls.

The government's programme lacked precision, to say the least, but even if the new prime minister was not to be drawn on how he intended to beat inflation and unemployment his determination was not in doubt. Having set himself the formidable task of learning Russian, a necessary attribute for the heir apparent to the presidency, he was clearly not to be easily overawed by an intransigent economy!

Norway

Something of the explosive impact of the Common Market issue on Norwegian party politics must have echoed across from the previous chapter. At the break in the story nearly all the parties were split on whether to join the Community. With the result of the referendum showing a clear rejection of Europe, the social-democrat government under Trygve Bratteli resigned, leaving the way clear for a right–centre coalition to make what it could of a free-trade deal with the EEC. Controlling only 38 seats out of 150, the government had no expectation of resuming office after the 1973 election. But the alternative was impossible to predict. All the established parties were threatened by dissident groups, not least the social democrats, who faced a major challenge from the socialist electoral alliance, a loose merger between anti-marketeers and communists.

On the right, the electoral risk of supporting EEC membership was brought home to the conservatives when Anders Lange, a fiery old-style nationalist, gave his name to a new party dedicated to cutting taxes and reducing the power of the state. As Vennamo and Glistrup (see page 186) were at first scorned by professional politicians, so Lange had to suffer the derision of practised campaigners who failed to see what he could achieve without organization or party workers. But against formidable odds Lange rallied the populist vote to return four members.

Though remarkable in itself, his achievement was overshadowed by other shock results, such as the collapse of the social-democrat vote to a mere thirty-five per cent, the party's lowest figure since 1930. Most of the renegades were in Telemark, a traditionally radical district dominated by large industry, and in the fishing villages and isolated industrial centres of the far north. They shifted their support to the socialist alliance, which acquired sixteen seats, and the chance of playing a critical role in any government of the left.

The other divided party, the liberals, did not have so far to

fall; but for them the drop was near fatal. They lost all but two
of their thirteen members, while the breakaway group, the new
people's party, had to be satisfied with a single representative.
Most of the liberal defectors, together with a much smaller
number of anti-EEC conservatives, transferred their allegiance
to the centre and the Christian democrats, or to Anders Lange.
Altogether sixteen parties took part in the election, double the
figure for 1969; but only eight achieved representation in the
Storting.

It was this huge proliferation of parties which saved the day
for the social democrats. Although themselves reeling from the
after-effects of months of family in-fighting, the divisions on the
right, debilitating at the best of times, made it more difficult for
the non-socialists to convert votes into seats. Even with a system
of proportional representation which makes every allowance for
minorities, a 52.5 per cent lead in popular support left the
bourgeois alliance – assuming such could be formed – in a
parliamentary minority of one. Put another way, Odvar Nordli,
the newly elected social-democrat leader, gained power by a
margin of eighty-four votes, the lowest majority in any
constituency returning his followers.

If the government was spared any further anguish on the
Common Market, there was an urgent yet much more delicate
issue which, if mishandled, promised a disruption in Norwegian
politics that would make EEC membership seem like a little local
difficulty. The discovery and extraction of oil from the bed of
the North Sea coincided with the realization by the leading
producers in the Middle East that by working together they
could control the world market for an essential product. Almost
overnight, the value of oil off the Norwegian coast assumed a
value undreamt of by the first prospectors.

When talks with the oil companies began in the early sixties
the sceptics were quick to point out that oil on the continental
shelf – if indeed it existed – would be expensive to drill, and that
potential buyers – assuming any could be found – would not be
prepared to pay an economic price. Highly favourable terms
including generous tax concessions were needed to attract the
initial investment for the exploration of 78 blocks in a patchwork
of 315 laid out south of the 62nd parallel. There followed four
years of disappointment, relieved only marginally by dis-

coveries of gas condensate. What little interest remained was beginning to fade when, just before Christmas 1969, the Phillips Group announced a major find in the Ekofisk field. The first oil was brought ashore in June 1971. By then there were several new finds to celebrate, and normally cautious forecasters were estimating that by 1976 total production would exceed Norwegian home consumption.

It was at this point that the government started to take a closer interest in what was obviously a valuable national resource. The early licences, in 1965 and 1969, were awarded to groups dominated by the large international companies, with the state retaining for itself only a small interest ranging from 5 to $17\frac{1}{2}$ per cent. But after 1972, when the publicly owned Statoil company was set up, a system of co-ownership and profit-sharing was developed which gave the state up to 66 per cent of the revenue from gas and oil production. It made an interesting contrast with the policy adopted by Britain, where the multinationals held on to their privileges and to most of the profits. It was not until the mid-seventies that a UK National Oil Company was founded on Statoil lines. However, for true generosity to commercial interests the prize had to go to Denmark, where a consortium headed by the shipping magnate A. P. Møller secured an exclusive fifty-year concession for the whole of the Danish continental shelf.

At the beginning of the decade Norway was ninth in the world league of wealthy nations. By 1975, her national income boosted by the rising price of oil on the international market, she was well on the way to overtaking the Swedes and the Swiss to enjoy the highest standard of living in the world. But this was not altogether pleasing news for a people who had lately rediscovered their regard for the simple virtues. There was a fear that oil riches would damage the social framework by inflating the economy, destroying old-established industries which would be unable to compete for labour and changing the commercial shape of the coastline to the detriment of fishermen and farmers. The theme of society at risk much preoccupied a social-democrat government dependent on far-left votes in the Storting and fearing more inroads into its traditional support in the north. A cabinet paper outlining the guiding principle for the development of the oil industry struck a cautious note and made depressing reading for businessmen who observed that, after oil, the most frequently recurring word in the document was 'problem'. In advocating a moderate scale of production and the gradual introduction of oil revenues into domestic consumption, the government failed to take the sting out of the environmentalist campaign while incurring the wrath of those who were still committed to a growth economy.

Occupying a leading place among the expansionists was Arve Johnsen, managing director of Statoil and an energetic and outspoken entrepreneur, whose claims on behalf of state enterprise frequently embarrassed the government. While fielding Johnsen's incessant demands for increased capital, ministers also had to contend with Statoil opponents, who claimed that other Norwegian companies in the oil business, such as Norsk Hydro, in which the state had a majority holding, and Saga, a private consortium, were barely given a chance to show what they could do.

The government dithered. There was no denying the advantages that oil gave to Norway. The simple fact that it was there, ready to be brought to the surface of the North Sea, was sufficient to guarantee the country enormous international loans (over £7,500 million by 1977), which staved off the worst effects of the mid-seventies recession. While most other countries were virtually powerless to stop the number of jobless rising, Norway enjoyed almost full employment, with the prospect of unlimited investment in new industries. Yet those who urged prudence were not entirely motivated by old-world nostalgia. Even assuming that agreement could be reached on the appropriate industries in which to invest – and this debate was far from over – the failure of the Volvo deal with Sweden (see Chapter 6) was soon to prove the difficulties of finding the right partner for commercial development. On the purely environmentalist issue, the 1977 Bravo blowout which, given less favourable weather, could have turned into a major disaster, underlined the risks of moving ahead faster than technical competence might reasonably allow.

What in the end swung the government towards a more liberal allocation of licences, apart from a broad commitment to economic growth, was the cutback on the first optimistic estimates of output from existing rigs, and the soaring costs of exploration and extraction which threatened to make some projects uneconomic if the go-ahead was long delayed. The biggest concession to the environmentalists – or, more particularly, to the fishermen's association – was to postpone exploration north of the 62nd parallel until summer 1980.

A sign of the government resolution to press ahead with North Sea development was the appointment in 1978 of a minister of oil and energy. With conservative backing in the Storting, the government's new man was given the brief of raising oil and gas production to an annual ceiling of ninety million tons. All other political parties favoured a much lower level. As if to belie their chances of getting their way, the very first well to be drilled in the golden block, (34/10) north-east of the Shetlands, confirmed geologists' views that the sector held great promise. Overnight, Norway had increased her known reserves of oil by five million barrels, almost as much again as had already been found.

While pumping into the economy money raised on future oil revenues to relieve pressure on hard-pressed industries, the government simultaneously brought its authority to bear on the unions in the hope of restraining wage demands. To make the sacrifice tolerable, concessions were offered in the form of selective tax reductions, increased social-security payments and a price freeze. Central to the strategy was the confident expectation that the recession would be short-lived and that Norway could soon expect to resume its export-led growth. Despite growing evidence to the contrary the social democrats stuck to this view throughout the run-up to the 1977 election. Inflation was slowing down from eleven to around seven per cent, the loss on employment was minimal and wage claims were modest. But the government's record of good economic management was under threat from several quarters. Industrial output was down; so were exports and, though the unions were co-operative, wages were up anyway because, cushioned by subsidy, employers in some sectors were actually short of labour and were prepared to pay high rates to make up the deficiency. Moreover, the black gold on which all hopes rested was proving surprisingly slow and expensive to extract.

That the social democrats were not particularly forthcoming on proposals for restoring balance to the economy reflected more the struggle between conflicting ideas than any lack of imagination. In the aftermath of the 1973 débâcle the left-wingers in the party tended to group around Reiulf Steen, a younger and more abrasive character than Nordli who, in 1975, was put into the uncomfortable position of having to accept Steen as party chairman. The dual leadership, though preventing an open split in the party, did little to assist decision-making at the top.

Fortunately for the social democrats the opposition parties also had their personality clashes to contend with, but the preoccupation with internal problems made for a lacklustre campaign. With the Common Market fracas all but forgotten there was an inevitable swing back to the two main parties. The social democrats increased their share of the vote from 35.5 to 42.5 per cent and their representation in the Storting by 14 seats to 46. Their advance was mainly at the expense of the socialist alliance, whose disparate membership, having achieved the objective that brought them together, now spent more time quarrelling among themselves than with the opposition. The desire for unity was more apparent on the right. Hopes of reviving the coalition were inspired by events in Sweden, where the bourgeois parties had recently cut short nearly a century of social-democrat rule. But who would lead a centre-right government? The likeliest candidate was the Christian democrat Lars Korvald, but neither his conservative nor centre-party allies could resist disclaiming him as their undisputed choice for the next prime minister. At the root of their difficulties was the expectation that the conservatives were set for a recovery from their Common Market defeat which meant that votes would switch away from the other opposition parties. It was only natural that they should try to prevent this by promoting their own distinctive philosophies. But their efforts were in vain. The conservatives did make gains, winning votes and seats from the centre and the Anders Lange party, whose leader had died between elections.

The final tally of votes was the most dramatic feature of the election. At the first count the government had a one-seat lead but the hopes of the right were restored when a re-check transferred one constituency from the social democrats to the Christian democrats. But then, yet another recount reduced the conservative total and brought an extra seat to the socialist left.

It was just enough to allow the social democrats to remain in office, though still as a minority government.

With the election over, the government felt sufficiently self-confident to remind Norwegians that they could not isolate themselves from the vicissitudes of the world economy. The Krone was devalued, credit controls were introduced to choke off private consumption, interest rates increased and public spending cut back. It was even acknowledged, if reluctantly, that the state could not act indefinitely as the paymaster for unprofitable enterprises. The change of policy was signalled by a new slogan: 'Dying industries must be allowed to die.' The long-term economic plan to 1981 was revised downwards.

The most critical issue was the future of the wages policy. The government was already deeply involved in all collective pay negotiations. Now it was proposed to give a sharper edge to the system of economic management by setting up a compulsory wages board. Some unions objected, and even called for protest strikes, but opinion polls showed there was popular support for strong action, and in the Storting the government could rely on the centre and right to compensate for any rebel votes on the far left. A moderate increase in the spring wages settlement was followed in September by a total price and wage freeze.

It was difficult for workers to accept what amounted to a real drop in living standards while the newspapers were full of stories of new oil and gas finds and soaring revenues from North Sea operations. More than a hint of the growing unpopularity of the government came in the 1979 local elections when the social democrats made their worst showing for over forty years. Nordli reacted by sacking over half his cabinet. The massacre was justified as making way for leaders who were more in touch with the people. These included LO's chief economist, who took over finance, and Reiulf Steen, who came in at trade. The immediate effect was to give a yet more radical edge to government policy which was reflected in a new collective pay agreement which ensured that all industrial workers received a minimum of eighty-five per cent of the average wage. This meant that the better-paid workers got as little as a five per cent increase while the poorer ones received up to thirty per cent. Any doubt there might have been that the government was engaging in short-term expedients was removed by the setting-up of a wage equalization pool, to which workers and employers in businesses paying above average wages were required to contribute. The funds were earmarked for supplementary handouts to workers in traditionally low-wage industries like fish-canning and textiles. Another squeeze on the richer end of the labour market came in the form of a rule that plant-level negotiations, which usually gave hard-pressed employers the excuse to pay above the going rate, should only take place once a year, and not lead to increases exceeding three per cent.

In confirming their reputation as the boldest of the Nordic social democrats the Norwegian party failed on this occasion to get a response from the voters. With an election due in the autumn of 1981, the opinion polls showed a continuing desertion to the right, a trend which was uninterrupted when Nordli retired on grounds of ill health to be succeeded by Mrs Gro Harlem Bruntland, Norway's first woman prime minister.

Denmark

For Denmark the first political surprise of the seventies was the resignation of Jens Otto Krag. It was a private decision, he explained: he simply wanted his life to himself for a change and that was a matter on which he did not feel the need for prior discussion with even his closest colleagues. Krag handed over to Anker Jørgensen, a hard-headed ex-trade unionist whose antecedents – son of a coachman, brought up as an orphan, a onetime worker in a tobacco factory – struck a welcoming chord with both wings of his party. But nationally he was unknown, and well before he could prove himself he was confronted by a formidable rival for public attention.

At first no politician was able to take Mogens Glistrup seriously. As a successful tax lawyer his admirers were at first concentrated in his upper reaches of Danish society – not the best launching-point for a populist leader. But that was before he went on television to proclaim that with a personal income of five million Kroner he made no contribution at all to the national revenue. His admission attracted wide interest, not least from Poul Møller, the conservative minister of finance.

The subsequent investigation into Glistrup's affairs led to 240 charges of tax evasion. More encouraging for Glistrup's was the reaction of small businessmen, farmers, shopkeepers and all those who felt their enterprise was stifled by the demands of a high-cost welfare state. For years they had been grumbling that, of all Europeans, the Danes were hit hardest by direct taxes which now accounted for fifty-six per cent of the average income, a burden made all the harder to bear by the recently introduced pay-as-you-earn system.

What had started with a simple demand to reduce taxes now developed into a full-scale electoral campaign, with Glistrup broadening his programme to include the phasing out of income-tax over five years, a massive cutback in welfare expenditure and the abolition of the Danish armed forces. He was quoted as saying that the only defence the country needed was a recording of 'We surrender' in Russian. Within weeks his newly formed progress party was topping twenty-five per cent in the opinion polls, with gains predominantly from the leading right-wing parties but also with a surprising number of social democrats lending support. The left, meanwhile, had its own internal troubles. With Jørgensen seeming to be oversensitive to the claims of the socialist people's party there were fears of a return to the Red government of the sixties. Criticism of the leadership led to a confrontation between Jørgensen and his strongest opponent within the party, Erhard Jacobsen. On a decisive parliamentary division, Jacobsen failed to put in an appearance and the vote was lost to the government. Afterwards he excused himself by saying that his car had run out of petrol; but if an apology was implied he rather destroyed the effect by going off to form yet another party, the centre democrats, which made its special appeal to middle- or lower-middle-class suburban voters. Deprived of his majority, and with his competence to govern seriously in question, Jørgensen called an election.

1973 was the year the Danish voters finally rebelled. With the press and television lending support to the already popular view that the established politicians were bumbling along without any clear idea of how to cure the country's economic ills, the electorate marched off to the polls determined to try something or someone new. Not one of the traditional parties escaped a severe hiding. The social democrats went from 70 to 46 seats

and, more surprisingly perhaps, the socialist people's party also
fell back from 17 to 11. The radicals, liberals and conservatives
together lost 30 seats. In 1971 the share of the total vote of the
two main party blocks was 46 per cent. In 1973 it was 32 per
cent. 40 per cent of all voters changed parties and 36 per cent of
all votes were cast for parties not previously represented in
parliament.

The first to gain from this turnabout was Mogens Glistrup.
Starting from nothing his progress party won twenty-eight seats,
making it the second largest in the Folketing. Although the
other leaders were determined to keep him out of office – if on
nothing else they agreed on that – it was no longer possible to
dismiss the man as a political buffoon.

There had been no one quite like Glistrup since the days
when Poujard rallied the small businessman's vote in pre-
Gaullist France. Points of comparison could be made with
Vennamo's populist movement in Finland; but Glistrup had a
much broader appeal, attracting a wide cross-section of voters
from all the other parties on the right. That Glistrup was able
to keep his following up to and beyond the next election was an
indication of the strength of anti-establishment feeling among
voters, and a tribute to his skill in offering beguilingly simple
answers to complex social questions.

Following the progress party on its protest excursion into
central government was another new right-wing group, the
Christian people's party, whose seven representatives wanted
nothing less than a moral regeneration to reverse what they saw
as the country's slide to the devil.

In on the far left of the Folketing came six communists whose
presence signified the revival of fortune for a party which had
not elected a single representative for almost a decade. But the
centre democrats, Erhard Jacobsen's breakaway faction from
the social democrats, scored even better with fourteen seats, and
this by a party which had not even existed three weeks before
polling day.

There were now ten parties in the Folketing, all disagreeing
on how best to run the country and each frightened of losing
face by seeming to compromise on a joint programme. After five
weeks of fruitless talks it was the negative line of thinking – what
was totally unacceptable leading by a process of elimination to

what was barely tolerable – which gave the job of forming a government to one of the least controversial figures in Danish politics. Poul Hartling, a mild-mannered theologian and liberal leader, accepted the challenge of putting together an administration, on the strict condition that the other parties of the centre and the right who felt unable to participate actively in government should look upon his efforts with benign understanding and tacit approval.

With the liberals holding just 22 Folketing seats out of a total of 179, Hartling's premiership gave a whole new meaning to the phrase 'minority government'. Yet he was remarkably successful. Making use of hitherto unsuspected negotiating talents, he survived for two years by painstakingly restructuring his majority for each item of the government's programme. Generally, he could rely on the conservatives and radicals to back him since their views on how the economy should be managed were broadly in accord. But the votes of the three parties combined left him thirty-two short of his objective, so that some sort of accommodation had to be made with the moderate left. At desperate moments, problems which did not allow for a compromise solution were simply ignored. As in 1974, when it was proposed to match a seven billion Kroner tax cut with a corresponding limit on public expenditure, no details were ever given of where precisely the savings were to be made.

The skill with which Hartling kept his balance on a swaying tightrope impressed the public, who gave him his best ever rating in the opinion polls. Hartling could now afford to be tougher in his dealings with the other parties, since it was they who had to worry about the outcome of a general election. And in another sense, the time was right for the prime minister to show his real strength. With inflation running at over fifteen per cent and the government resorting to yet more foreign borrowing to cover the twelve billion Kroner trade deficit, another effort was needed to hold down prices and home consumption and to stimulate exports.

Hartling believed that for action to be effective it also had to be dramatic. He proposed cutting across the current round of wage negotiations which, following recent precedent, showed every sign of getting out of hand, by declaring a total freeze on all increases. The 'zero solution', as the policy was soon to be called, failed to attract the social democrats, who wanted a compensatory rise in social expenditure to reduce unemployment, now rising to seven per cent, and to ensure that the worse-off did not suffer a fall in living standards. This was no deal at all for Hartling who, by accepting, would have lost support on the right. The only alternative was to press on doggedly and, when it was clear that it was just not possible to put together a majority on his terms, to appeal to the country.

Hartling knew very well that the election would not free him from strong parliamentary pressures outside his own party. What he hoped for was, as he put it, 'a handshake with the voters', a show of confidence which would make it harder for the other parties to demand concessions. He almost made it. Liberal representation nearly doubled, from twenty-two to forty-two seats. But it was the old story of votes shifting within instead of between power blocks, so that Hartling made most of his gains at the expense of his closest allies, the conservatives and radicals, who lost six and seven seats respectively. To make matters worse, the widely expected collapse of the progress party did not take place. With the loss of just four seats, Glistrup returned to parliament with his authority confirmed as leader of the third largest party. As the liberals' major competitor for power, the social democrats also improved their standing, taking back much of the support they had previously lost to the centre democrats. Still, with fifty-three seats, Jørgensen was not so far ahead as to insist on Hartling's dismissal.

The incumbent premier soon found that his electoral success counted for little. His enemies, such as Glistrup, were more than ever determined to get him out, while his erstwhile friends who had lost seats to the liberals were persuaded that further association with Hartling was tantamount to political suicide. Regretting perhaps that he had not attempted to bind other parties closer to him before he went in for an election, Hartling resigned.

Next the speaker of the Folketing, acting as 'royal investigator', was asked to try his hand at constructing a coalition. The solution which had the strongest appeal outside parliament was a government shared between the liberals and social democrats, but irreconcilable differences on economic policy, aggravated by a personal antipathy between Hartling and Jørgensen, soon ruled out that possibility. Other permutations failing almost as soon as they were suggested, it was back to a minority administration, but this time with the biggest party, the social democrats, as the natural successor. Jørgensen accepted when he was assured that the liberals and radicals would soften their opposition role to one of benevolent neutrality. Thus Denmark returned, if reluctantly, to what was now popularly known as rule by negative majority.

The new government had to combat the effects of the first round of oil price increases – a burst of inflation, a rise in unemployment to six per cent (the highest in Norden at that time) and a dramatic deterioration in the balance of payments. Whatever Jørgensen's earlier views of Hartling's efforts to manage the economy, he was soon following much the same line of reasoning. Having frozen rents and prices, he called the Folketing into emergency session in the middle of the 1976 summer vacation to push through an incomes policy limiting increases to six per cent for the next two years. Hopes that LO would support the government were disappointed, and the strikes that winter, including one by petrol-tanker drivers, nearly brought the country to a standstill. Despite the privations, or possibly because of them, the electorate rallied to Jørgensen as the strong leader who gave every impression of knowing what he was doing. They had paid the same compliment to Hartling; but the social democrat had two advantages over his predecessor. He was backed by the largest party in the Folketing, yet he was no real threat to the smaller parties on the right, whose tacit support he canvassed. There was even some advantage for them in isolating the liberals, from whom they could hope to regain votes in the next election.

When in 1977 Jørgensen appealed to the country to endorse his record, including incomes policy, he may not have been too certain of how many extra votes he would gain but he was reasonably confident that the liberals would lose ground. They had obstructed the government (it was their refusal to support a change in housing policy which caused the election), yet, without allies, they were unable to present themselves as a viable alternative. In the event, the social democrats did very well indeed, putting up their share of the vote by seven per cent and increasing their representation to sixty-five seats, while the liberals fell right back to where they stood before the 1975 election, winning only twenty-one seats.

Once again the joker in the political pack was Mogens Glistrup. The election came at a good time for him, since polling was on the very day by which Danes had to complete their income-tax returns. This fact alone was calculated to arouse sympathy for a politician who was currently facing the prospect of a jail sentence for tax evasion. But Glistrup gathered in more than the anti-tax vote: he was the channel of protest for those who thought there were too many state regulations, too many bureaucrats and too much government interference in their everyday lives. The progress party gained just two seats in the 1977 elections, but with the collapse of the liberals it was now once again the second largest party in the Folketing.

Glistrup's central position in Danish politics was confirmed the following year when the Copenhagen City Court, finding him guilty of wilful tax evasion, nonetheless rejected prosecution demands to disbar him from parliament and to send him to prison. Instead he was let off with a hefty fine, the impact of which was lightened by some caustic judicial observations on the laxity and incompetence of the tax authorities.

Judging by the division of votes between the party blocs the Danes wanted power to go the centre right. Yet, ironically, it had to be taken as a measure of Glistrup's personal success that an anti-socialist government was now less of a possibility than before he entered politics. Since no one would co-operate with the man who could make or break a centre–right coalition, the advantage went to the social democrats as the only party capable of sustaining a working majority.

To keep that advantage Jørgensen broadened his programme to appeal to the centre. In his 1977 economic package, limits on pay and prices were reinforced by a rise in value-added tax from fifteen to eighteen per cent, and higher taxes on spirits, tobacco, petrol and other consumer products. This pleased the opposition, who wanted to shift some of the tax load from incomes, but upset the left, who did not feel adequately compensated by the promise of industrial expansion and measures to reduce unemployment. When there was a demand for further concession from the right, the government agreed to reduce employers' obligation to pay sickness benefits from five to three weeks. It was a token offer but it secured the vote.

It was soon evident, however, that stronger measures were needed. For a country importing ninety-eight per cent of its fuel, the ever-mounting cost of energy put a huge strain on the balance of payments. In the long term, say by the mid-eighties, there was the hope of meeting up to one third of total energy needs from oil and gas fields in the Danish sector of the North Sea, but for the immediate future there had to be an alternative to greater dependence on foreign loans. 'We cannot continue along this path,' warned Jørgensen, at the same time acknowledging privately that unless he somehow consolidated his power base he would not have the political muscle to tighten the screw on wages, credit and spending.

Approaches to possible coalition partners brought a constructive response from the liberals. At first they favoured a grand alliance including the conservatives to deal with the crisis, but then came round to the idea of a two-party arrangement on condition that the social democrats quietly buried some of their more controversial plans, such as employee shares in industry and a capital-gains tax on property. The partnership caused great bitterness among trade unionists, who staged demonstrations and strikes to protest at what they saw as their party's swing to the right. But in neutralizing the opposition – there was now no immediate prospect of a right-centre bid for power – Jørgensen had bought time to make painful adjustments to the economy.

A VAT increase and public-spending cuts went through without much trouble, but the big test was the general wages agreement due to be renegotiated in early 1979. This quickly degenerated into a trial of strength between the government and LO. Both sides wanted to stimulate exports but the unions' solution, to embark on a massive investment programme, seemed to ignore the immediate problem of keeping costs down at a level where the existing export performance could be maintained. The threat of a national strike in vital services and the counter-threat by employers of a general lockout brought in the labour mediator, who forced a settlement by extending the existing agreement by two years. This standstill compromise hardly measured up to the government's expectations, though remedial action soon came in the form of increased taxes and further cuts in government spending. In a try-anything mood,

Jørgensen held out an olive branch to the unions by offering to look again at LO's proposal for an investment fund to be supported by a ten per cent profit tax. The controversial aspect of the scheme was that the unions wanted part control of the fund, an implied challenge to management that so offended the market principles of the liberals that they scuttled back into opposition.

If Jørgensen was so far failing in his primary objective he still appeared to the voters as the politician most likely to get things done. In the election called soon after the break-up of the coalition the social democrats made modest gains. More significantly, perhaps, the first sign of a retreat from Glistrup was recorded, with the loss to the progress party of six seats. The electoral verdict was a clear enough instruction to Jørgensen to persevere in his efforts to confound the cynics, among whom must be counted a Norwegian journalist who gained notoriety for his observation that 'Denmark is going to the dogs, albeit on a first class ticket.'

Iceland

While economic uncertainty for most of Norden represented a mild affliction, Iceland qualified for the critical list. Foreign reserves were dangerously low, and inflation riding at giddy levels, even before the oil price increases hit the industrialized nations. If in the sixties consumer prices rose at an average annual rate of 12 per cent as compared with 4.5 per cent for western Europe, in the following decade the Icelandic average curved up to over 30 per cent.

The root of the problem was the imbalance in overseas trade caused by a general rise in import prices, at a time when Iceland was having to bear a fall in the value of her primary exports – fish products and aluminium. The standard remedy, which to varying degrees the other Nordic economies tried to apply, was to cut back on consumer and public spending until the country was living somewhere close to its real income. But to attempt to achieve this was to defy the first rule of Icelandic industrial relations, that increases in the cost of living had to be compensated almost immediately by a corresponding increase in wages. Indexation was a common feature of labour agreements in all Nordic countries, but only in Iceland was it raised to a level of holy writ. The principle was enshrined in all settlements between the federation of labour (ASI) and the employers' associations, who were used to handling things in their own way and disinclined to pay much attention to government pleas for restraint. It was this general weakness of government in the face of what seemed to many to be the threat of national bankruptcy that led to a sharp break in the voting pattern in 1971.

The election was preceded by the longest unbroken coalition period in Icelandic politics. Having survived for twelve years, the independence and social-democrat government approached its third encounter with the electorate with confidence. The signs of dissatisfaction were not misread but the opposition was divided and apparently unfit to offer an alternative administration. The strongest attack came from Hannibal Valdimarsson and a group of left-wing dissidents whose politics were somewhere between the social democrats (thought to be too conformist) and the communists (too dogmatic). Valdimarsson had broken away from the social democrats in the mid-fifties to form the people's alliance. Now, in rejecting the communist-dominated leadership of the people's alliance he was heading a union of liberals and leftists (UCC). His aim was eventually to bring together all groups on the democrat left, but meanwhile he took the lead in berating the government for its failure to hold inflation, its timidity in claiming offshore fishing rights and its supplication in dealing with the American forces.

Valdimarsson's energetic and popular style of electioneering was a strong attraction to social democrats frustrated by their long association with a right-wing party. In collecting ten per cent of the vote the UCC was counted as one of the victors in the election, as was the people's alliance, which, despite the split caused by Valdimarsson's defection, maintained its parliamentary strength. The government parties fell back dramatically, with the social democrats suffering the greatest loss. Any doubt as to the general disillusionment with the ruling coalition was removed when even a joke party created by university students to satirize the pretensions of serious candidates collected a respectable two per cent of the vote.

Unable to govern on their own, the UCC and PA persuaded the progressives to join them in coalition. That party had not done well in the election, the protest vote having passed it by to move further left, but it still represented the biggest single party from the previous opposition and was the only possible recruitment area for a prime minister. In heading the three-party coalition Ólafur Jóhannesson quickly earned himself a reputation abroad as a politician who was determined to upset all the political conventions. But the threat to terminate the defence treaty with the United States did not materialize and the extension of the offshore fishing zone to fifty miles soon paled against the subsequent two hundred-mile limit set by a right-of-centre government. The biggest disappointment, however, was the failure of Jóhannesson to take a grip on the economy. He was unlucky in that the oil price rise made a hard task yet more difficult; but with no agreement within the government on how best to contain inflation, now rising to fifty per cent, he was unable even to make a start on proposing remedies. As a result the experiment in left-wing government came to an abrupt end in the 1974 election, when the voters gave a boost to the fortunes of the independence party. Its leader Geir Hallgrímsson took over as premier but with the progressives staying on in government, albeit in a secondary role.

The first year of the new administration was almost entirely preoccupied with labour disputes, as the ASI and employers tried to reconcile their interests while listening to the almost desperate appeals from the government to acknowledge the national interest by abandoning full indexation. Eventually, in the shadow of a general strike, a compromise was put together which allowed for indexation only when the cost of living crossed an agreed threshold. This union concession was matched by tax reductions, which in turn were balanced by promised cuts in public expenditure. The policy was successful to the extent that by the end of 1975 inflation was held at thirty-seven per cent, a figure which would be guaranteed to throw other economies into sheer panic but which in Iceland was read as a signal of imminent recovery. Confidence was further inspired when an IMF loan supplemented the foreign reserves – at one stage so low as to cover only one month's imports – and when a favourable trend in the terms of trade was further improved by two devaluations. Unemployment, always low in Iceland, fell close to zero.

On balance, 1976 was another encouraging year. This time a general strike did occur, but it lasted only ten days and was followed by a national wage agreement which again limited indexation to certain threshold payments. Inflation dropped another step, to thirty-three per cent, and investment in the country's generous reserves of geothermal energy brought a welcome return in the form of reduced oil imports.

But the unions were impatient. If things were getting better, what need was there for restraint? With an election not far off, the government could not hold out against a united labour movement. The 1977 wage agreement with the ASI, finalized in June after eighty-four days of negotiations, linked increases of between twenty to thirty per cent to an expansion of the social services, tax cuts and a special boost for the lower paid. With the restoration of full indexation giving another twist to the inflation spiral, the government promised not to increase income tax, cut social welfare expenditure, devalue the Krona or change the policy of indexation for the period of the agreement. There was still the possibility of raising indirect taxes to dampen consumer spending, but since putting up the tax on anything except the most inessential products was certain to be reflected in the cost of living and so trigger automatic wage increases, the exercise could only be self-defeating.

Unions not affiliated to the ASI, notably the civil servants and the bank employees, naturally followed on with claims that were equally extravagant. On paper they won pay increases of between thirty and thirty-five per cent but in practice, what with indexation and overtime, the bank employees, for example, were able to add seventy-six per cent to the value of their pay cheques.

The government did what it could to keep some sort of hold on events. To tighten up the system of tax collection a PAYE scheme was announced for early 1979 together with the replacement of the sales tax with a value-added tax. But with the level on inflation threatening to swing back into the higher thirties and beyond, these long-term measures seemed almost of academic interest – though it says much for the underlying strength of the Icelandic economy and society that there was still time to think about averting at least a temporary collapse of the monetary structure.

In the first weeks of 1978, election year, Hallgrímsson re-asserted his authority by declaring that the wage agreements had to be modified to prevent a seizing up of the economy. Union reaction to what was seen as a blatant disregard by a right-wing administration for labour interests – not to mention the solemn undertakings made just a few months earlier – was a series of wildcat strikes. Undeterred, the government pushed through a thirteen per cent devaluation, ruled that wage index-ation would be limited to just half the increase in the cost of living and announced a sharp cutback in public expenditure. On the government's debit side, a proposal to alter the rules of indexation so that no compensation would be made for changes in indirect taxes aroused such furious hostility it was quickly withdrawn.

In the midst of crisis, a state commission appointed in 1976 to study the inflation problem came up with conflicting opinions on the immediate control of prices. But taking the longer view, there was agreement on three fundamental defects of the Ice-landic economy: its overwhelming dependence on the export of fish products; the lack of an adequate counterbalance to the centralized power of the unions; and the failure of the state to develop some of the more sophisticated techniques of financial management. It was suggested that an incomes board should be set up to co-ordinate the interests of government, labour and business.

It was one thing to offer remedies, but quite another to implement them. Hallgrímsson's failure to restrain inflation – it was well on its way to fifty per cent by the time he had to face the electors – led directly to his downfall. The likeliest alterna-tive, a return to a left-wing coalition in which, according to the opinion polls, the people's alliance would hold the dominant position, revived fears among Iceland's NATO allies of another tussle over the American base at Keflavík. Ever sensitive to jibes about their status as occupying forces, the Americans tried harder than usual to remain inconspicuous. In addition to the basic rules never to wear uniform or to take goods from army shops on their restricted excursions outside the base, the US services TV channel was switched to close circuit to prevent local inhabitants from seeing it. More positively, help was offered in building a new passenger terminal at Keflavík to segregate civilian travellers from the military.

Whether or not these concessions influenced the campaign, the swing to the left in the June election fell short of giving the people's alliance a commanding position in the negotiations for a coalition. The independence and progressive parties each lost five seats, which on a simple count would still have left them with a mandate to continue in office. In practice, however, the progressives wanted out. All other feasible permutations had to take account of the pro-NATO social democrats, who surprised everyone by gaining nine seats and recovering their position as a leading party. But in refusing to accept Ludvík Jósefsson, the leader of the people's alliance, as prime minister while rejecting overtures from Hallgrímsson to join with his party in a government of moderates, the social democrats frustrated the resumption of normal government service. The impasse was ended only when Jósefsson cleared the way for his party to enter a coalition with the social democrats and progressives by declaring himself no longer a candidate for office. A condition of participation by the people's alliance was that its members should not press for withdrawal from NATO. At the head of this uneasy alliance was Ólafur Jóhannesson, prime minister of the ill-fated left-wing administration of 1971–4.

To make a start in restoring a sense of order to the economy, the Krona was devalued by fifteen per cent; but that was it. The rest of the government's short life was occupied in trying to reconcile the tough stance of the social democrats, who wanted, among other things, a five per cent ceiling on the seasonably adjusted cost-of-living index, and the people's alliance, who resisted all efforts to deflate the economy. This was by no means pure awkwardness on the part of the left-wingers. There was a genuine conviction that, with serious attempts to cut back on the fish tonnage for conservation reasons, measures to slow down the economy might push the country into serious recession. With next to no prospect of achieving even part of their programme the social democrats pulled out in October 1979 and the government collapsed soon afterwards.

The latest appeal to the electorate brought a substantial advance to the progressives at the expense of both its allies in government. But it was an inadequate basis on which to try yet again for a progressive-led coalition. Several candidates for the premiership stepped forward and as quickly retreated in the face of a less than enthusiastic reception, until a leading member of the independence party, Gunnar Thóroddsen, broke with his colleagues to emerge as the leader of a coalition embracing the people's alliance, the progressives and a few rebel independents. His victory was a tribute to the flexibility of Icelandic politics, but the solution he offered to his country's problems – wage restraint in return for social reforms – begged the question as to whether Icelanders were prepared to accept tough anti-inflation measures. The incentive was to bring a semblance of control to a cost-of-living index which in 1979 climbed over sixty per cent.

Sweden

When Erlander retired in 1969 after twenty-three years as social-democrat leader, there was only one serious contender for his job: Olof Palme, an intellectual and a visionary whose forthright pronouncements on the shortcomings of Swedish society put him to the left of most of his colleagues. His radical image contrasted somewhat with his personal background – the son of a wealthy, upper-class family who had married into the social élite – and for all those who criticized him for his over-energetic pursuit of social and economic equality, a corresponding number thought that he failed to sympathize or communicate with the ordinary voters. But Palme could afford a few knocks. What counted strongly in his favour was that he had the backing of the outgoing prime minister. He had served a ten-year apprenticeship as personal assistant to Erlander and then, after entering parliament in 1963, had quickly advanced to ministerial status, first in communications and latterly in education.

Within months of his taking office Palme was leading his party into one of the bitterest election campaigns in living memory. The mere fact that Erlander had gone seemed to act as a release on frustrations which had been bubbling away beneath the normally placid surface of Swedish democracy. An unofficial strike in the state-owned LKAB mines at Kiruna, led by relatively well paid skilled workers who were protesting against the general levelling of incomes, was a warning to the party and to the trades union confederation (LO) that their efforts on behalf of the lower-paid workers were by no means universally applauded. But Palme stuck to his ideals. Quoting the findings of a commission of inquiry into low incomes which showed that nearly a third of the workforce and well over fifty per cent of pensioners lived below what LO regarded as the poverty line, he supported a campaign for greater equality and for a 'low-income profile' for future wage settlements.

If Palme was under attack from the right, including the right wing of his own party, matters were hardly more settled at the other end of the political spectrum. The new prime minister might reasonably have expected to win favour with the left. He understood and sometimes spoke the language of Marxism and he had taken up the most cherished course of the highly organized and vocal student movement – opposition to US involvement in Vietnam. But it was a hopeless task to expect to win the active support of those who wanted 'socialism now' and for whom even the communist party was too placid. Some of his fellow campaigners feared that in helping to revitalize the left by giving them a sympathetic hearing, Palme was putting the entire election in jeopardy.

The risks were all greater because 1970 was the first election to be fought under the revised constitution. Hitherto Sweden had had a two-chamber parliament, with an upper house elected indirectly by the local authorities. The system had a built-in advantage for the social democrats. One-eighth of the upper house came up for election each year, so once established it took a long time to shift the balance of power away from the ruling party. Since the government needed a majority in the two houses, voting together to stay in office, even reversals in the direct elections to the lower house could be neutralized if there was a favourable margin in the second chamber.

The need for constitutional reform had been evident for some time. A special commission set up in 1954 had taken nearly ten years to consider its recommendations, but eventually reported in favour of unicameral parliament. Even then the social democrats moved slowly, and another committee was set up to review all the arguments. By the end of the decade they had run out of delaying tactics, and agreement was reached on a single-chamber Riksdag of 350 members elected by proportional representation.

The opposition took heart, though their revival of confidence did not go as far as to come to terms on a joint programme. Hedlund declared roundly that collaboration was unrealistic, while Ohlin argued that the formation of a non-socialist bloc would only help the social democrats, because liberals and centre would be accused of condoning the extremist views of the conservatives. But if the campaign proved anything it was that the opposition parties had more in common than they had expected – not least their antipathy to Olof Palme, whom they saw as an intellectual dogmatist, too clever by half. Ironically, some of the strongest attacks on Palme came from Gunnar Hedlund, the man whose close association with Erlander had kept the social democrats in office in the critical post-war period. Now he was telling his audiences that the young and inexperienced Palme (at forty-one the new premier was Hedlund's junior by thirty years) had taken on more than he could handle. As evidence, his diplomatic recognition of North Vietnam and his attacks on US foreign policy, which led to the withdrawal of the American ambassador, were frequently cited. Even his closest associates were worried that Palme had over-reached himself when he likened the American bombing in Vietnam to Nazi war crimes.

Posters were displayed showing Palme walking side by side with Sträng, the solid and dependable finance minister, as if, to quote a commentator, 'to remind voters that the elder statesman was on hand to keep the new boy in check'. The association was not entirely beneficial to Palme. With skilled workers showing dissatisfaction with their rewards, the traditional right-wing election-call for tax reductions to stimulate individual and corporate initiative was put with renewed vigour. Inevitably, it was the finance minister who took the brunt of the attack; and his defence, that the government intended holding taxation at its existing level while giving aid to those sectors of the economy really in need, sounded less than usually persuasive. The possibility was mooted that this time round Sträng might be a vote-loser.

Dagens Nyheter called the election 'a struggle on a knife's edge'. That the social democrats would fall back was taken for granted, but would they also lose their majority? On the day, the government's share of the vote dropped by nearly 5 per cent to give them 163 seats. The parties of the right collected 170 seats between them, with the centre moving ahead strongly to return 71 members. But there were also the communists to take into account. They had been expected to fall victim to the new constitutional rule that to qualify for representation in the Riksdag a party must secure 4 per cent of the national vote or 12 per cent in any one constituency. But since condemning the Russian invasion of Czechoslovakia and dissociating themselves from Moscow, the communists, now preferring to call themselves the left communists, had rediscovered some of their old vitality. Carried forward on a wave of anti-capitalist and anti-American sentiment, chiefly among young voters, they won 17 seats, enough to put the social democrats back into office, only this time as a minority government.

Since the communists gained largely at the expense of the social democrats, it could be argued that yet more votes would have been lost had Palme not shown sympathy for the left. The 1960s' rejuvenation of Marxism, a phenomenon of Western dimensions, was not to be ignored. Even in Denmark, where the social democrats were more hostile to activists on the left, they were forced to accommodate them in the power structure. But insofar as Palme was capable of tempering his views to suit his immediate advantage (and by European standards he was a refreshingly honest politician), it seems probable that he would have done better by his own people if he had followed more closely in Erlander's footsteps. Despite his much published courtship of the left he failed to win their wholehearted support, yet at the same time he antagonized the right and frightened them into thinking seriously, for the first time, about the prospects for a centre–liberal–conservative coalition.

Events following the election stimulated the spirit of togetherness in the opposition camp. Dissatisfaction among skilled and professional workers was soon shown to extend well beyond the iron-mining region of the north, indeed well beyond Sweden, because there were labour disputes and strikes throughout Scandinavia. At home the trouble really started when the two

biggest white-collar unions, the federation of professional associations (SACO) and the national federation of government employees (SR) put in for salary increases of up to twenty-three per
cent. What worried the government was not the claim itself,
though it was far in excess of what they had expected to pay,
but the accompanying demand for separate bargaining machinery. Here was a major revolt by middle-class unionists against
the whole concept of centralized wage negotiations; and the
employers' federation (SAF), which had long symbolized the
strength of the Swedish economy, was now the object of contempt for white-collar workers, who knew that if the policy of
minimizing pay differentials was to be effective it was they who
had to make the sacrifices. In deciding to go it alone they
challenged both the government and the LO.

Palme, the inexperienced leader whose authority had been
diminished by an unsatisfactory election, surprised everybody
by reacting quickly and strongly. He flatly refused to compromise, and a limited strike was countered by a lockout which
affected the railways, schools, welfare services and even the
armed forces, and threw the country into chaos. The fact that
there was a strike at all, in what was normally held up to be a
model industrial environment, attracted wide attention. But
there were aspects of the dispute so extraordinary as to make
what was in any case a strong story, front-page news round the
world. Among those threatened with lockout were the church-
men, who, as state employees, were as entitled as anyone else to
their union cards. The prospect of the clergy being denied
the use of their own churches made the government look
faintly ridiculous, as did the battle – a purely verbal one –
with the army. Fearing that the officers might use their membership of SR as justification for doing less than their normal
duties, the government threatened to retaliate by locking out
the military, a move which was thwarted by the supreme
commander, who announced that if his staff were prevented
from doing their work, the army conscripts would be sent
home.

After nearly two months of fruitless exchange between unions
and government, Palme tightened the pressure. Relying on
middle-class regard for authority he rushed through emergency
legislation which banned all strikes and lockouts for six weeks.

Union resolve crumbled and a settlement was patched together which did little to satisfy white-collar aspirations.

If anything, middle-class complaints became more vocal over the following months. This was not so much a reflection on Palme's radical policies – though his promise to bring democracy to the shop floor raised a few managerial hackles – as a reaction to a general downturn in the economy which had a mild but noticeably depressing affect on the standards of living. Like their colleagues in Norway the social democrats held to the tried and trusted Keynesian remedies. The reserve funds which companies had set aside for just such a rainy day were released to maintain the level of investment, and loans were raised on the international money market, but Sweden already had a balance-of-payments problem, and with near-full employment pushing up labour costs the prospects for renewed growth were almost entirely dependent on international market forces outside Swedish control.

With an uncertain economic future, and evidence of a voting shift away from the social democrats, the approach to the 1973 election was taken cautiously. The time was not right for Palme to prove himself the great social reformer. Industrial democracy, when it was discussed at all, was projected well into the future and, fearing a loss of confidence in the finance market, the party played soft on an LO-backed proposal to use the state pension fund to buy shares in private enterprise. With Palme failing to live up to his reputation as a socialist ogre the opposition tried a more general attack on what they saw as the underlying contradictions of social democracy. Though professing the freedom of the individual as the first objective of the welfare society, the social-democrat party, it was claimed, had come to behave like an arrogant big brother – fussy and over-protective, telling others how best to run their affairs and then, if frustrated, resorting to bullying tactics. It was an argument which had to be put across with some care, since it implied that Swedish voters had been too feeble to stand up for themselves. Yet curiously, the politician who gained most from the discomfort of the social democrats was one for whom the very concept of subtlety was as incomprehensible as a man-powered flight to the moon.

When, in 1972, Gunnar Hedlund stepped down as leader of

the centre party, he was succeeded by Thorbjörn Fälldin. There were a lot of jokes made about Fälldin. Closely identified with his northern rural background, he was more often photographed messing about on his farm than in dealing with political business. His small-town image, accentuated by a fondness for home-spun philosophy delivered in a ponderous monotone, put him at the other end of the political line from Palme, the sophisticated internationalist. But that did not make him a nonentity.

The same people who worried about Palme's cleverness found Fälldin's honesty refreshing and endearing. So obviously not part of the Stockholm establishment, he was a persuasive advocate of decentralization and a convincing defender of the rights of the individual against state bureaucracy. For those Swedes who felt constrained by a welfare system which seemed to offer only a single, straight path from cradle to the grave Fälldin offered a way of escape. Where he was weakest was in his relationship with the other right-wing parties. To become prime minister he needed their support, but though they had much in common the liberal and conservative leaders were unwilling to risk all on what could be a short-lived populist crusade. For the 1973 election they each fought for their own programmes but agreed that if the results were in their favour they would set up a coalition.

The social democrats played on this weakness, making it a central theme of their campaign that if the bourgeois parties could not put together a joint platform they were incapable of exercising effective government. But they were sensitive to the charge that they were unresponsive to the voters' wishes. Palme was frequently defensive, stressing that 'this is a good country' and that to elect Fälldin was to risk a fall in living standards. A social-democrat poster urged, 'Do not vote away social security.'

The turnout of over ninety per cent was the highest ever recorded in Swedish election history. The centre party made a great advance, particularly in the metropolitan areas, but the gain of nineteen seats was mainly at the expense of the liberals, who also lost badly to the conservatives. The social democrats fell back yet again, but the dramatic polarization that many had expected did not take place. Instead there was deadlock, with 175 members elected to each side. Pausing only to wonder how they came to approve a constitution which allowed for an even number of representatives (an amendment was soon passed), the politicians talked their way to a solution, albeit an unsatisfactory one. What evidence there was of electoral preference suggested that Palme should try to keep his government together, at least until the Riksdag decreed otherwise. He was the leader of the largest party and the popular vote marginally favoured the social democrats who, with their communist allies, had a majority of 77,000 in a total count of 4.9 million.

Despite misgivings that a programme broad enough to attract votes from the opposition would damage the confidence of party activists, Palme kept his sharp words for the conservative leader, Gösta Bohman, and was polite to Fälldin and extremely accommodating to the liberal leader, Gunnar Helén. He was helped by a grass-roots revolt in the centre party against Fälldin's plans for a merger with the liberals, who were correspondingly more attentive to government overtures. Since the voters had refused to reward them for their pre-election solidarity with the other non-socialist parties, an understanding with the social democrats offered the best hope of recovery from their low point in the polls. Helen continued to assure the public that his party remained anti-socialist; but it was no secret that he was influenced in his thinking by the example of the German free democrats, who participated constructively with the social democrats in the Bonn government.

Having lost the initiative, Fälldin adopted a wait-and-see policy which disappointed his supporters but was almost certainly the best tactical decision. The way was thus open for a government of compromise – or chance! In the first year no less than sixteen parliamentary decisions were made by lot, a practice which gave rise to much ill-received fun at the expense of the politicians.

On basic issues, however, the government could usually patch together a majority. An urgent package of economic measures – a liberal-inspired demand for a cut in VAT was accepted in return for votes in favour of selective subsidies – was followed by a series of all-party consultations to discover what other proposals might win broad acceptance. The first, held at the Haga Pavilion outside Stockholm, led to a social-democrat-liberal deal on further tax cuts. Haga II, which followed a year later in March 1975, produced a social-democrat-liberal-centre agreement on an eight to ten per cent ceiling on wages. Haga III brought no constructive results, but by then another election was due and the parties were keener to point up their differences than to show how well they could agree. The main question was how the economy could absorb the doubling of oil prices. Sweden ranked first in the world in energy consumption per head of population, and with seventy per cent of her needs met by oil imports the price spiral of 1973-4 added some eight thousand million Kronor to her trade bill, more than enough to wipe out any gains from the recent export recovery. Sweden kept up her investment rate by using her creditworthiness on the international money markets and by encouraging industry to keep up production levels even when sales were low. As a result unemployment was held down and living standards continued to improve, though far less dramatically than hitherto. But with wages increasing three times as fast as in Germany, stocks piling up at home and market shares falling in the traditional export areas, the economy remained in deep trouble.

In the sure knowledge that world demand for oil would continue to outpace supply for the foreseeable future and that further price rises could be expected, the first priority for the government was to find a substitute for imported energy. One possible solution was to accelerate the expansion of nuclear power. Sweden was further ahead than most with plans for a network of reactors. A state-controlled atomic energy company had been set up in 1947, and before long a number of large private firms were also putting up capital for research and development. One of these was the electrical engineering company, Allmänna Svenska Elektriska (ASEA) which pioneered the boiling-water reactor in opposition to the heavy-water reactor favoured by its state rival. The BWR used more uranium but it had the edge in terms of cost, a factor which presumably weighed heavier with a consortium of private-sector electrical supply companies who in 1966 gave ASEA its first order. When their lead was followed by the state power board, the government decided to tip all its eggs into one basket and refused to fund the efforts of the atomic energy company to exploit the heavy-water reactor. Instead money was put into an ASEA offshoot, which came to a commercially attractive deal with the American company Westinghouse to build light-water reactors under licence.

Up to this point there was no hint of public nervousness about a major shift to a source of power with an unproven safety record. Opponents later claimed that this was because everyone outside a magic circle of scientists, civil servants and business-men was singularly ill-informed. But the Riksdag debated the issue in 1970 and 1971, and on both occasions the government's plans for phasing in nuclear energy were approved unani-mously. It was a different matter when, in the wake of the oil crisis, the expansion programme was revised upwards to allow for a chain of fifteen reactors to be completed by 1985. Suddenly the country realized the extent of its commitment and the hazards involved. Critics like the writer Eva Moberg and the Nobel prize-winner Professor Hans Alfvén, who had been accus-tomed to speaking into thin air, now found themselves with eager audiences. And to Thorbjörn Fälldin, the arch-opponent of the centralized decision-making process which allowed the nuclear lobby to flourish, the spokesman for rural Sweden and the champion of the anti-pollution movement, they offered a cause into which he could throw himself body and soul.

He toured the country calling for the end of a government which, by its shortsighted policy, was prepared '. . . to endanger our children and grandchildren for thousands of years to come'. His almost religious devotion to the anti-nuclear crusade – 'No government post is so important to me that I will hedge on my conviction in this matter. . . . I will not take part in a government that starts one more reactor' – re-established Fälldin as the leading alternative for the premiership even though his poten-tial coalition partners, the liberals and conservatives, were much more sympathetic to nuclear development.

Fälldin's emotional appeal was scorned by the social demo-crats, but with hindsight even those in government at the time admit that the centre-party leader had a point. In a society which prided itself on its openness, important matters had been resolved without the public having any idea of what was going on. If the lines of communication had not been blocked was it likely, say, that one of the earliest reactors, Barsebäck, would have been built just eighteen kilometres from Malmö and twenty from Copenhagen? The oil crisis gave weight to the government assertion that it would have been irresponsible to ignore the nuclear option, but that did not explain why a socialist administration had delegated responsibility for future energy policy to a private-enterprise consortium. If it had been otherwise, argued the anti-nuclear lobby, Sweden might have avoided the commitment to light-water reactors which had the strategic disadvantage of requiring home-mined uranium to be taken first to the US for enrichment.

With the election fast approaching, what was left of the social democrats' reputation for open democracy was further tarnished when in January 1976 the film director Ingmar Bergman was taken from rehearsals at the Royal Dramatic Theatre in Stockholm to be interviewed by the police about his taxes. What they thought they had was a clear case of tax evasion involving payment to film actors via a production company in Switzerland. But whatever the evidence – and its weaknesses were later revealed by the ombudsman, whose investigation led to Bergman's receiving a sizeable tax refund – the authorities were at best clumsy in their handling of the affair.

After spending some time in hospital recovering from what he described as 'nearly unbearable humiliation', Bergman announced he was leaving Sweden to work abroad. Before doing so he launched a blistering attack on the social democrats' 'ideology of grey compromise' which pointed up the virtue of expensive programmes of social reform while ignoring the dangers of a bureaucracy spreading 'like a fast-growing cancer'. If they did not know it before, Swedish taxpayers were now aware that revenue inspectors could enter their offices and homes (the former without even a court order), require banks to surrender statements of accounts and even see private medical records – all with the law on their side. The real problem for the government was that deep down even the most honest and respectable citizen felt that tax evasion was not a crime. On the contrary, anyone who found a way of holding on to a bigger share of his earnings was commended for his ingenuity.

For the opposition the tax issue was their strongest electoral card. Industrialists complained that workers were staying away because they were expected to pay well over fifty per cent in marginal tax. The position was even worse for small businessmen and the self-employed, who had to pay their own social security. Their plight became a matter for public debate when Astrid Lindgren, the much-loved children's writer, was assured by the tax board that she was bound to pay them 102 per cent of her year's income. This bizarre calculation was the result of bad mathematics and a one-off change in the way payroll taxes were charged, but this was no consolation either to Miss Lindgren or to many employers who found that in real terms they were often less well off than those who worked for them. The writer of fairy tales responded by publishing in a popular daily a charming story about a never-never land where the rules of logic were infinitely adaptable to allow people as many per cents as they wanted. The news value of these events was enhanced by the knowledge that both Bergman and Astrid Lindgren were life-long social democrats.

The prime minister faced another embarrassment in his dealings with the unions. The 1976 LO congress approved a scheme whereby industry was to set aside twenty per cent of profits for the purchase of shares on behalf of employees, or more specifically the unions. The plan was essentially long-term; it would be a matter of decades before the unions could expect to dominate a major business. Still, it was a commitment to workers' control. Ideologically Palme was sympathetic, but, given the unsettled state of the economy, the timing of the proposal could not have been more inappropriate. Fälldin was quick to take the point. At his party conference in June he signalled the official opening of the campaign with a bitter attack on what he saw as the trend towards a planned and centralized economy, hinting at a parallel between social-democrat policies and the economic philosophy of the eastern-European bloc.

Still, the social democrats recovered strongly in the run-up to the election; and it was not until the final week when Fälldin made his famous pledge to abandon nuclear power within ten years that public attention refocused on the centre party.

The social democrats lost just less than one per cent on their share of the vote but it deprived them of their majority and gave Fälldin his chance. Although Palme blamed his defeat on Fälldin's attack on nuclear policy, the centre actually lost four seats but this was more than offset by the liberals' five-seat advance and a gain of four by the conservatives. As leader of the second largest party Fälldin remained the natural alternative as prime minister.

For voters and politicians it took a little time to get used to the changes at the top. Defeat for the old ruling party had been expected yet held off for so long that even when the results showed clearly that power was passing to the right, few could believe it was actually happening. One senior member of the new administration distinguished himself in parliament by referring to Palme as prime minister several weeks after that gentleman had become leader of the opposition.

The shaping of the coalition took a little time but was surprisingly painless. Throughout the campaign Fälldin had maintained that any government which he headed would be bound by the middle-of-the-road principles of the centre party and liberals. But he took care not to fall out with the conservatives, who assumed along with everyone else that if their claims to power-sharing were reasonable they would be welcomed into the new administration. Once the question ceased to be hypothetical the conservatives asked for, and got, one more cabinet post than the liberals, who were the smallest of the three parties, and the job of minister of economic affairs for their leader, Gösta Bohman. The liberals were compensated by the appointment of their leader, Per Ahlmark, as deputy prime minister as well as minister of labour. Three more diverse characters to be in charge of government it was difficult to imagine – Fälldin, the slow-talking rural philosopher and chief mediator, Bohman, more the crusty elder statesman, outspoken and stubborn, and Ahlmark, at thirty-seven the youngest, clever but mercurial.

Of the policy deals to be made, the most urgent was in the sensitive area of nuclear development, where Fälldin had cried 'Stop!' too often to be allowed to forget his commitment – or so it was thought. Despite mumblings of discontent in his own party and accusations of betrayal thrown at him by the social democrats, he settled for allowing Barsebäck II to be loaded and for the rest of the nuclear programme to remain on the drawing board while a special commission – that much-favoured Swedish palliative for political ills – examined future energy supply and alternatives to nuclear power.

The rest of the government's programme was positively radical by any but Scandinavian standards. The promise to encourage competition and to increase individual freedom and choice was quickly translated into lower taxes on small businesses and the appointment of four committees to study ways of relaxing the bureaucratic grip. But the cynics noted that the first non-socialist budget in forty-four years allowed for thirty-five thousand more public-sector jobs. And there was no understating the commitment to 'carry on a policy of social reform', which included new measures to help the underprivileged, better working conditions and further moves towards sex equality. In the international sphere, where else but in Scandinavia could a government of the right pledge 'increased support to the struggle for liberation in southern Africa'?

There were, however, signs of a toughening attitude towards the unions, whose deal with the outgoing government had guaranteed increases of over forty per cent in 1975 and 1976. The chairman of the employers' federation was first in with a warning that there was no room in the economy for any immediate improvement in real wages – an opinion endorsed by the government, whose declared policy was to hold back on production costs to give the export industries a chance to catch up. There was no doubt in anyone's mind that wage-induced inflation was the main cause of Sweden's fading appeal in the international market place. Other Europeans – the Germans notably – were steadily turning out quality goods at a lower price.

But though the coalition was prepared to weather a strike by white-collar workers – the first ever to result from a failure in national wage negotiations – rather than break its own wage guidelines, the strategy adopted by the Germans of keeping the domestic economy in check by allowing unemployment to rise was never seriously considered. Instead, Per Ahlmark as minister of labour led a substantial effort to keep unemployment below two per cent, a policy which required a record level of state intervention to help companies ride out the latest crisis. One industry after another – shipyards, steel, textiles, glass, shoes – asked for and received loans and grants which soon reached an annual total of three billion dollars, an outlay about equal to the country's total industrial profits. By the end of its life the coalition had accomplished more nationalization than all previous administrations put together – quite an achievement for a supposedly right-wing government, and one which may well have accounted for unions' tacit conversion to wage restraint. They also accepted the need to hold down consumer spending, allowing a VAT increase and a double devaluation – six per cent in March 1977 and ten per cent in August – without much in return except a price freeze. With wages pegged, the combined effect was to reduce the real living standards. As part of the second devaluation, the coalition took Sweden out of the European snake, the linking arrangement for a group of currencies which had effectively over-valued the Krona by tying it to the Deutschmark. The unions were rewarded for their forbearance by news of order books refilling and an impressive reduction in the trade deficit.

But if the government deserved credit for a bold economic policy there were few other signs that the three parties could work constructively together. On energy policy, Fälldin found himself fighting a lonely and an increasingly desperate battle. A new law making permits for reactor construction dependent on government approval of measures for disposing of radio-active waste was accompanied by a stern warning from Fälldin that unless the industry could offer stronger guarantees against accidents further development could be discounted. The law did not apply to the five reactors already in operation – presumably because if it had the entire nuclear programme would have come to a halt, and that was unacceptable to his coalition partners. But if the risks were as serious as Fälldin claimed, how could he remain head of a government which was prepared to gamble with the safety of the people? It was a question the prime minister frequently put to his own conscience but without getting any easy answers. His hope was that given a little time his energy advisers would come up with a solution.

There was no shortage of experts ready to plead their own special cases. Voices were lifted in praise of hydro-electric power. But most of the country's rivers had already been harnessed, and in the north, where there was spare capacity, environmentalist groups were strongly opposed to dams and power stations intruding on the last great European nature reserve. The only realistic prospect was for those rivers already providing HEP to be exploited more intensively.

There were hopes for a Swedish oil find, but searches off the coast tapped only small reserves near Gotland and in the south.

Nor had prospecting abroad brought much success, though Swedish enterprise was involved in projects as far removed from home as Ireland, Egypt, Tunisia and Spain. Curiously, Swedish Petroleum AB was slow to bid for exploration rights in the North Sea, though a deal securing five per cent of the output of the Thistle Field in the UK sector and the right to buy a share of the output of the Norwegian consortium NOCO marginally reduced the country's dependence on the Middle East.

Generous provisions were made for research into the development of solar and wind energy, and a report from the secretariat for future studies made bold predictions for the conversion of marsh and secondary woodland to feed fired electric power and heating plants, but common sense ruled that the best prospect for the short term was to secure a share of the more than adequate North Sea oil reserves. There was no lack of Norwegian enthusiasm for an energy agreement, but the Swedish part of the bargain, to provide technical and commercial help in building up her neighbour's industrial base, proved to be less easy to secure than politicians on either side had expected (see Chapter 6).

Fälldin's strenuous efforts to find a way out of the nuclear dilemma met with another setback when his own energy commission decided by a clear majority that radio-active waste could be safely treated and stored. The leader who not two years earlier had pledged that nuclear power would be phased out by 1985 now had to decide whether to go ahead with fuelling two new reactors. While he was agonizing with his conscience the coalition was further weakened by the resignation of Per Ahlmark. It was no secret that he found it difficult to work with his conservative opposite number Gösta Bohman, or that he was contemptuous of Fälldin's simplistic style of politics. But it came as a shock to his colleagues when 'for deeply personal reasons' he abruptly walked out of the government and out of politics. His successor, the young-looking forty-six-year-old Ola Ullsten, who advanced from minister for overseas aid to the second job in the government, was a less ebullient character; but insofar as he had better relations with the social democrats than Ahlmark, who saw too many personal rivals in their ranks, he added another source of friction to an already shaky government.

Criticized and satirized on all sides, Fälldin showed signs of losing his nerve. When the Stockholm daily paper *Aftonbladet* jokingly implied that he was not altogether right in the head, he over-reacted and sued for libel. He lost the case, as everyone said he would, but his disappointment was such that he thought seriously of resigning, doubting, as he put it, 'whether the post of prime minister is worth the personal price it demands'. True to his popularist style of leadership he talked openly about his disillusionment, embarrassing some voters who were used to their politicians behaving in a more reserved fashion but im pressing many others by his apparent sincerity. Eventually, however, he allowed himself to be persuaded by his party to stay on while agreeing with his conservative and liberal colleagues to delay loading the two latest reactors until a special geological study had been made on the safety of storing nuclear waste in rock chambers. The general assumption was that he would eventually be forced to authorize the fuelling of Ringhals 3 and Forsmark 1 and yet two more reactors then in the last phase of construction. The prospect was anathema to the hardliners in the centre party, who were not prepared to budge at least until the popular view had been tested. Fälldin was told to reopen negotiations with a demand for a referendum. But this was the sticking point for Ullsten and Bohman who, while not opposed in principle to a referendum, were not prepared to concede it as a priority. Fälldin was trapped. Just two years after he had achieved one of the most remarkable victories in Swedish election history, the virulent anti-nuclear campaigner fell victim to his own success.

His resignation and the fall of the government put the social democrats into a quandary. They were riding high in the opinion polls, yet were unwilling to push for an election when they were constitutionally bound to repeat the performance in less than ten months' time. The alternative of a coalition with the liberals on the West German and latterly the Danish model was not even considered by a party hierarchy which remained convinced that the 1976 defeat was an electoral aberration soon to be corrected without the need for ideological compromise or even a serious reassessment of immediate policy. On the right, it was conceded that the centre party had to remain out of government until the current parliament had run its course.

Fälldin let it be known that he would give tacit support to a liberal-conservative coalition but the social democrats were up in arms at the prospect of a government which had the conservatives as the dominant partner. Nor were the liberals keen on identifying themselves so closely with the ethics of the free-market economy.

Palme and Ullsten concluded that the only possibility was for the liberals to govern alone. It was an extraordinary turn of fate that the most junior of the party leaders, heading the second smallest parliamentary group (only the communists had fewer seats), should be asked to run the country. The immediate circumstances could not have been less propitious. In the Riksdag vote, Ullsten received only thirty-nine votes of approval – those of his own party. The conservatives and communists voted against him and everyone else abstained, the social democrats having promised not to oppose if the liberals kept to the left of centre and were not too adventurous. On paper, therefore, he headed one of the weakest minority governments in Europe. But looking beyond parliament the prospects were more encouraging. Just a few days before his departure Fälldin detected the first signs of economic recovery. Industrial production had started rising again, the trade balance was once more in surplus and, with devaluation aided by wage restraint, Sweden had regained the edge in international competitiveness. The scene was set for the liberals to stimulate private consumption with a package of tax cuts and improved family allowances – all good vote-winners.

To the man in the street it was Ullsten, a personable and self-assured leader, who showed every intention of governing as if he really had a majority behind him, who was responsible for the change in the country's fortune. A sharp rise for the liberals in the opinion polls infuriated the conservatives, who resented being pushed out of office just as Bohman's tenure at the economics ministry appeared to be bearing fruit, and it worried the social democrats who suddenly realized that if they wanted to win the 1979 election they could not afford to dawdle at the starting-line, waiting for others to make the running. In February they launched a nation-wide debate on a ten-point programme for change hailed by the party press as 'an election platform on which tens of thousands of social-democratic

217

election workers can stand'. Independent observers wondered if it could bear the weight. The policy-makers had rightly identified taxation as a major theme for the election but, bravely or foolishly depending on political view, the social democrats argued that a real tax cut was impracticable. Selective concessions such as a reduction in income-tax for those on low and middle earnings had to be paid for by new forms of taxation. That was the bad news. The good news was that the social democrats believed they had found a painless way to raise more revenue. The idea was to bring in a production-factor tax – really a tax on company wage bills and capital. The effect of this on employment and production costs had serious implications for the export competitiveness which Swedish industry had only recently regained. But the immediate problem for the social democrats was to sell the proposition that the state genuinely needed to hold on to its share of the national income. Excepting the communists, the other parties put more emphasis on savings than on extra spending and, following the conservative lead, held out the hope of substantial tax cuts.

Back in the social-democrat programme was the proposal to set up employee funds to buy shares in industry. It was given low priority, Palme having persuaded the party executive to proceed cautiously. There were those on the left who wanted to know how long they could hold back issues like workers' control and still retain their socialist credentials. But the party had not enjoyed its experience of opposition, and wanted badly to regain office. It was not the time for bold experiments which were more likely to frighten off the floating voters. The basic appeal was to the idea of *Folkhemmet* (the people's home) – the caring, welfare society which the social democrats had built up and which only they could be entrusted to preserve.

For a few weeks after the fall of the coalition the nuclear-energy debate lost its sense of urgency. By agreement with the social democrats and conservatives, the minority government drafted an energy bill which allowed for a stop on the expansion of the nuclear industry once twelve reactors were operating. Meanwhile, the experts appointed to examine the safety aspects of loading Forsmark 1 and Ringhals 3 gave the go-ahead in the face of continuing opposition from the centre party. It seemed as if the humiliation of Fälldin was complete. But, before the government had a chance to act, an event on the other side of the world caused the whole of Swedish nuclear policy to be thrown back into the melting pot.

The reactor leak at Three Mile Island near Harrisburg, Pennsylvania, made a stronger impact in Sweden than in the United States. That the crisis was competently handled insofar as no one suffered any ill-effects was barely detectable in Swedish reports, which dwelt almost exclusively on the sobering if self-evident observation that accidents could happen – and if in Harrisburg, why not in Sweden? The affair was like a tonic to Fälldin; but before he had the chance to recover fully, Palme reacted in a very calculated way to prevent a split in his own ranks and to stop short a centre-party revival. In April the social-democratic leadership conceded that a referendum on nuclear energy was not such a bad idea after all, as long as it was held after the election.

Meanwhile, it was accepted that the contents of the energy bill and the decision on loading any new reactors should wait on the nation's verdict. In conceding to the social-democrat initiative the government had the embarrassment of justifying its volte-face to its recent partners in coalition. No doubt reflecting that if Harrisburg had happened a few months earlier he might still have been prime minister, Fälldin turned on the liberal leader, claiming that he had lost all credibility the moment he allowed Palme to decide the government's energy policy. It did not look that way to Ullsten, who felt very much alone in solving the immediate problem of negotiating an adequate supply of oil to last the country through the winter.

In the wake of two OPEC price rises and an oil shortage on the international market, Sweden was paying out more for less. With the major companies refusing to step up deliveries, buyers resorted to the Rotterdam spot market where every new bid set a record. Most of the price increases were passed on to consumers to try to cut consumption while hopes were pinned on an exclusive deal with one of the oil-producing nations. But the best that could be secured was an offer of three hundred thousand tons from Iraq, a fraction of the country's needs. As rumours strengthened of petrol rationing by winter, liberal popularity slumped.

With the centre party and the liberals in the doldrums the

way was clear for the conservatives to present the free-market economy as the only real alternative to social democracy. Gösta Bohman mounted an energetic campaign against bureaucratic restrictions and excessive public spending. The other non-socialist parties tried hard to dissociate themselves from what they regarded as Bohman's extreme views while maintaining interest in reviving the coalition. But having a cause to fight gave the conservative leader the same advantage as Fälldin had enjoyed in the previous election, when nuclear energy had been the central issue. The opinion polls showed a marked swing away from the centre towards the conservatives – ironically the party most strongly in favour of holding to the nuclear programme.

The election was exciting because everyone expected a tight finish, but the campaign lacked substance. With the all-important decision on energy policy postponed until the following spring there was no basis for constructive discussion on wages, tax reforms or social expenditure. Not surprisingly the electorate found it difficult to make up its mind. A gentle swing to the left brought the social democrats a gain of two seats and the communists another three. This was thought at first to put Palme just in front, but the contest was so close that the final result turned on the distribution of forty thousand postal votes. These turned out to favour the right and to give the partnership (assuming it could be formed) a one-seat advantage. The lasting image of the election is of the non-socialist leaders waiting for the declaration. Pictures show Ullsten and Fälldin to be passive, almost depressed, at the prospect of a return to power while Bohman beams a happy smile. It was, after all, his victory. The conservatives jumped eighteen seats, largely at the expense of the centre, to become the largest of the non-socialist parties, with the liberals barely holding on to what they had.

There followed a month of party wrangling when frantic attempts to find a leader to hold the centre-right together inspired rumours that Fälldin was about to be replaced by someone more acceptable to the other two parties. But from this low point in his fortunes Fälldin gradually reasserted his authority, as Gösta Bohman, himself rejected as a candidate for the premiership, declared his preference for the centre-party leader. It was then only a matter of time for Ullsten to accept that his expectations of continuing as premier were to be disappointed. Having reached that decision the ruling triangle barely had time to agree ministerial appointments and to promise a mildly reformist programme before they were plunged back into electioneering on the narrow but vital question of energy policy.

The nuclear referendum took place in March 1980. All parties accepted in advance that the result would be binding, but they were less direct on formulating a set of options which enabled the voters to express a clear choice. Three proposals were offered, two of them advocating a doubling in the number of reactors but nevertheless projecting a long-term phasing out of nuclear power, while the third called specifically for a phasing out within ten years. Thus the referendum gave Swedes who believed in the lasting utility of nuclear power no chance to express their belief. Equally, those who were convinced that nuclear power was a threat to human survival were faced with it for the rest of the decade even if the anti-nuclear proposal won.

The most telling statistic in the campaign was the cost to Sweden of doing without nuclear power, which an independent study put at eight billion pounds. Were the environmentalists prepared to sacrifice living standards for their beliefs? Much also was made of the impact of a 'no' vote on employment in areas where reactors were sited. Officially the social democrats and the liberals backed proposal two, which differed from proposal one (the conservative preference) only in stipulating that all new power plants must be publicly owned. In wanting an early phase-out as in proposal three, the centre found itself an ally of the communists, an unlikely association which gave the far left a new respectability.

Split three ways on an issue that was central to economic strategy, it seemed unlikely that the coalition could long survive the referendum, whatever the result. But when the voters gave the decisive yes to nuclear development – the first two proposals got respectively 18.7 and 39.3 per cent – Fälldin did not follow the line of least resistance and resign. His centre-party supporters referred hopefully to what was described as the Norwegian precedent when the social democrats accepted the referendum vote against joining the European Community. But on that occasion prime minister Bratteli, whose devotion to Europe was every bit as strong as Fälldin's enthusiasm for clean air, took his government out of office. The main difference perhaps was that joining the EEC was an immediate question for the Norwegians, whereas the expansion of nuclear energy was not a matter on which a definitive policy could be quickly decided. In sticking to his job Fälldin could comfort himself that after activating the two new reactors which were ready for service, it would be some time before other sensitive decisions were required. Meanwhile a complex and potentially dangerous technology needed careful political handling, and there could be no doubt in the centre leader's mind as to who was best suited for that task.

If others in the government had their doubts, they were deterred from expressing them by the sure knowledge that open disagreement would undermine the coalition and bring demands for an early election that would be difficult to resist. The urge to make something of their narrow majority was reinforced by the conviction that they were alone capable of dealing with Sweden's economic problems, notably the challenge of trying to apply a wages policy at a time when the country's high labour costs were causing her to lose badly in international competitiveness. The 1979 negotiations between LO and SAF led to an initial moderate award but failed to set limits to the following year's increase. With inflation moving back over ten per cent, the unions pitched their demands at the same level. The employers wanted to pay much less, arguing that the economy could stand an increase of not more than three per cent. An attempt to bridge the gap was made with a government offer to freeze prices for nine months and to reduce taxes if the unions temporized. Their refusal inaugurated the biggest labour conflict in Sweden's history, with strikes and lockouts shutting down most of the country's industry and public services. Recourse to the official mediators, which in normal circumstances should have provided a way out of the impasse, was blocked by the employers, who refused a recommended compromise settlement of nearly seven per cent. The mediators then resigned, a cue for Fälldin to intervene once again, this time with a dramatic summons to SAF representatives to present themselves before a full meeting of the cabinet. He then warned the employers that if they remained obdurate the government would impose sanctions to end the dispute. SAF gave in and the mediators' judgement was endorsed by both sides.

It was, said Palme, like the ending of a bad operetta. But there was more to it than that. Clearly, the industrial relations machinery which had served Sweden so well over the years was proving inadequate for an economy where growth could no longer be assumed to be a constant factor. It was not so much tinkering with the system that was needed as a wholly new philosophy of political management.

Conclusion

Each Nordic country had its own particular reason for registering an anti-establishment vote in the early to mid-seventies – the Common Market issue in Norway, taxation in Denmark, the poverty of the regions in Finland, inflation in Iceland and over-government in Sweden. As the leading party the social democrats suffered most, but there were also dramatic changes on the right, with extremist parties making their strongest advances in Norway and Denmark.

So was it just coincidence that all of Norden should be thrown off political balance at about the same time? Ignoring for a moment the occupational groups with special grouses, studies of those who changed allegiance point to the newly affluent as the most easily deflected from their normal loyalties – typically the youngish couples on the suburban housing estates, those who had done well out of social democracy but who now feared that any further moves towards the egalitarian society could only be achieved at their expense. It had to be accepted on the left that its working-class foundation was fast contracting, and with it the number of voters who were prepared to take the system as they found it.

But there was a deeper problem. In central Scandinavia, where the social democrats had enjoyed a long run of uninterrupted power, there was an uncomfortable feeling that the party had taken on a life of its own, controlling and directing the nation's affairs as best suited its own interests. It was an interpretation of events which the left angrily rejected. In the age of the computer and the centralized data bank it was natural to assume that the state had too much power to manipulate and control. But by international acclaim, Norden boasted the most open system of government in the world. Hardly any official activity was closed to public scrutiny, and consultation with relevant interest groups was assumed to be an essential preliminary to decision-making at all levels.

Yet something was lacking. The middle-class Danes who complained that their taxes were too high did not feel adequately represented in the power structure; nor did the Swedish anti-nuclear campaigners or the Norwegian farmers and fishermen, who resented the assumption that they were bound to do well out of the Common Market. Ideas for extending the freedom of the individual soon figured on every party agenda. Then in the second half of the seventies Nordic government concentrated all their efforts on holding off the worst effects of world recession. Departures in ideology took a poor second place to efficient economic management, and the old political pattern started to reassert itself. But the problem of the individual's being able to make his presence felt in a complex and sophisticated social organization remained and would not go away. It promised to be one of the foremost political questions of the following decade.

6
Nordic co-operation in economic recession

The mid-seventies recession was a great stimulant to Nordic co-operation. Though its effect varied in intensity from one country to another, it was a problem shared and one that clearly could be mitigated by joint strategy. But first reactions to OPEC's application of the laws of supply and demand, which put up the price of crude oil by nearly four times between 1973 and 1976 and disrupted international trade, led to a policy split in the Nordic bloc.

Norway and Sweden chose to ride out the crisis with direct support for industry and employment while at the same time holding down consumer and public spending. They were fortunate in being able to rely on the international money market to help them along. As good credit risks, they took full advantage of their borrowing powers. By the end of 1978 Norway had accumulated a net foreign debt of almost twenty billion dollars, or close to half her GNP. She was, of course, a special case. With North Sea oil on tap to supply her energy-hungry neighbours there was really no limit to her borrowing capacity.

Sweden too was in a strong position. Though not having any oil of her own she did have a well established industrial base supporting advanced technology for which there was a lively demand in many of those countries with oil to spare.

It was less easy for Denmark and Finland to spend their way out of the recession. Though prosperous by western standards both countries were already heavily in debt as a result of diversifying exports in the sixties, a massive operation of industrial redirection financed largely by the international bankers. Now, any spare borrowing capacity was held in reserve to pay for oil at inflated prices. Making a virtue out of necessity, it was claimed by the two governments that subsidies to industry would merely delay the structural change needed to increase competitiveness abroad. It was an argument at first treated lightly in Norway and Sweden, but as the recession wore on they acknowledged that the conventional remedies for hard times in industry were, of themselves, no longer adequate. Leading areas of the economy were coming under pressure from low-cost competitors in the developing countries like Brazil, Hong Kong, Korea and Taiwan, a feature of international commerce that was likely to get more serious in the years ahead. It came to be recognized that support for ailing industries was an unproductive as well as an expensive exercise unless it was accompanied by a reappraisal of future demand.

A prime example was shipbuilding, important to Sweden, Denmark and Finland, where it accounted for up to ten per cent of total exports, but more so to Norway where the figure was more than twenty per cent, without including revenue from her merchant fleet, the fifth largest in the world. After heavy investment, mostly in bulk cargo carriers and tankers, in the early seventies, to cater for the expected growth in trade and increase in oil consumption in the west, all four countries had spare capacity. Then, as the depression cut into the profits of shipping lines, the construction side of the business saw the gaps in the order books widening to frightening proportions. The Norwegian and Swedish governments rushed in with loans and subsidies to assist a hard-pressed industry. By the end of 1977 Sweden had put in over a billion dollars, while Norway contributed four hundred million dollars in that year alone. But this was only the beginning. By 1979, demand was running at under one third of potential output. A Norwegian royal commission estimated that 1985 might be a realistic date to expect a recovery in shipping, and even then it was not likely to be easy. The time had come to think about adapting the industry to take account of real world demand.

At first, admiring glances were directed towards Denmark, where the big firms had put more investment into liners, a part of the business that was giving better returns than tanker construction. Burmeister and Wain, one of the world's leading producers of marine engines, was in difficulties, with losses close to two hundred million dollars in 1974; but optimism was generated by the assertive and unorthodox financier Jan Bonde Nielsen, who took over the company and within two years turned it round to make a small profit. The role of government in the industry was limited to a scheme to attract domestic orders by offering generous credit terms while providing retraining to the six thousand or so shipyard workers, about a third of the total labour force, who lost their jobs between 1972 and 1978.

The virtue of letting free enterprise take the lead in sorting out the problems was less apparent after Burmeister's new owner came under police investigation for sharp business practice. The company was pitched into a boardroom fight to get rid of Nielsen which ended with him using his power as the biggest shareholder to sell off a majority holding in the profitable diesel engine division to MAN, the West German commercial-vehicle and engineering group. The deal was promoted as the only chance for saving the great Copenhagen shipyard, a prospect which slowly receded to a point where, in the closing months of the decade, bankruptcy proceedings were started against Burmeister.

A more encouraging example of what could be achieved without heavy intervention from the state was provided by Finland, where no yards were closed and where, between 1973 and 1978, the labour force fell by less than one ninth. A big factor in the survival of Finnish shipping was the steady flow of orders from the Soviet Union; but early specialization in the building of icebreakers, arctic offshore vessels, container ships and – the most promising bet for the future – oil and gas drilling rigs and ships also played a major part in maintaining a healthy industry.

In 1978 Norway started to let the air out of the subsidy cushion with a reduction of state support from an average of twenty per cent for each contract to twelve to fifteen per cent. At the same time it was acknowledged that the merchant fleet would get smaller, tumbling from its fifth place in world ranking. To ease the shock, the shipping companies were helped to buy second-hand vessels, many of which were available on the international market at knock-down prices, with loan guarantees of up to thirty per cent of the purchase price. The Swedish government took a similar line, offering generous grants to Svenska Varv, the holding company for state-owned yards, which now took over Kockums, the last big privately owned shipbuilder, while tempering generosity with hard commercial sense by proposing to hand over two of the largest yards to maintenance and repair work and adapting others to some sort of heavy engineering. In both countries employment in shipping and shipbuilding, having dropped thirty per cent from 1975 to 1978, was to continue its downward slide.

Before the end of the decade there were further moves to cut output in those parts of the industry where losses were heaviest. In Sweden the state-owned Svenska Varv proposed the closure of several yards, including one of the biggest at Landskrona, entailing overall the loss of seven thousand jobs out of a total of twenty thousand. At the same time an appeal was made for government aid to enable the industry to adapt to specialized products such as offshore prefabricated plants, gas and chemical carriers, ferries and naval vessels. Union opposition to the cutback extended the life of the Landskrona yard until new jobs had been created for the redundant workforce but the government pressed ahead with a shipping bill which projected the phasing out of subsidies over a three-year period. The structural reorganization package included liberal terms for loans and guarantees, increased investment in training and research, and the sale of all tonnage owned by the state.

It was much the same story with other staple industries, including steel and engineering, textiles and even pulp and paper, where the effects of over-capacity at a time of recession were magnified by the dramatic advance of American competitors. Exploiting the virgin forests of the southern states was made easy by cheap labour and capital, not to mention huge economies of scale, so that by the mid-seventies American exporters could land chemical pulp in Europe at prices which threatened to put the Scandinavians out of business. The Nordic market share in Europe fell from fifty-six per cent in 1977, when most mills in Norway, Sweden and Finland were operating at less than forty-five per cent capacity. Efforts to hold down prices restored some of the competitive edge but also bit deeply into profits, so that companies could not afford the investment they said they needed to rationalize and modernize plant. State support was forthcoming for some of the most exposed firms, but a reluctance to move too far too fast turned on evidence that paper and board consumption could be slowing down in absolute terms. The packaging industry was turning to plastics and other new materials, while printing was coming under pressure from electronic forms of communication. The Boston Consultant report on the future of Swedish industry pointed to a decline for forestry, which could not be expected to contribute to long-term economic growth.

Although the finance and economic ministers met regularly to share ideas, it would be wrong to suggest that the Nordic countries advanced with some sort of telepathic precision towards a common solution of their economic problems. To identify one major difference which emerged after the first optimistic forecasts were abandoned, Norway, Sweden and Iceland continued to make full employment the highest priority even if this meant mortgaging the future with a high foreign debt, while Denmark and Finland chose to allow unemployment to approach the European average. Sometimes the countries were drawn together despite themselves, as in 1977 when Sweden devalued her currency against the Deutschmark and the others felt bound to follow.

At first, enthusiasm for cross-border co-operation seemed to be strongest among industrialists, who saw that if nationalization was to be the rule, then it made sense to pool ability and resources, the better to meet strengthening competition from outside the Nordic group. Finland led on making the case for sub-contracting schemes which allowed each country to put its specialist skills to best use. Thus parts for nuclear power stations built in Sweden were made in Finland, and Saab set up a new car plant in association with the Finnish firm Valmet. On the Norwegian side, co-operative enterprise with Sweden extended from investment in the production of aluminium, which was much in demand by Volvo as a basic material for its cars, to the joint venture of the Swedish chemical firm Kema–Nobel and the Norwegian Dyno Industrierer to create a new company based in Oslo to manufacture binding agents for fibreboard.

These initiatives were backed by the respective governments, even occasionally prompted by them. But as the crisis deepened the governments themselves took to exploring the prospects for wider co-operation, linking the rejuvenation of industry with the all-important question of energy supply. This seemed to give the advantage to Norway. She had all the oil she needed and more, while the other Nordic countries had none. But the costs of extracting the oil from the North Sea were high, and even at OPEC prices, the economic case for continuing to take in Middle East oil was overwhelming – just as long as it kept flowing. Norway was the insurance against the day when OPEC might decide to be really difficult. What still had to be established was whether her clients were able to afford the premiums. There was much that Norway wanted in industrial investment and know-how, but she insisted on careful negotiations to establish the advantage to her of any long-term deals. If the Nordic countries could not satisfy Norway's demands then there were others, notably West Germany, eager for a partnership.

Norway's sense of urgency was partly motivated by the need to reconstruct her industrial base to allow for increased output of finished goods and technically advanced products, not least to take account of the decline of some of her traditional revenue-earners such as shipping and shipbuilding. But she was also aware that her bargaining strength could be shortlived, lasting not more than the twenty years or so it would take to develop alternative forms of energy.

Sweden had long since mounted an ambitious nuclear programme, and though she pulled back a little when the centre-right coalition came to power in 1976, environmentalist opposition to charging more reactors faltered under economic pressures. The main achievement of the anti-nuclear lobby was to inspire the inventive Swedes to explore other energy resources. While there was little prospect of tapping more hydro-electric power (it accounted for twelve to fifteen per cent of the country's total energy needs), the sun and the wind had yet to be harnessed. In the longer term, there was the prospect of converting a share of Sweden's capacious marsh and forest land for the production of biomass or plants specifically cultivated to transform insolation to organic matter. The hope was that these energy forests could be used either for electricity and heat generation by direct combustion or to produce a fuel like methanol.

But it was in Iceland where, relative to the size of her economy, the strongest effort was made to increase the supply of domestic energy. Opportunities were there in plenty. Not much more than five per cent of the hydro-electric potential was utilized, and there were vast untapped geothermal resources created by volcanic activity just below the island's surface. That most of Iceland's imported oil came from the USSR gave a sharper political edge to what was regarded elsewhere in Norden chiefly as an economic problem. A rapidly mounting foreign debt was worrying enough, but for a small country that was also strategically sensitive, owing so much to the Russians was especially hazardous.

From 1974 to 1976, no less than six per cent of the country's gross national product was invested in the exploration, production and distribution of electrical power and in geothermal heating and water supply. At the beginning of this period, forty-five per cent of the population used natural hot water systems; by 1976 the figure had increased to fifty-seven per cent and was expected to rise to eighty per cent by the end of the decade. There was still a long way to go before geothermal energy could be adapted to industry on any scale – aside from any other considerations, geothermal plants had to be built in the volcanic zone with the consequent risk of major eruptions – but there was no reason why hydro-electric power could not support industrial development. Iceland was not a potential energy exporter – the distances were too great – but having a huge potential of surplus power (there was even a chance of finding oil off the north and north-west coast), she was able to offer attractive incentives to foreign investors.

At first glance, Denmark was more vulnerable to pressure from the major energy producers. Hope of a substantial oil strike in the Danish sector of the North Sea had been disappointed, as had forecasts of an energy bonanza off the west coast of Greenland. But the known reserves of oil under the ocean bed, together with plentiful supplies of natural gas, promised to satisfy up to one-third to one-half of the country's needs until the end of the century. Moreover, an energy conservation programme, one of the most successful in Europe, based on the conversion of oil-driven power stations back to coal, was destined to provide two-thirds of Denmark's electricity by the mid-eighties. Atomic energy was ruled out after the Swedish government's mauling by the anti-nuclear lobby, but the decision was made less dramatic by renewed optimism among oil experts that oil and gas development in the North Sea and off Greenland still had a long way to go.

National inhibitions were no part of the Finnish political scene. The heavy dependence on imported oil, most of it from the Soviet Union, and the shortage of domestic resources pushed the country towards the nuclear option as early as 1965 when four power plants were ordered, two from Sweden and two from Russia. At about the time that the first of these plants was coming on line, work had started on a power station for the United Paper Mills at Simpele to be run on peat, a fuel which was in plentiful supply, if difficult to transport from its largely northern location. Though no one doubted that imported oil would continue to be the main source of Finnish energy consumption, its share was expected to fall from fifty-two per cent in the mid-seventies to about forty-five per cent in 1985.

In late 1976 a joint government committee was formed to study the prospects for closer links between the Norwegian and Swedish petroleum industries. The report was held up by the Swedish uncertainty on the future of nuclear power and by a temporary lull in the oil-price war, but it soon became clear that Norway was prepared to satisfy Swedish needs only if there was an adequate return traffic in technology and marketing expertise. There were also prospects of a deal with Finland, linking investment in the petro-chemical industry to increased quantities of timber for the Norwegian pulp mills. With Denmark there was no easily identifiable area of common interest, but that country was busily discussing with Sweden the possible joint exploitation of natural gas, and at the same time trying to work out a joint approach to Norway, from whom any supply lines to Sweden might equally well serve Danish needs.

The precedents for energy co-operation were encouraging. Nordel, a system for co-ordinating electricity production for Sweden, Norway, Denmark and Finland, had been operating successfully since 1963. With some dozen transmission lines linking the four countries, the world's largest current cable was opened between Norway and Jutland in 1977. These lines allow for surplus electric power to be quickly diverted to any region where it is urgently required or where local production entails higher costs. What makes this something more than a simple sharing agreement is the different methods used for generating electricity – Norway, Sweden and Finland relying heavily on hydro-power while Denmark depends exclusively on oil- and coal-fired plants. The hydro group generally has an excess of electricity in wet years and can export to Denmark; but in dry years support is needed the other way. A change in relationship came with the development of nuclear power in Sweden and Finland. This was a Nordel bonus for Denmark, since it strengthened confidence in maintaining a full electricity service even in the event of another and more serious oil crisis. Nuclear energy also made Sweden into an electricity exporter to Norway after more than a decade of taking in hydro-power from her neighbour. One of the factors which helped to ease negotiations on oil supplies was Sweden's decision to raise the limit on the production of electricity specifically allocated for transmission to Norway.

Given the long-established reciprocal arrangements for topping up the energy supplies it was perhaps surprising that Sweden did not take an earlier interest in North Sea exploration; but it was not until OPEC started forcing up prices that drilling off the Norwegian coast became economically attractive. Sweden's own oil company, Swedish Petroleum AB, which was set up with government money, spread its efforts on prospecting in Ireland, Tunisia, Egypt and Spain, in addition to searches off Gotland and the southern coast, all without success. Even after the Norwegian potential was recognized there was a natural reluctance to get involved too quickly and too energetically in case the smaller country complained about big-brother tactics. But when the invitation to talk came from Oslo, the response was enthusiastic. The two industry ministries quickly got together to assess the value of a long-standing guarantee on oil deliveries in terms of a Norwegian share in the expansion of a diverse group of industries ranging from wood processing to petrochemicals and electronics.

The first stage of an agreement was settled in mid-1977, with the promise of sufficient Norwegian oil to satisfy about twenty per cent of Sweden's total annual needs by the early 1980s. It was accepted that the Mongstad refinery in Norway should be expanded from a capacity of four million tons to ten to twelve million tons a year, and to launch this project in a highly competitive business the Swedes said they would not go ahead with a proposed state-owned refinery at Brofjorden. This was a substantial concession at a time when energy experts were suggesting that Sweden should protect herself against another oil crisis by reducing her dependence on imported processed oil, which was then running at nearly forty per cent of annual requirements.

Other clauses in the agreement were couched in less specific terms, suggesting only that 'market developments' should determine the future of the petrochemical industry in both nations and that progress in other economic growth areas must wait on detailed studies and negotiations within the co-operation committee. Though it was early days, opinion on the Norwegian side held that events were moving too slowly, a criticism which might have been put more forcefully had not the possibility been raised of securing for Norway a major interest in the next round of Sweden's economic expansion, by circling the co-operation committee and dealing directly with the industrialists. The proposal, which turned out to be the boldest and certainly the best publicized of recent exercises in Nordic co-operation, was a Norwegian buy into the previously wholly Swedish-owned Volvo company.

Ironically, the idea might never have taken off or even merited serious discussion had not a plan for a merger with the other big Swedish vehicle manufacturer, Saab–Scania, foundered on the apparent inability of industrial leaders in one country to overcome their natural rivalries. The starting point was Volvo's need for a broader operating base. The largest commercial enterprise in the Nordic area, accounting for nearly eight per cent of Swedish exports, and a highly profitable company for the first half of the decade, it suffered reverses as the European recession stretched towards Scandinavia. A small home market contracted still further, with competition from imported cars that were cheaper and more economical to run than the Volvo models. The need to hold prices at a time when labour costs were jumping ahead put a severe strain on the company's resources. Moreover, attempts to strike out for new markets were largely unsuccessful. The takeover of DAF in Holland, which was supposed to give Volvo a stake in the booming small-car business, looked like turning into an expensive disaster. The grafting of the solid Volvo image onto the tiny DAF failed to impress the customers, and the company was set for bankruptcy until the Dutch government stepped in with a massive subsidy. A move into the leisure-boat business – always a promising market in Norden – petered out, while heavy investment in safety and pollution controls calculated to appeal in the US was not translated into higher sales. Plans for an assembly plant in Virginia were abandoned.

Despite the setbacks, Volvo could count on its highly lucrative truck division. In this the company was in a similar position to Saab–Scania, which supported an ailing car business with the profits from an expanding market for heavy lorries. Perhaps together the two firms could rationalize their operations to match the competition from their big European, Japanese and American competitors. The idea appealed particularly to Dr Marcus Wallenburg, the seventy-seven-year-old Saab–Scania chairman and the most influential personality in Swedish industry for over forty years, who saw the coming together of the giants as a fitting culmination of a prestigious career.

An agreement in principle was quickly settled at chairman and managing-director level but, looking to avoid stock exchange rumours, nothing was said to the management of either company or to the unions before the public announcement on 6 May 1977. First reactions were sympathetic if not enthusiastic. If there had to be a retrenchment of the country's motor-car industry then the deal, in the words of its promoters, looked 'good for Sweden'. But it soon emerged that opinion among those who had to make the agreement work was by no means unanimous. The management of the powerful Scania truck division, who believed, reasonably, that it was their profits which had kept Saab alive ever since the merger in 1969, resented the implication that they now had to prop up Volvo cars as well. As for the money-making side of Volvo, it was argued that not enough attention had been given to the technical problems of joining the two truck operations. Worse still, the whole affair was beginning to look like a Volvo takeover, with Pehr Gyllenhammar, managing director of Volvo, nominated as managing director of the new holding company, whose head office was to be Gothenburg, Volvo's headquarters.

What observers found surprising was that differences of opinion were allowed to develop into major issues of confidence without, apparently, much effort being made to point up the opportunities or to reconcile management to the new ways of thinking. The same might be said of the unions, who were bound to be consulted under Sweden's worker-participation laws. Nearly all favoured the merger, but there was some ambiguity in the conditions made on future employment. The interpretation at Volvo was that the unions were prepared for a reduction in jobs; at Saab–Scania the opposite was inferred and objection was taken to union efforts to strengthen their director representation. No attempt was made to clarify these points, and the two companies were still at loggerheads in midsummer when Pehr Gyllenhammar, clearly exasperated by what he regarded as Saab–Scania obstruction, used the occasion of his half-yearly report to announce that the merger was off.

Still seeking the means for an aggressive expansion which Gyllenhammar believed was the only way for Volvo to survive, he turned next to the Swedish government, suggesting a product-development fund which could be used to help finance a new car for the 1980s. But the Fälldin coalition, though sympathetic to business interests, was having a hard time controlling its finances and was in no mood to assume extra commitments. In any case, the views of Saab–Scania had to be taken into account and, in this respect, recent precedents were distinctly unfavourable.

What was left? Certainly the possibilities in Sweden were all but exhausted. Across the border, however, in Norway, there was unlimited oil money and an administration eager to exchange capital for technical and business expertise so long as it resulted in more industrial employment for Norwegians. In May 1978 Gyllenhammar, the young Harvard-trained businessman whose reputation for commercial originality was unrivalled in Sweden (it was said that the only traditional thing he had ever done was to marry his chairman's daughter), revealed his most imaginative scheme to date. Volvo was to go into partnership with the Norwegian government. A restructuring of the company would release forty per cent of the shares for purchase by Norwegian interests producing an immediate capital injection of nearly nine hundred million Swedish Kronor, with much more to come. In return Volvo was to develop and produce aluminium and plastic components for automobiles in Norway, and to create there a prototype car for the environmentally conscious 1980s. A move to Norway was promised for the head office of Volvo Penta, a major producer of marine engines, to precede the setting up of a factory to produce a new series of marine diesels (a big concession, since it gave Norway the chance to convert some of her spare shipbuilding capacity). All this was to create three to five thousand new jobs to add to the four thousand-strong workforce Volvo already had in Norway. An October deadline was set for the signing of a firm contract.

It was an indication of the change in the style of government since Palme's days that Gyllenhammar was able to go so far without directly involving senior ministers. But the second part of the agreement, which set out Norway's offer of extending Volvo activities into oil and gas prospecting, was bound to involve the government. Access to North Sea prospecting was a long-cherished goal of Swedish politicians, but one in which they had been baulked time and time again. A five-hundred-million-Krona investment in the Norwegian Oil Consortium NOCO was nearing agreement, but this was expected to produce little more than six million tons for the Swedish market over a fifteen-year period. True, there was no guarantee that the drilling concessions to Volvo would produce better results; but the Norwegians were unlikely to hand over the potentially dud blocs to their new business partners. In any case, there was the prospect of linking the Volvo deal to an assurance of increased deliveries of oil from existing fields. The Norwegians were undoubtedly sympathetic, now that real progress was being made on the industrial front.

After an unpublicized trip to Oslo in April to give formal approval to what Volvo had already negotiated, Fälldin used every chance to confer with Nordli on the wider implications of the agreement. Even at a conference on the economic future of Lapland attended by all the Scandinavian prime ministers, the two were inseparable; and though their conversations remained secret, no one was fooled about the likely subject of their discussions. But later in the year, with Fälldin's coalition close to disintegration as his colleagues fought out their differences on nuclear energy, the headlines were taken over by the Volvo critics with, invariably, Nordli in the lonely role of defender and cheer-leader for Scandinavian co-operation.

First it was the Norwegian Federation of Industry which raised questions – some of them difficult to answer directly. There were many doubts as to Volvo's commitment to job creation in Norway. Did the company really intend to set up more factories to manufacture a new car? If not, the target of up to five thousand additional jobs could not be met. Again, if Norwegian industry was to be a supplier of components, it had to be said that cut-throat competition in the car market had cut margins so hard that several firms were now deciding they could well do without that sort of business.

Pehr Gyllenhammar added force to the NIF argument by telling the Norwegian press that, contrary to general opinion, Volvo's car factories would remain in Sweden and Holland for the foreseeable future. Production costs were too high in Norway, he said. The Norwegian government protested sharply and with some effect. Before the end of the year Nordli was able to announce that a new car would be built in Norway and that the development work was due to start in 1979.

Then it was Sweden's turn to complain. Compensation to existing shareholders was inadequate, ran the argument; the Norwegians were getting a major share of the biggest commercial concern in Scandinavia at cut-price rates. Attitudes varied according to the value put on the oil concessions and, naturally enough, the Norwegians tended to emphasize their own munificence. Indeed, an opinion poll in *Dagbladet* revealed that a majority of Norwegians felt they had gone too far and that the wily Swedes would reap most benefit from the deal.

The debate might have got out of hand had the government crisis in Sweden not been resolved by Fälldin's resignation and the replacement of the centre–right coalition by a minority liberal government. The new prime minister, Ola Ullsten, made completion of the Volvo agreement an urgent priority, and his first official visit outside Sweden was to Oslo to talk out the problems with Nordli and his ministers. Of the three questions to be settled, two were relatively straightforward. The compensation to Volvo for reorganizing as a binational concern (a strong point with Swedish shareholders, who thought that they were being asked to subsidize Norwegian development) was fixed at 200 million Swedish Kronor. This was to top up the 750 million already promised by Norwegians for new share capital. Secondly, the matter of just how much oil was to go to Sweden and at what price was resolved by linking it to a reciprocal arrangement for timber – though not without complaints from Swedish mills, where they were trying, often unsuccessfully, to maintain their own supplies. Oil deliveries to Sweden were to be stepped up to 4 to 5 million tons annually by 1985, while Norway was to receive 1.5 to 2 million cubic metres of timber a year.

More difficult to settle was the Norwegians' claim that since they now owned – or would soon own – forty per cent of Volvo, that proportion of the company's profits should be taxed in Norway. In the end the argument was conceded by Norway – not because they felt the justice of the counter-claim, but because they realized that any arrangement of that sort would require special legislation and an indefinite postponement of any firm agreement.

With the political issues largely resolved it looked as if the deadline for signing the treaty, already postponed once from October to 8 December, would now be met. But it was too early to talk about certainties. There was still much dissatisfaction, particularly among Volvo shareholders, whose support was as critical as that of any of the other participants. The shareholders felt badly treated, not just for financial reasons – though the advice from their managing director to adopt the long-term view and not to expect any early dividend increases was hardly cheering – but because no one had bothered to ask them if they wanted their company to be part of the give and take of Nordic relations.

So, while the politicians were putting their signatures to what Nordli described as 'an agreement on industrial and energy policies in the broadest sense' and what Ullsten greeted as 'a breakthrough for Nordic co-operation', the Volvo shareholders threatened to break ranks by rejecting the forty per cent sale to Norway. Their champion was Håkan Gergils, Chairman of the Swedish National Shareholders' Association (SARF), who generally prefaced his criticism of the way the Volvo deal had been managed by claiming that he was capable of winning more than half the votes at the company's next general meeting due in January 1979.

Since he needed only one-third of the votes to be able to block proposals Gergils could not be ignored. His initial attack centred on an undoubtedly weak spot of the negotiations. Although Norway was committed to putting at least fifty per cent of her shares into private hands, little interest had so far been shown outside the main banks. The risk, said Gergils, was that in one disguise or another the Norwegian government would become the largest single shareholder. A shift in the balance of power on this scale had to be against Swedish interests.

In reply Nordli blamed the prices and incomes freeze for the apparent lack of investors, and argued that all would come right when the economy improved. His Swedish critics were not convinced. The wide-ranging terms of the Volvo deal and its importance for the future of the Norwegian economy was bound to engender optimism on the side of the purchasers. But if they were as keen as they sounded for the deal to go through, did this not tend to confirm the widely held Swedish view that Volvo was being sold too cheaply? Why, asked Gergils, should the company shareholders be asked to subsidize an international agreement, important aspects of which, such as oil deliveries to Sweden and the supply of timber to Norwegian mills, were totally divorced from any return that could be expected on their investment?

The SARF challenge was taken seriously by the Volvo directors. Gergils had shown what he could do at the previous annual general meeting when he had collected twelve thousand proxy votes, enough to get a SARF representative appointment to the main board. There was also a suspicion that the association was receiving unofficial backing from investment companies close to the Wallenberg-controlled Enskilda banken. It was no secret that Dr Wallenberg was still smarting from the failure of the Saab–Volvo merger and had not entirely given up hope of bringing Volvo back to the negotiating table.

While the Volvo board started to collect proxies on its own account, and the unions, much in favour of the Norwegian agreement, launched their campaign accusing shareholders of putting short-term profits before national interests, the opposition took heart from developments on the Norwegian side, where doubts were setting in as to Nordli's ability to secure a favourable majority in the Storting. His trouble started when his allies, the left socialists, came out against the package. The value of the two votes thereby lost became apparent as, one after another, the non-socialist parties took the same line. The biggest shock came when the Christian people's party, which had backed the government in committee, reversed its decision. Grass-roots fears that the giant Volvo was about to take over Norwegian industry were partly responsible but, on a less emotional level, there were serious reservations as to the wisdom of the Norwegian state's entering into an agreement with a private Swedish concern.

Confusion as to who precisely was guaranteeing what came into the open with a terse exchange on timber deliveries. The two sides gave different interpretations, the Swedes arguing that they were not committed to supplying a specific amount, while the Norwegians asserted that unless they received close on two million cubic metres a year, oil exports would be reduced accordingly. Before the timber issue could be settled, however, and before Nordli had to test his brave claim that with the help of a few opposition renegades he could still put together a parliamentary majority, news came of the success of the Swedish Shareholders' Association in attracting a sufficient number of votes at Volvo's AGM to block the agreement. The board cancelled the meeting and conceded defeat.

Immediate thoughts were about what could *not* now happen. Volvo Penta would not move to Norway; there was to be no agreement on increasing oil deliveries to Sweden and timber supplies to Norway; Volvo Petroleum, set up in the expectation of drilling rights in the North Sea, seemed destined to remain a paper company; a new car would not be developed by Volvo in Norway. The disappointment of the two governments, not to mention the Volvo managing director, was all too evident. Pehr Gyllenhammar came in for the harshest criticism for over-stretching his company's managerial and technical resources. But without Norwegian capital, how else could he modernize his industry? A government-commissioned report on the automobile industry postulated that Volvo and Saab–Scania required more than four billion Swedish Kronor over three to five years to develop new car models. It was assumed that financing of this order could not be achieved on the open market. The alternative was to revive the idea of a merger between the two companies as a preliminary to a strict programme of rationalization. Inevitably, it was said, Gyllenhammar would soon return cap in hand to Saab–Scania.

But the commercial forecasters lost some of their confidence when Volvo, taking advantage of the general improvement in car sales in the early part of 1979, went determinedly for volume growth while Saab came to a joint investment agreement with the Lancia branch of the Fiat group. There were more surprises in store. In December Volvo sold a twenty per cent share in its car-making business to Renault, the eighth largest car manufacturer in the world. The advantage to Volvo lay in gaining access to Renault's revolutionary ideas on fuel saving. The heavy, thirsty car for which Volvo was famed was to give way to the light-weight, high-strength, advanced-technology vehicle. In mapping out this expansionist plan for the eighties no one thought to involve the Norwegians.

1979 saw an impressive if temporary recovery in Nordic growth rates; but the rising cost of imports helped to push up the cost of living, and with another great spurt in oil prices (the increase had been tenfold since 1972), there was renewed pressure for the five countries to work together to find a way out of the economic cul-de-sac. A proposal from Nordli for the setting up of a Nordic economic research council to examine the possibilities for closer integration was quickly accepted by the other premiers. At the same time, Norwegian–Swedish negotiations were resumed on oil and timber supplies and on industrial cooperation.

In holding to his view that discussions had to progress from the general to the specific before any agreement could be signed, Nordli waited for the Swedes to come up with proposals. Eventually thirty companies were persuaded to detail projects which could benefit from a collaborative effort ranging from marine technology to methods of utilizing methanol. Evidently the Norwegians had been looking for something more ambitious and exciting, but in expressing mild disappointment they also acknowledged that in the short run it was probably the best that could be expected. From advocating the expansion of constructive employment, to assessing what businesses were likely to be successful in ten or twenty years' time, was a step that the most daring futurologist would hesitate to take. As in

Sweden, so in Finland and Denmark, industry reported on the virtual impossibility of deciding, at a time of great economic uncertainty, how best to allocate its resources.

The Norwegians signalled a change of tactics with an assurance that, in the event of another energy crisis, the oil supply to Nordic countries would not be tied to their levels of investment in co-operative ventures. Greater interest was shown in engaging Nordic companies in North Sea energy development without at the same time insisting on participation in the broader aspects of Norway's economic plan. Volvo was first in, with plans to collaborate with Statoil on deliveries of natural gas to Sweden; but there were also talks with Danish companies on linking up gas supplies, and a cautious welcome was given to outside bids for North Sea exploration rights.

Industrial democracy

There was another respect in which Nordic thinking on industrial questions was coming together. It is a widely accepted maxim of industrial society that mass production is inseparable from a mechanical, isolating and mind-destroying routine for most employees and that, as a consequence, important decisions can only be taken by those who, setting themselves apart from the main workforce, acquire the skills and knowledge which entitle them to be managers. The Nordic countries were among the first to challenge the assumption that, for the majority, work must be a necessary evil performed without real responsibility. The new cultural policy made work a cultural act. Releasing creative talents and bringing a greater sense of fulfilment to the lives of ordinary people meant that the nine-to-five existence had to give more room for individual initiative and intellectual satisfaction.

In many ways Nordic industry was an ideal laboratory for experiments in industrial democracy. The transformation to large-scale enterprise was a recent phenomenon. Many workers could recall or had had experience of small units of production, and individual skills were still highly valued. The general level of education assumed an ability, if not an immediate willingness, among workers to take on additional responsibilities. Against these advantages had to be set the tendency towards centralization which had led to a decline in union initiative at factory level and the sometimes exaggerated but deeply engrained respect for the views of 'experts'.

The idea that employees should take a bigger share in company decision-making was advanced by the Norwegians in the early sixties. Hoping to build on the experience of the advisory production committees and works councils – both a familiar part of the post-war commercial scene – a joint committee of the social-democrat party and the federation of trade unions (NFTU) was set up to report on democracy in economic life. Agreement on basic principles was a foregone conclusion. After a short deliberation it was declared unacceptable that '... the place where men are required to spend a third of the day must be excluded from the general democratization of the rest of the community'. In factories and offices workers 'ought to feel themselves to be members of a democratic society, and not just units in a production process'.

Specific proposals followed a few months later. Employees were to be given freer access to company information and to be educated in business procedures as a preliminary to the main recommendation that company law be amended to put employees on an equal footing with shareholders. This did not go down well with the employers, who believed that neither the cause of industrial democracy nor management efficiency would be served by a compulsory allocation of worker representatives at board level. Their alternative was a strengthening of the existing bodies of co-operation by means to be freely negotiated without the assistance of the courts.

When pressed, both sides agreed that they were short on evidence to back up their arguments. The discussion needed to be brought down from the dizzy heights of political ideology to a level where conflicting claims could be tested by practical research. A joint approach was made to the Institute for Industrial Social Research at Trondheim, which in turn sought the aid of the Tavistock Institute of Human Relations in London. Together they set up a programme to study the impact of worker directors and, looking at the problem from the opposite end, to investigate ways in which employees could have a greater say in the running of their own jobs.

A preliminary report published in 1963 confirmed the management view that access to the board would, in most cases, prove to be an anticlimax for the employees. Either they would be overawed by the greater knowledge of the permanent directors or they would quickly lose interest in matters not immediately relevant to everyday work. A more constructive outcome was expected from the second phase of the research, which concentrated on extending the democratic principle to shop-floor organization.

Meanwhile, the recommendations of the joint NFTU–social-democrat committee on industrial democracy – which included representation at board level – were endorsed by their respective national conferences. In the wider political context, worker-directors were seen as playing an essential part in persuading industry that employee participation had to be taken seriously. Shortly afterwards, towards the end of 1965, the social-democrat government suffered an electoral defeat. The conservative members of the succeeding centre–right coalition opposed industrial democracy, but in varying degrees the other partners were sympathetic to reform. A compromise was sought in the appointment of a commission which started to collect evidence in 1968. Its report, published three years later and just one month before the social democrats were returned to power as a minority government, was sufficiently radical in tone for Odvar Nordli, then prospective labour minister, to describe it as a 'valuable first step in developing a comprehensive system of industrial democracy'.

Working with the NFTU, the social democrats launched a public debate which produced a strong reaction in favour of worker involvement in the higher reaches of management. This principle became the centre point of the 1972 bill to amend the companies act. Henceforth, in firms of more than fifty employees, a majority could demand that up to a third of the members of the board should be elected from their ranks. For companies with a staff of over two hundred a new concept of authority was introduced, that of the corporate assembly. Consisting of one-third employee and two-thirds shareholder representatives, the assembly was to have as its prime task the election of a board but was also to act as the final authority on matters radically affecting the company's future, such as investment or rationalization plans. As with smaller businesses employees could elect up to one third of the directors.

Taking their lead from the Norwegians, social democrats in Denmark and Sweden adopted the cause of worker-directors, though with variations to suit their own commercial environments. The Danes were perhaps best prepared for the change, having a two-tier system of company administration which allowed for the easy acceptance by senior management of a stronger employee voice in general policy-making. All but the smallest companies are required by law to have a board of directors, elected by the shareholders, and a management board, appointed by the directors. The division of functions is only loosely defined and can vary widely from one firm to another (in contrast to Germany where the same basic system operates), but broadly speaking the management board has the responsibility for the day-to-day running of the business. The legislation of 1974, which allowed for workers in companies with a staff roll of fifty-plus to elect two directors, was therefore not seen as a possible source of disruption by executives, whose dealings were mostly with the board. Decisions by the directors, worker or shareholder, would undoubtedly affect them but not in a way that was likely to cause abrupt or unexpected reversals in their professional lives. In practice, of course, the same was true of Norway; it was simply that the psychology of change was less of a problem for the Danes.

They could also claim useful experience in the working of joint consultative committees. Introduced in 1947 as part of an industrial reconstruction policy agreed by both sides of industry, the committees are composed of equal numbers of worker and management representatives. Though not empowered to make unilateral decisions, their status was such that, in most companies, changes in work schedules, safety and welfare conditions and employment policy were dependent on consultative committee approval.

By contrast, the Swedes with their stronger industrial base and highly centralized system of labour relations were used to hearing the workers' view from trade-union officials, who invariably related more closely to national policy than to purely local needs. Worker-directors made their first appearance in the sixties, but on the initiative not of the unions but of far-sighted companies like Gränges, the big mining and engineering combine. Though this was welcomed by many social democrats, the reaction of blue-collar workers as put by LO was to play down the importance of board representation. Access to company decision-making, it was argued, could only be achieved by central negotiations between the unions and employers and by supporting legislation on specific issues. The generally poor record of works councils in Sweden was used to support the case. But there was a suspicion here that the LO leadership was acting defensively, having come under recent attack for deciding policy in a high-handed way, ignoring the interests of particular groups of workers. To permit employees to elect board representatives whose first allegiance was not to a union was to concede that existing relationships with management were inadequate. LO sensitivity was duly noted by the government when, in 1972, a bill allowing for worker-directors on the boards of companies with a hundred employees or more specified that they should be union appointments. Another bill extending employee representation to boards of smaller firms was promised for the future.

Nordic experience so far tends to confirm the view that on their own, worker-directors can achieve little. Subject to the same rules of confidentiality as other board members, they often feel themselves cut off from the people they represent. Frustration arises from not having all the relevant information – a problem frequently shared by ordinary directors, who can find themselves bypassed by powerful chairmen or managing directors. This was the case when Volvo and Saab tried to merge, though stock exchange considerations were given as the excuse for not keeping the two boards fully in the picture. There are additional problems where real power is concentrated on a holding company which by its size may not qualify for employee representatives, or where an international concern is controlled by a board outside Norden.

But worker-directors were never expected to find a way through all the complexities of modern industry. At best they have widened the channels of communication, increasing general understanding of company finances and the functions of senior management while reassuring other board members that they all have interests in common. In this they have helped prepare the way for more far-reaching experiments in industrial democracy.

In 1969 the results of the second phase of the Trondheim–Tavistock research in Norway was published in a report called *Towards a New Company Organization*. It tackled the question of industrial democracy from shopfloor level, detailing four experimental projects aimed at increasing the scope for individual responsibility and choice in work routines. Six basic principles of job satisfaction determined the shape of the exercise: the need for variation; the opportunity to learn something; the ability to make decisions; the chance to gain respect and a degree of mutual support; the importance of believing that one's work is useful and valuable; and the wish to reconcile the job with a desirable future without this necessarily entailing promotion.

It was a philosophy which, given practical application, required a paper mill in southern Norway to reorganize its chemical pulp action so that a one-man, one-machine pattern gave way to a system in which small groups each monitored several machines. Split into four shifts, the workforce was trained in quality control and communication so that they could pass on information about plans and targets without the help of supervisors. Over six years, productivity doubled, staff turnover fell from twenty-five to six per cent and the group system was extended to other departments. Results almost as encouraging were recorded in two of the other projects.

But the research was by no means conclusive. Employers were too quick to assume that job enrichment led to increased productivity. Subsequent experiments, notably in Sweden, showed that this was not always the case; in fact it only happened in rare circumstances. Special factors were associated with the Norwegian study. The work units were mostly small – only thirty-five men in the paper mill project – providing circumstances in which relations between managers and employees were already conducive to friendly co-operation. It was surely no coincidence that the least successful experiment was carried out in the largest of the four companies involved, where contact between employers and labour was more remote and relations were characterized by mutual suspicion. The expectation of failure was overwhelming.

Despite its limitations, however, the Norwegian research

pointed the way towards achieving a more personally satisfying working environment, and this had implications for change going way beyond any single firm's marginal costings. Interest, then, was strong when two of the largest Nordic firms, the Swedish car-makers Saab and Volvo, determined to move away from conventional assembly-line techniques to enable small groups of workers to complete a succession of related operations such as fitting a car's electrical equipment. At Volvo's Kalmar plant, which was transformed in 1974, individual carriers, each loaded with a car body, travelled along a magnetic tape to twenty-eight assembly groups of fifteen to twenty workers. Each team had its own specified task and an agreed time in which to carry it out. The discipline of the assembly line was retained by the carriers moving at computer-controlled speeds, varying from three to thirty metres a minute depending on the difficulty of the job.

The process was taken a stage further at Saab–Scania's engine plant at Södertälje. There, teams of three or four workers, stationed in small bays, each finished a complete engine, which came to them with cylinder heads, crankshafts and connecting rods already fitted. The engines came off the conveyor and were stationary while being worked on, but the freedom this gave to vary routines was limited by the time factor: the allocation for completing an engine was just twenty-seven minutes.

The Volvo and Saab experiments were criticized by other car manufacturers, who claimed that multi-assembly groups could not succeed in the larger factories of America and Europe. Their workers, too, were not easily persuaded of the virtues of the new systems. A visiting US delegation to the Saab plant concluded that the boredom of the Detroit assembly tracks was easier to endure than the social challenge of a group operation. But the initiating companies' reaction on the shop floor generally favoured the extension of freedom. This is not to say that the extra investment undertaken by Saab and Volvo was offset by increased productivity. According to a report on the Volvo experience sponsored by LO and SAF, the quality of cars produced by group assembly techniques was not as good as management had hoped and the rate of assembly was no different from that achieved in the traditionally run factories. Even Volvo's major objective of reducing absenteeism and turnover among its workforce fell well short of target, though savings were made on the cutback on supervisory staff.

It says much for Swedish as for Norwegian employers that interest in measures to improve the work environment was kept alive even when hopes of securing associated gains in output had long since faded. Each year there was a steady increase in the number of firms engaged in experimental schemes. Union influence was, of course, a significant factor. Their links with employers on work environment questions remained close. For example, in the late sixties the Swedes set up a joint research and development body on the Norwegian model. But the unions took care to play it both ways by working with politicians as with employers. The centre and liberal parties were broadly sympathetic, but contact was closest with the social democrats. There was no essential difference in ideology, both sides immediately associating improvements in work environment and job enrichment with industrial democracy, which was plainly the next stage in social-democrat progress towards equality.

The result, in Sweden, was a series of laws challenging the employer's long-established right 'to engage and dismiss workers at his own discretion; to direct and allot work; and to avail himself of workers belonging to any organization, or to none'. Safety at work, security of employment and the promotion of opportunities for older and otherwise disadvantaged workers were covered in a rapid succession of measures which were then overtaken in 1977 by a comprehensive Working Environment Act, the product of lengthy negotiations between unions, employers and government. What makes this law a milestone in labour legislation is the emphasis it puts on a worker's right to job satisfaction – a frustratingly vague concept, but one which is basic to industrial democracy.

The corresponding Norwegian law (also passed in 1977) made a brave attempt to set out rules for management guidance, specifying that work should be organized so that 'employees are not subjected to unhealthy physical or mental strains'; that they should be given 'a reasonable chance of personal development', and that in the planning and the nature of the work, regard must be paid to possibilities for employees to exercise initiative. In summary, 'every effort must be made to avoid monotonous, repetitive work and work which is controlled by machine or assembly line in such a way as to prevent employees from varying their work routines'. The Swedes followed up with a co-determination law which opened to negotiation those previously exclusive managerial rights to determine conditions of employment and the allocation of work. All important changes in organization, including investment decisions, were now to have union approval before they could be implemented. The new law also put paid to the works councils, which could no longer be justified now that employers had the obligation to inform and negotiate with the unions.

Another aspect to industrial democracy, but one that is seldom connected in the mind of the average voter, is the question of ownership and employee sharing in company profits. Though nationalization has never figured prominently in the Nordic political debate, the vastly increased scale of industrial operations over recent years and the necessity for governments' closer involvement in the finance of private companies have given the subject renewed topicality. It was a great talking-point in Sweden, for example, that the centre-led government which came to power in 1976 with the defence of free enterprise as one of its central campaign themes was responsible for taking more firms into public ownership than any previous administration. That world recession was responsible for this uncharacteristic disregard for the market economy merely emphasized how urgent it was to evolve a policy on the future relationship between government, shareholders and employers.

The left, of course, wanted no excuse to think about changes in the power structure of industry, though traditionally the idea of profit sharing was opposed by the unions, who did not want to cloud the division between capital and labour. Attitudes began to change when collectively the workers entered the capital market in a big way with their contributions to government-administered pension funds. The question naturally arose as to why these funds should not be used as a tool of industrial policy. For moderate social-democrat governments the proposal sounded too much like workers' control and, though it became a popular talking-point, nothing constructive emerged until the end of the sixties. It was then that the need for incentives to divert savings into industry inspired thoughts of creating investment funds supported by a share of the profits

251

from every major firm but controlled by the employees or their union representatives. Again, the parliamentary wing of the labour movement reacted cautiously, though in Denmark a co-ownership bill was narrowly lost in 1973 when the social-democrat government decided on an early election.

One encouraging sign was the less than hostile response from employers and managers. That the principle of promoting a wider spread of ownership was not discounted out of hand (even if union control was hotly opposed) was largely a result of the growth of white-collar unions. With their middle-class member-ship they were not greatly attracted to the removal of income differentials or to higher taxes to pay for advances in public welfare, but they were sympathetic to schemes for decentraliz-ing power in industry. Quickly taking the hint, liberal and centre parties set their minds to work on finding ways for em-ployees to be involved more closely in the achievements, or failure, of their companies.

But even if industrial democracy could be assumed to be a following stage in the development of Nordic society, the disap-pointing results of many of the early experiments show that it cannot succeed in isolation. It must be part of a wider process of preparing citizens to combine social responsibility with mak-ing the best use of their individual talents. How far Norden has progressed in this direction is the theme for the final chapter.

7
Towards cultural democracy

In the beginning there was political democracy; then came social democracy; and now the movement is towards cultural democracy, though the distance from the goal and the speed at which the Nordic countries are travelling is a matter of contention. One difficulty is the lack of an agreed definition. What is culture? A survey of American literature came up with 164 different meanings ranging from culture as an exercise in sophisticated living – taking in food, drink, dress, stimulating conversation and travel – to a concept of intellectual and spiritual purity, to culture as 'a state of mind ... a competence to communicate and express sufficiently for mastery of life's situations and for finding personal creative fulfilment'.

This confusion over terms is of recent origin. A century and more ago European culture was generally held to represent the highest achievement of man's artistic talents and the lifestyle associated with their appreciation, which could be enjoyed only by the few. There was something suspiciously tidy about this élitist theory, even in an age when literacy was confined to a small minority who could afford to indulge their interests in art, music and literature. If creative genius was not exclusively reserved for the learned and wealthy (and no one seriously suggested that it was), they could hardly claim the recognition of excellence as their sole prerogative.

Élitist culture met its first serious challenge in the emergence of capitalism. In an industrialized society governed by the principle that what is profitable is virtuous, common sense ruled that the true worth of any cultural experience could more accurately be judged by its general popularity than by the arbitrary standards of taste set by a small privileged group. Unashamed élitists like Nietzsche wrote contemptuously of entrepreneurial pandering to mass demand, fearing it would undermine respect for high culture and so weaken, perhaps even destroy, the foundations of civilization. This was a prospect that was only too apparent to those who witnessed the bludgeoning impact of industrialization on urban life in Britain and Germany. But Nietzsche and his followers reckoned without the insecurity of the middle classes who needed, above all, acceptance from those whom they saw as their social superiors. It was, therefore, to the old values that they paid their respects. Even while applying strict utilitarian logic to their businesses by giving the people what they wanted, or what they could afford, they had no faith in mass culture. The best that could be expected of the common people was that in acquiring basic literacy they would come to show proper respect for the discriminating judgement of the élite. Thus coccooned within the class structure, the proponents of high culture gained in strength and arrogance.

Scandinavia was not entirely immune to these social forces; but distance from the centres of European power, the absence of natural resources which elsewhere set the pattern for mass production and a relatively broad dispersal of land ownership allowed for important differences in the cultural pattern. The aristocracy was fully attuned to European thought, generally adapting the intellectual fashion of Germany as its own, but it was an élite without a strong power base, and by mid-century it had all but lost its dominant role in the civil service, army, Church and the universities. At the other end of the social scale, the farmers and rural proletariat were scattered in small, often isolated and inward-looking communities which remained true to their rustic origins, even in the rare circumstances where factories, mills or mines provided the main source of income. A sense of belonging extending further than the next valley or forest came from a shared language and religion and from a pride in a common history.

This feeling for the past expressed in story and song attracted the interest of political and intellectual leaders, who saw in the exploitation of folk culture the best prospects for arousing nationalist sentiment. In Sweden and Denmark it was chiefly a reaction to a declining influence in international politics. While the big powers measured their greatness by the strength of their armies or the scope of their territorial ambitions, the two leading Nordic countries tried to compensate for their lack of military muscle by glorifying the achievements of their ancestors. Thus Swedish patriots sought consolation for the loss of Finland by throwing their energies into the Gothic Society which promoted an idealistic view of the nation's history. And it was no coincidence that the first folk high school was in north Schleswig, where revival of the Danish heroic spirit accorded with the need to resist the encroachment of German culture. The creator of the folk high schools, the theologian turned educationalist N.F.S. Grundtvig, had as his first objective the popular awareness of and pride in Danish heritage. His students, mostly youngsters from the farms who might otherwise never have progressed beyond elementary instruction, learned something of Danish culture and history from teachers who were themselves already imbued with enthusiasm for the Nordic achievement.

Rediscovering the past appealed just as strongly to the subordinate members of the Nordic family, but for them cultural self-respect was linked to a specific objective – the achievement of independence. Central to their cause was the promotion of language as a symbol of national identity. The revival of interest in Finnish, which over the years of Swedish sovereignty had been held in contempt by the educated classes, was promoted by the publication in 1835 of the *Kalevala*, a volume of folk poems collected by Elias Lönnrot on his trips into the rarely travelled Finnish hinterlands. It is difficult how to appreciate the impact of the *Kalevala* on the intellectual imagination. But for a country with little in the way of recorded history, except as a subject state, it came as a revelation to read of the adventures of Finns who, in pagan times, had owed allegiance to no one outside their own community. That the *Kalevala* was also judged to be a literary masterpiece proved what had hitherto been seriously in doubt – that the Finnish language had a soul which could inspire the finest artists. Other folklore collectors soon followed in Lönnrot's footsteps, urged on by nationalist politicians like Johann Snellman, who acknowledged the debt owed to the peasants as the custodians of true Finnish culture. 'So long as a nation loves its own history, its own antiquity, so long will it also have hope for its future,' he told his followers.

With patriotic fervour still rising against the evicted overlords, the Swedes, whose cultural influence long survived their physical departure, and against their successors, the Russians, few paused to question the authenticity of the *Kalevala* or of other folk literature. It was left to a later generation of researchers to show that Lönnrot had given as much to the *Kalevala* as had the ancients whose thoughts and beliefs he sought to recapture. Without his literary talent the poetic fragments which formed the basis of his work would have remained just fragments, and while it was widely assumed that he had restored the poems to their original form not even Lönnrot believed this to be true. However, by the time such matters came to be discussed seriously the nationalist cause was less dependent on the infallibility of folklore records.

The idea of using language as a nationalist weapon found strong favour in Norway, another subject country which had lately exchanged masters. There the source of colonial authority had shifted from Copenhagen to Stockholm. Efforts to establish a national language by the gradual modification of Danish were not discouraged by the Swedes who, like the Russians in Finland, saw an opportunity to wean their recently acquired citizens off their traditional cultural loyalties. But the concept of a separate linguistic identity attracted such enthusiasm that the advocates of *riksmål*, or 'language of the realm', soon found themselves upstaged by those who favoured the creation of a wholly national language based on Old Norse as preserved in the rural dialects of the remote fjord country of western Norway. *Landsmål* ('language of the land') attracted nearly a third of the population, a victory for regionalism which set off a long-running dispute between urban and rural Norway.

Even the *landsmål*-speaking Norwegians did not go the whole way in their search for linguistic origins. If they had done so they might well have ended up making common cause with the Icelanders. In boasting the oldest and the least adulterated of the Nordic languages, the Icelanders had to concede that it was almost certainly acquired from the Norwegian colonizers who came to the island in the ninth and tenth centuries. In fact, the Icelandic and Norwegian languages did not become markedly different until the fourteenth century, when Norwegian started adapting first to Danish and then later to Swedish influence. Though Iceland was governed by the Danes it was more isolated, and so protected from linguistic innovation. Where Danish was spoken it was generally as the language of commerce.

Icelanders therefore had no difficulty in preserving their spirit of individuality – only in asserting it politically. The first tremors of nationalism in the early years of the nineteenth century, when war between England and Denmark nearly brought ruin to the country, gained force with economic recovery and the weakening of Danish rule. Poets and scholars from the Icelandic Literary Society, the National Library and the Northern Text Society, all founded within a few years of each other, explored the Norse heritage, to reveal that from the tenth to the thirteenth centuries the literature produced by this tiny country ranked with the best in the world. Moreover, it had stood the test of time not just as poetry but, in the sagas, as a vivid and dramatic early history of an extraordinary nation. The significance for the nationalists was quickly recognized, and it is no coincidence that Jón Sigurdsson, Iceland's popularly acknowledged leader for most of the second half of the century, combined political work with a study of the saga literature, bringing it to a wider public at home and abroad.

But it would be a mistake to think of the Nordic folk culture renaissance solely as an aid to nationalism. The view that it was more naturally a force for Scandinavian unity was advanced by those who, delving back into the past, pointed out common origins and showed that the family distinctions prized so highly by the nationalists were invariably artificial and of recent creation. As a leading popularizer of folk culture Grundtvig tried to have it both ways, advocating for each of the Scandinavian countries the setting up of folk high schools to promote an understanding and love of national literature and history while simultaneously inculcating a respect for the Nordic heritage. The wider loyalty gained precedence at university level where there were clear advantages in pooling resources. Grundtvig was among the early supporters of a Nordic university to take over from all existing institutions of higher learning. Politically also, Grundtvig recognized the practical sense in the Scandinavian states' working closer together to strengthen their position in European affairs. But then the German thrust on the southern border made every patriotic Dane an enthusiast for Nordic power.

That the philosophy of the folk high school found early favour with Denmark's neighbours said something for the potential of

Scandinavianism; but each country gave its own individual stamp to the style and content of the teaching, and in the formative years promotion of the Nordic idea was counted as secondary – if it was counted at all – to knowledge of the provincial cultural tradition. As the first outsiders to adopt and adapt Grundtvig's ideas, the Norwegians suffered a conflict of emotion when the folk high school at Sagatun closed in 1892 because it was said to be too liberal and too Danish. Radicalism was strong among those who were attracted to the schools, but they were as keen as anyone to remove themselves from Danish influence. Teachers continued to find themselves in trouble for preaching advanced ideas (grants were denied and government-administered schools were set up in competition), but there were no further cases in which folk high schools were accused of neglecting the nationalist cause.

The Nordic idea was more attractive to the Swedes, who were confident of their central role in Scandinavian culture; but it was not a major theme in the high-school curriculum, which departed from the Danish model in being weighted towards science and mathematics. A more fundamental difference was the rejection of Grundtvig's pedagogic techniques, which corresponded more closely to revivalist preaching than to formal teaching. Said P.A.Güdecke, principal of Östergötland's folk high school in the 1870s,

A nation as predominantly sober and practical as the Swedes is not to be won by words alone. ... The best representatives of our youth are too hard-working, too energetic to be able to sit for five months on a bench, merely to look and listen passively, while the teacher uses all his physical and mental strength to collect and present all the best he knows. ... The young want themselves to lend a hand to the work. ...'

In Swedish folk high schools the main teaching aid was the book.

As a nation 'conceived in and born of folklore' Finland was receptive to Grundtvig's philosophy but only in so far as it gave support to national ideals. Perhaps without even realizing his debt, Snellman frequently echoed the Dane in his appeal for an intellectual awakening among the common people. But the means to the end was the extension of popular education, already well established in Denmark, where the folk high schools supplemented the elementary teaching provided by the state. It was not until the end of the century that the first high school started in Finland, and this specialized in household skills for girls. The school for Swedish-speaking Finns, opening a few months later, was closer to the Grundtvigian model in that most subjects were taught by lectures. On the other hand, history was not given the same high status as in Danish high schools, because in the opinion of the principal, obviously not a Snellman convert, too much was left to the teacher's subjective views.

Though part of the Danish kingdom, Iceland managed to do without high schools. The reason was not resentment against a Danish initiative – quite the opposite in fact, because it was the Icelanders who led the way with their own form of extended education. Long before Grundtvig came on the scene it was customary on remote farms for families to join in readings of the sagas, an occasion known as the *Kvöldvaka*. These domestic study circles were the only opportunity for most children to learn to read and write, but first-hand acquaintance with the sagas was also valued as moral education, the handing on from one generation to another of a respect for established social standards and a pride in the national character. Grundtvig simply adapted the *Kvöldvaka* to serve a wider community.

To describe the development of high-school education by numbers of buildings and students is to risk understating Grundtvig's achievement. Even in Denmark itself where, after the loss of Schleswig–Holstein, the folk high schools were given official blessing as schools of national recovery, the highest number of students recorded in a single year rarely exceeded five thousand out of a total population of over two and a half million, and this in a country where state-financed elementary schooling started as early as 1814. And yet it was precisely because Scandinavia put a high value on literacy – Sweden introduced free education in 1844, with Norway following in 1860 – that Grundtvig's philosophy made its impact, and not just on the formal structure of Scandinavian education. The rifle clubs, which proliferated in response to Grundtvig's appeal for an alert citizenry ready to defend their country, created a demand for village 'meeting houses' for training sessions and gymnastics (another Grundtvigian passion). These centres soon attracted adult education groups who, eager to tap the cultural treasury opened by Grundtvig, organized lectures on religious, political and literary topics. By the end of the century lectures and study circles were a popular feature of social and professional organizations in all the Nordic countries.

Inspired by the Grundtvigian idea of culture as the binding force of society, people developed the habit of working together; whether it was in the agricultural co-operative organizations which, against all the odds, transformed Danish farming into a modern, highly productive industry, or in the Church-led campaigns for moral regeneration such as the temperance movement. By 1914, in Sweden alone, more than 350,000 had taken the pledge, a conversion rate closely matched throughout Scandinavia at a time when a supply of schnapps was cheaper than a thick coat for keeping out the cold and alcoholism ranked with poverty as the most virulent social disease.

In contrast to the experience of the big European powers, the Nordic countries embarked on the twentieth century with a strong sense of cultural identity which embraced all classes. Superbly effective as an instrument of nationalism, folk culture was also a great equalizer. The convictions that culture emerged from, and so rightly belonged to, the people, made Scandinavia fertile ground for egalitarian politics, and was a commanding influence on the development of contemporary art which appealed across class barriers. The early collections of folk tales sparked the imagination of Hans Christian Andersen, and for Grieg and Sibelius inspiration came from the folk melodies of their respective countries.

Inevitably there was a reaction against folklore as the first source of artistic endeavour. Too much delving back into the past, it was said, diverted writers from their proper function of making statements about contemporary society and its need to adjust to the challenge of industrialization. In the 1870s the literary movement known as naturalism reached northern Europe. It was made fashionable by a young Danish critic, Georg Brandes, who argued that political and social controversy was the life force of literature. The unashamedly radical edge Brandes gave to his lectures and writing was sharpened by the election to the Folketing of his brother Edvard, an outspoken atheist who started a controversial career by refusing to take the oath. For the old guard – not least the moderate left with its Grundtvigian and Christian associations – Brandes represented a dangerous influence on young people and a threat to accepted standards of decency in public life. When Georg was nominated as by far the best qualified candidate to fill the chair of literature at Copenhagen, the establishment blocked his appointment.

The prospect of turning away from the cosy security of the folk heritage to face the uncertain and in many ways disagreeable present might understandably have inhibited the latest generations of writers; instead it acted as a liberating force. It was as if the folk tradition was a form of cultural apprenticeship, preparing the way for something more exacting. If Strindberg and Ibsen were often too demanding for audiences still tentatively exploring the borders of theatrical propriety, there were other writers, less well known today but famous in their own time, who contributed to a greater sense of realism on the literary scene and invited questions about public affairs which the politicians and Church leaders were too cautious to raise. One such was the Norwegian Bjørnstjerne Bjørnson, first director of the national theatre and winner of the 1903 Nobel prize, whose novels and problem plays rivalled Grundtvig's essays as generators of public debate.

The 'modern breakthrough', as it was known in all the Nordic countries, was identified with the challenge to constraints on middle-class society – established religious beliefs and sexual morality, republicanism and, specifically, the 'decency controversy' which revolved on the question of women's status in the home and the community. But beyond the world of Ibsen, Strindberg and Bjørnson there were writers who responded to the challenges of industrialization and its impact on ordinary people. Martin Andersen Nexø, who was born in the Copenhagen slums, vividly portrayed working-class conditions in *Pelle the Conqueror*, an epic sequence of novels which inspired a generation of proletarian authors. There was a move here away from naturalism with its preoccupation with ideas towards a more imaginative form of social realism which tried to get closer to man's inner feelings. Knut Hamsun who, next to Ibsen, ranks as the most influential Norwegian writer of modern times, sought to capture the 'whisper of the blood, the entreaty of the home, all the unconscious life of the mind', in his depiction of the individual caught up in the degeneracy of industrialization and urban life.

Literary realism was not unique to Scandinavia: Dickens made his impact on Britain; Balzac, Flaubert and Zola on France and Turgenev on Russia. But in few other western countries was the movement as powerful as in northern Europe, where books containing a strong social message were the most widely read type of literature amongst all classes in the period up to the Second World War. This is not to claim an all-pervading cultural awareness, but it does separate Norden, where by the early years of the century cultural democracy had taken firm root, from the rest of Europe where, even with the advance of socialism, cultural élitism survived virtually unchallenged.

Many European leaders were from privileged backgrounds and, though they recognized that their working-class followers had their strongly entrenched set of values, there was no expectation, or even hope, that it could measure up to competition from the cultural establishment. Though patronizing in their assumption that what they knew best was best, socialist visionaries were bold enough to proclaim their faith in the popular intelligence. Education would open the minds of the people, so that in recognizing quality when they saw it they would naturally reject the mediocre and plain awful. The problem was to eradicate poverty and to create the social conditions in which citizens could freely exercise their powers of discrimination. It was not an argument which could be stressed too forcefully in an election. Calling for equality of opportunity in education was one thing, but to tell voters that their taste, though inferior now, was likely to improve when they entered the welfare society was to risk unnecessary offence. Yet few working-class voters missed the point or even disagreed with it. It was taken for granted that the life enjoyed by their social superiors was more satisfying in ways that could not be assessed by counting material benefits. Why was it then that, with all the evidence of popular respect for the cultural hierarchy, fear of domination by the masses and the imminent destruction of traditional values continued to preoccupy conservative writers? Critics like Ortega y Gasset (*The Revolt of the Masses*, 1930) revived the Nietzsche complex, worrying less about what socialists might attempt than about fifth columnists in the middle class who, protesting their concern for maintaining standards, put their money and energy into the technology of mass production to satisfy the public's crude desire to be amused. A sensationalist press, cheap romantic fiction, tawdry advertising and escapist films were thought to dull what sensitivity the common people had acquired in the days before the élitist principle was put at risk.

Insofar as there was a reaction from the left it was to welcome those sections of the mass media which clearly extended opportunities to ordinary citizens to broaden their range of cultural experiences. Thus radio was credited with encouraging appreciation of drama and classical music, and paperbacks were the means by which the pleasures of literature could be shared more widely. If in the early days cinema appeared to be dedicated to escapism, there was the thought that much of what was presently commended as élite culture was originally dismissed as ephemera. There could be no sure way of telling in advance what would prove to be most durable. The thirties aesthetes who refused to have paperbacks on their shelves echoed a prejudice first heard in the fifteenth century when the Duke of Urbino declared he would not have a printed book in his library. But even conceding that a large proportion of what passed for entertainment was indisputably rubbish, if welfare and educational expenditure increased as the left demanded the level of cultural discernment would rise accordingly. In other words, if the social and economic priorities could be got right, culture would look after itself.

In Norden too, where the social democrats enjoyed a wider measure of power than their counterparts elsewhere in Europe, economic questions took precedence. In an age of real and threatened recession and mass unemployment it could not have been otherwise. But while it was taken for granted that the first priority was to raise the standard of living for the mass of the people, it was less obvious that material and cultural affairs could be quite so clearly distinguished. To the extent that for the majority a comfortable home and a decent education were essential prerequisites to a greater appreciation of the arts, it was accepted that culture followed in the wake of economic progress. At the same time the actual process of making society richer was seen as a partly cultural activity.

Nowhere was this more apparent than in building and design.

The functionalist concept, inspired by the aim of the Deutsche Werklund to create 'more beautiful things for everyday use', made its first impact on Scandinavia in 1917 when the Swedish Society for Industrial Design organized a Home Exhibition in Stockholm. The purpose was to show how working-class homes could be structured and furnished in a way that was attractive, practical and inexpensive. Interest was lively but there was no immediate follow-up because many of the best designers were making a good living turning out exclusive high-price items and were not yet ready to put their talents to wider use. But there was a groundswell of support from those who saw themselves as part of the peasant handicraft tradition and who wanted to carry over the values of individual craftsmanship to the era of industrialization and mass production. It was not long before they found a leader. In 1919 Walter Gropius founded the Bauhaus school of functional design. First in Weimar and later in Dessau he gathered a staff of highly gifted architects, painters, sculptors and technicians whose varied imaginative skills were brought to bear on the problem of combining efficiency with beauty in manufacturing and construction. By the time Gropius left Germany to escape the Nazis his movement had attracted disciples in all European countries. But without doubt the strongest concentration of support for domestic functionalism was to be found in Scandinavia, where young designers vied to create new forms for household products – clean, smooth lines in furniture, colourful and easily manageable kitchenware, unfussy ornaments. Support for the movement among opinion leaders was overwhelming, and aroused envy among modernists abroad who had to fight off a strong rearguard action from sections of the cultural élite who were appalled at the association of art with the manufacture of household implements.

The lead in promoting what was soon recognized everywhere in the world as Scandinavian design was quickly taken by Finland, where functionalism had the added attraction of symbolizing the release from Soviet political and cultural hegemony. It was in architecture where Finnish influence was pre-eminent, with the work of Alvar Aalto arousing as much interest and controversy as that of Le Corbusier. Aalto had started to make a name for himself with conventional classical-style buildings when, in Norway and Sweden, he detected signs of a change in architectural fashion. By 1927, when the first Scandinavian functionalist building, the Skansen restaurant in Oslo, was completed, he was travelling widely in Europe absorbing the radical ideology of Le Corbusier and Gropius. Aalto himself was established as one of the masters of the modern movement with the construction of the Paimio Sanatorium, memorable for the long tiers of balconies – emphasizing the dominant role of light and air – rising like decks of a ship out of a forest setting. Though functionalism became respectable for residential buildings, and even stirred social-democrat visionaries to advocate collective housing units as part of a grand design for egalitarian living, Aalto and his contemporaries put their best efforts into the construction of factories and various public institutions. The 'mighty goal', as Aalto put it, 'was to bring industrialization step by step to the position, which it will no doubt one day achieve, of being a factor for cultural harmony'.

This concept of 'harmony' which remains dominant in all Nordic design led Aalto to set his imagination to work on the contents of his buildings. He and the Danish architect Arne Jacobsen were chiefly instrumental in popularizing the elegant lightweight furnishings which soon became standard in ordinary homes. One of the wonders of Scandinavia was the widespread regard for improving the domestic environment. 'Nowhere in the world', wrote an English writer, 'can one find such uniformly charming taste in every household, where the commonplace object is treated more pleasingly by designer and workman, and where that object is so appreciated by the average purchaser.' What made this discovery all the more interesting was that it really was popular taste which the writer had encountered – not standards imposed by an administrative or class élite. In small homogeneous societies ideas travelled fast, and public reaction to something new could be gauged quickly and accurately. Governments were sympathetic to the principles of functionalism but their role was limited to commissioning young architects with imagination and, in Sweden, to agreeing that one per cent of the cost of construction should be spent on decorating public buildings – an initiative followed in the other Nordic countries after the war.

But there was one area of Nordic life where élitism was as strong as anywhere in Europe. The traditions of an intellectual meritocracy founded on the supremacy of the universities made education a deeply conservative profession, and one which socialist thinkers, being products of the system, were mostly reluctant to challenge. In the pre-war era of social reform the priority of the left was to invest more in schools and teachers, so that every child could advance beyond basic literacy. After that, it was difficult for even the most advanced reformers to imagine how, in practical terms, education was to be organized other than as an open competition. The winners – those with the best talent for passing examinations – could then be dispatched to higher learning secure in the knowledge that by dint of hard work and natural ability they had earned the right to influential, interesting and rewarding careers. The problem, therefore, was not so much the system itself, even though it clearly supported a social hierarchy, but the way it was organized to favour a small minority of contestants. Children from moneyed families who could buy the best of everything including education inevitably outmatched their clever but poorer contemporaries who were dependent on scholarships and sympathetic teachers. Equality of opportunity was the first commandment of those who believed that if the learning resources were made available, clever children from working-class families would automatically advance to the ranks of the achievers.

The testing time for this thesis was in the period after post-war reconstruction when rapid economic growth coincided with a dramatic increase in the school population. Education overtook other social services to take a lion's share of government expenditure. In the countries of the OECD, the allocation to schools advanced by an average of fourteen per cent in the 1960s and the number of teachers rose by more than a third. It was the age of optimism, when education was confidently expected to chart the way to a just society in which every individual could realize his intellectual potential. That it did not happen quite like that was in large measure a result of trying to equate equality of opportunity with the administrative convenience of dividing children into two broad groups - the thinkers and the doers. The simplistic assumption that it was possible to divine the nature and strength of a youngster's abilities often before he had started on the critical years of learning gained credence on the evidence of psychologists who believed they had found objective ways of measuring intelligence. But even with the hindsight of knowing that intelligence is not a fixed property to be identified and assessed by a once-and-for-all test, it is extraordinary that many on the political left should for so long have accepted that variations in educational achievement, which common sense showed were closely in line with environmental influences, gave strength to the theory of an unequal and unchanging distribution of inherited ability.

The segregation of children into two grades of school offering either an academic or a practical education proved to be unreliable and wasteful. It was bad enough that many young people were directed away from educational opportunities from which they might reasonably have expected to benefit, but that most of these came from working-class backgrounds emphasized how little education was contributing to the achievement of social equality. Moreover, it was a system which more than anything helped to reinforce the hierarchical distinction between 'them' and 'us'. Naturally the educationally advantaged took to high culture as part of their justification for being picked out as very clever people, while those who learned practical skills and who counted themselves as educational rejects were made to feel more at home with the pulp culture offered by the mass media. To 'them' belonged the theatre, concerts, art galleries, museums, hardback fiction and the serious press: to 'us' the cheap romances and thrillers, cinema spectaculars, newspapers with big headlines and lots of pictures, light comedy and endless musical variations on the theme of unrequited love.

One did not have to take literally the Marxist view of mass culture as a form of capitalist manipulation to keep the workers passive to realize that there was something seriously wrong with a democracy which could offer freedom from want without at the same time facing up to the question, 'Freedom to do what?' C. Wright Mills touched a sensitive nerve when he described western society as '. . . passive, indifferent and atomised in which traditional loyalties, ties and associations become lax or dissolve completely . . . and in which man becomes a consumer, himself produced like the products, diversions and values which he absorbs'.

The Swedes were among the first to realize that school

selection – whether based on intelligence-test scores, attainment-test scores, marks or teacher ratings – was inefficient, socially biased and culturally divisive. With its first secure majority the post-war social-democrat government could afford to challenge the conservative philosophy of education, and it did so with two objectives: to support the growth economy with an increased flow of technologically proficient school-leavers and to prepare the ground for social equality.

The claim that the selection was wasteful of talent was bolstered by studies at home and abroad which showed that of the minority picked out as potential high fliers, up to one-third left school without passing examinations. That the overwhelming majority of drop-outs were working-class children suggested that, however impartial the selectors claimed to be, it needed more than a lively brain to achieve intellectual fulfilment. There was also a feeling that teachers who discarded so many of those who were by common consent the cleverest of their generation could hardly expect to be recognized as competent. The alternative to selection was comprehensive education, offered both as a more productive method of tapping the national pool of talent (though this was widely disputed and difficult to prove) and, in mixing children of different abilities in the same classroom, as a means of instilling a sense of social justice and unification. Forecast of another industrial revolution, bringing with it a shorter working week and increased leisure time as unskilled labour was made obsolete by automation, underlined the risk of staying with an education system which was so obviously attuned to the interests of a small minority.

In 1950 the government won approval for a large-scale experiment in comprehensive schooling as a preliminary to the reshaping of the whole structure of education. Selected areas replaced their variously named primary and secondary establishments with comprehensives catering for all children from seven to sixteen, the period of compulsory attendance. Seven years later the results were assessed. By then, however, almost one-third of the population was involved in the project; and though much of the research into the scholastic benefits was dismissed as inadequate or invalid, there could be no going back on what was essentially a political commitment. In 1962 comprehensive education was made the rule for the entire country, with time allowed for the administrative changes to be implemented.

It took another ten years before pre-sixteen selection was finally abandoned. This somewhat cautious advance must be set against the far-reaching social implications of educational reform in Sweden. In the larger European countries, where rigid selection procedures came in for heavy criticism, change was more apparent than real. Rote-learning, military-style discipline, the dominance of examinations and not least the shaping of the curriculum to match the traditions of the universities and the learned professions, all remained central to secondary education as practised in France, Germany and the United Kingdom. To contrast a specific feature, comprehensive schools in Britain were invariably streamed, so that those who were thought likely to achieve academic distinction were still creamed off at an early age and frequently even taught in separate buildings. In Sweden streaming was prohibited by the 1962 act, though in the focal subjects like languages and mathematics older pupils were graded. At the same time a start was made in constructing a new curriculum which emphasized the development of the personality to cope with the problems and challenges of a society undergoing a social and economic transformation. The freedom of students to pursue their own interests was confirmed, and they were encouraged to work more on their own or in groups without supervision. The hierarchical relationship between teacher and pupils was to give way to an informal and relaxed partnership.

Educational thinking in the rest of Norden followed the same broad pattern, though in Norway the first priority was not the creation of the comprehensive school as such – with a small thinly spread population few districts could contemplate the organizational luxury of providing alternative forms of teaching, let alone special premises for pupils with intellectual promise – but the extension of basic compulsory education from seven to nine years and the equalization of opportunities for rural and urban areas. The nine-year target was made a matter for local option in 1959 and obligatory ten years later, by which time only a few remote districts had failed to achieve the new minimum standard. Adherence to the egalitarian principles of comprehensive education was evidenced in the decision to eliminate all forms of grading in the first six years of schooling and to extend this policy across the entire range of compulsory education.

Testing and grading the very young was rejected in Denmark when comprehensive education was adopted in 1958. That same year Finland also went in for some restructuring of the school system, but with an administration shared by supporters of right and left the compromise was on extending compulsory education while retaining selection at eleven. It was not until 1970 that the comprehensive principle was accepted for the pre-sixteen age group, and even then it was to start in Lapland and to progress gradually to the south.

By that time, those Nordic countries which had led the way in providing all young people with the same basic education were coping with pressures for reform in the upper secondary and university sectors. It was bound to happen. Teaching in the comprehensive schools promoted the social-democratic ideal of equality and mutual respect. 'The new school rejects individuality, and teaches children to collaborate with others', said a junior education minister in the Swedish government. 'It rejects competition, and teaches co-operation. Children are taught to work in groups. They solve problems together, not alone. The basic idea is that they are considered primarily as members of society, and individuality is discouraged. We want to produce individuals who are integrated into society.' More circumspectly, Danish educationalists saw their role as 'preparing pupils for taking an active interest in their environment and for participation in decision-making in a democratic society, and for sharing responsibility for the solution of common problems ... so that ... teaching and the entire daily life in school is based on intellectual liberty and democracy.' But it came to the same thing.

Opponents saw this as a deliberate attempt to engage in social engineering – which, of course, it was. The views of minister Sven Moberg, quoted above, were used by Roland Huntford, a severe critic of Swedish society, to support the title of his book, *The New Totalitarians*. What he and other European liberals who feared school indoctrination chose to forget was that conventional education, with its emphasis on transmitting received culture, might equally be described as propagandist – in the cause of conservatism. Nordic politicians were distinguished by their courage in recognizing education as a powerful instrument for social change and using it accordingly.

But if equality was to mean anything, there had to be concessions in those sectors of education hitherto reserved exclusively for the élite. Up to the early seventies all post-sixteen-year-old students in Norden were firmly segregated. Those who wanted academic courses, usually the children of the professional class, were directed away from the majority, who were judged to be intellectually more attuned to practical, vocational work. The conflict between egalitarianism as preached in the schools and the version of equality of opportunity practised in advanced education was for a time masked by the huge expansion of places in the colleges and universities. In proudly acknowledging, for example, that the number of students in Swedish universities increased from 37,000 to 117,000 in the 1960s it was easy for the authorities to skate round the disturbing fact that by the end of the decade only one in ten of those students came from working-class homes. Norway was unusual in that the teacher-training colleges, which attracted a high proportion of working-class applicants, enjoyed strong regional loyalties and a prestige equal to and sometimes higher than that of the universities. But in the rest of Norden, as indeed in the rest of Europe, the class bias in higher education was no less pronounced than in Sweden.

Left to themselves, traditionally cautious academics, already made nervous by the pace of university expansion, might have tolerated the injustice, at best hoping that it would fade away as social changes lower down the system had time to work their way through. But there came a point in the mid-sixties when even the most sheltered professor recognized that he could not behave as if he were somehow apart from the real world. Criticisms had to be answered because it was the students themselves, the privileged minority who were supposed to have a vested interest in maintaining the status quo, who called into question the way the institutions of higher learning handled their responsibilities.

They did so from a variety of motives. There were those who, quite simply, were disappointed in their expectations. They had been brought up to be front runners and were now frustrated to discover that the race track was overcrowded with competitors.

The unprecedented boom in higher education, which was a feature common to nearly all the industrial nations, was intended to satisfy the technical and managerial needs of the growth economy. But the relationship was hardly ever formulated in precise terms, partly because the demand for different types of qualified personnel was at best uncertain, but also because the universities were jealous of their freedom and did not want to be seen as the servants of commerce. The result was that some disciplines, notably sociology, were vastly oversubscribed in relation to the number of responsible and well-paid jobs available.

The resentment of those who had got so far only to find that employers were no longer falling over each other to recruit graduates found expression in support for the new left attack on the materialistic values of the affluent society and the institutions, like the universities, which were its main prop. Capitalism, they argued, even in the modified form approved by the social democrats, was still an undignified struggle for personal gain in which all but a small minority were doomed to disappointment. Even where, as in Europe, it could be shown that the economic standing of the average citizen had improved enormously in the previous decade, happiness could not be measured by counting his possessions. Where, it was asked, was the logic in man's striving for more and more things without stopping to ask himself if he had a genuine use for them?

Herbert Marcuse, the elderly Marxist intellectual who, somewhat to his embarrassment, was ordained the high priest of student protest, taught that capitalism thrived on promoting 'false needs' that 'perpetuate toil, aggressiveness, misery and injustice' in a world where work has become an 'exhausting, stupefying, inhuman slavery'. With the subservient majority unable to imagine its future in terms other than those of capitalist ideology, Marcuse held that genuine opposition was confined to the privileged intellectual élite who alone were capable of seeing beyond their own experiences, an assertion which naturally confirmed his popularity with university revolutionaries.

Less virulent critics who recognized that capitalism, suitably managed, had its virtues nonetheless acknowledged that there remained deep deficiencies in the quality of life of ordinary people. It became a commonplace to observe the growing isolation of the family, the lack of popular interest or involvement in community affairs. In searching for causes, an education system set up to cater for a minority, to pass on mainly middle-class values and to deal with a given quantum of knowledge, was identified by many as a repressive force, dedicated to full conformity and deterring all but a privileged élite from realizing their abilities. Well-intentioned but half-hearted efforts to shift the balance in favour of the masses – such as the abolition of selection in early secondary education – served only to point up the intractability of the problem. The affluent society was largely a passive society. And if, outside the élite, there was minimal interest in the potential for individual and family enrichment extending beyond the acquisition of a new car or washing machine, it was because state investment in education and culture had failed to act as a release to imaginative energy.

This was certainly the prevailing view in Norden, where reaction to the students' vendetta with the establishment – a succession of demonstrations reached its peak in 1968, with widespread violence in France and Germany raising fears of democracy in danger – was to press ahead more urgently with reforms aimed at achieving greater social equality and cohesion. Sweden led the way with a plan for merging the academic and vocational branches of post-sixteen secondary education. In place of various specialist institutions, integrated upper secondary schools were to be set up to accommodate two-, three- or four-year courses (the last two leading to further or higher education) within the context of a broad-based curriculum. The motivation for change was unambiguously social, any educational or economic benefits being regarded as purely secondary to the declared intention of levelling the status of academic and practical subjects. Students would end up in different jobs enjoying greater or lesser rewards according to the scarcity value of their talents and the importance placed on their work, but by sharing in education it was hoped they would acquire mutual respect and concern for the wider interests of the community.

But the objective could not be achieved by organizational reform alone; social attitudes were shaped by what was taught and the way it was taught, and both called for a radical rethink. Taking advantage of a highly centralized administration which could even control the publication of textbooks, the government set about revising the curriculum in a way that made teachers aware of their role as agents of social change. Egalitarian ideals were pursued wherever subject content allowed, for instance by discussing 'socially committed writers' in literature courses, or by emphasizing the problems of the third world in history and international affairs. As part of the effort to instil a sense of individual responsibility for corporate well-being, the protection of the environment, with all its implications for the control of manufacturing and limitations on the freedom of the consumer, featured regularly in the teaching of science and social studies.

Sometimes education was expected to be unashamedly propagandist, as in the campaign against alcohol, drugs and tobacco. 'Teaching', said one observer, 'is not only aimed at giving pupils a knowledge of the facts, but also at developing certain attitudes and establishing patterns of behaviour'. It was policy which resulted in at least one notable achievement: the sharp decline in the number of smokers among school attenders, though, interestingly, the drop was more marked for boys than girls. Female resistance to the warnings of the anti-smokers may have been stiffened by the knowledge that tobacco had 'manly' associations and so offended the principle of sex equality. Taught to believe that almost any form of sexual discrimination was illogical, some girls possibly took to smoking to assert their independence. No doubt with unconscious irony, a sex-equality poster which appeared on many school notice boards actually showed a woman smoking a cigar. But the purpose of the advertisement was not to persuade girls to take up the tobacco habit. The caption read,

Girls are not supposed to smoke cigars. What else is it they are not supposed to do?

The answer was in smaller type.

A girl is not supposed to think she is anything except a girl. A girl is not supposed to take charge of anything. A girl is not supposed to care about an education because she will only want to get married and have children. A girl does not want a technical career, so she should study art, history, or literature. These subjects are much more ladylike.

And the punchline:

The prejudices are many but it is possible to break them.

The campaign for sex equality represented a true meeting of minds in politics and education. It was supported on grounds of social justice, economics (with full employment for men, women represented a valuable labour reserve) and personal fulfilment. One survey showed that over two hundred thousand mothers with children under ten were eager to extend their interests beyond the home if only they could get help with looking after their infants. The government contribution was to increase by fifty per cent the allocation for nursery-school development, to reform the tax system in favour of married women and to support the activities of pressure groups like the Sex Equality Commission, a co-operative venture of the trade unions and the employers' federation whose representative vigilance on behalf of women's rights extended to a protest against Punch and Judy shows. They complained that Judy was too frequently knocked about by an archetypal violent male.

But since everyone agreed that the core of the problem was education it was here that the reformers put their best efforts. The 1969 curriculum stated unequivocally, 'Schools should work for equality between men and women – in the family, on the labour market, and within society as a whole. They should give instruction on the sex role question and should stimulate pupils to debate and to question existing conditions.' Though it did not sound like it, in fact the schools had a creditable record in encouraging sex equality. It was a long-established rule that all subjects should be taught to both sexes, so that boys saw nothing unusual in attending domestic-science classes and girls were quite accustomed to trying their hand at carpentry and metalwork. That natural sexuality was rarely frustrated by prejudice or intolerance was also much to the credit of the schools, where sex instruction was comprehensive and compulsory. But there was still some way to go before teachers could genuinely satisfy the requirements of the new curriculum. There was a call for sex roles to be discussed more frequently in courses as diverse as history, biology, religious knowledge and geography, which depicted girls as conscientious, dutiful and helpful about the house but at the same time passive and timorous,

275

while portraying boys as aggressive, untidy and forgetful. The old stereotypes were to be replaced by a more balanced assessment of personalities and their domestic roles. Appearing in a draft text, an illustration showing mother baking cakes was withdrawn in favour of a kitchen scene with father helping to prepare breakfast. It was the last time anyone made that sort of mistake.

The rush to accommodate the radical ideals of the sixties was hardly less energetic in neighbouring states, where the social democrats, the main force for social change, were on somewhat weaker ground. The great debate on education in Denmark climaxed with a decision to impose stricter limits on the grading of pupils and virtually to abolish examinations. This policy was reversed in 1974 by the liberals, whose minority government favoured a revival of the competitive spirit in education. A year later, a minority social-democrat government compromised by permitting streaming in core subjects – maths, English, German and science – for pupils over the age of fourteen but left it to the local school boards, on which parents were strongly represented, to make the final decision. Whether or not to sit examinations was left up to the individual student, who was allowed to make up his own mind after consultation with parents and teachers. The minimum leaving age was fixed at fifteen but every pupil could stay on at school for an extra year as of right. It was a system which effectively reconciled freedom of the individual – a powerful element in the Danish political tradition – with the demands of the left for greater equality.

At the upper-secondary stage, reforms which followed the Swedish pattern were obstructed by those who feared that all would be educated down to the same level. The academic or grammar schools which catered for fifteen to twenty per cent of the relevant age group were kept distinct from the vocational institutions, though the route to higher education was broadened by recognizing a new two-year primary teachers' course as an alternative entry qualification. By 1976, the number of students going to university with a teacher's certificate instead of a pass in the grammar school examination had increased to seven thousand.

In Norway too the theoretical and practical branches of upper-secondary education were kept apart, but this did not mean that the exclusiveness of higher learning was sacrosanct. One of the simplest but most dramatic reforms in Nordic experience was the recognition, in principle, that all Norwegians were entitled to at least three years' compulsory post-education, either immediately on leaving school or after work experience. The universities were asked to admit all applicants over twenty-five who had been in employment for at least five years – and not necessarily paid employment in the conventional sense, because housewives were specifically included. The same rule applied in Sweden, though here the qualifying period was reduced to four years in 1977.

This bold attempt to open up the most privileged and politically influential sector of education did not produce the flood of students some academics had expected and feared. They had assumed that the growth in university attendance would follow the American pattern, that once the professors had accepted their role as popular educators the system would soon adapt to taking in thirty, perhaps even forty per cent of school-leavers. In fact, attendance peaked at twenty per cent in Sweden and at slightly lower levels in the rest of Norden, an achievement which was by no means outstanding in comparison with other developed countries. The familiar argument that reforms at pre-university level still needed time to work their way through the system was wearing thin, even though, for instance, a decade after the formal integration of Swedish upper-secondary education, there were still many authorities where vocational courses were accommodated in separate buildings. But it was the failure in economic calculations which really confused the forecasters. The realization in the early seventies that full employment and rising standards of living were not, after all, self-perpetuating, tended to confirm the working-class assumption that a university education with its rather obscure associations with the labour market was inappropriate for their children. The pressure was for vocational qualifications with good prospects for retraining or supplementary instruction as necessary.

In Scandinavia there already existed exceptional opportunities for combining study with work or for returning full-time to education after a period of employment. A strong tradition in adult education founded on the pioneering efforts of the voluntary movements and the folk high schools was bolstered by generous state support including, frequently, provision for paid study leave. Changes in the definition of adult education from country to country and even district to district, and the blurred distinction between vocational and leisure learning, make accurate statistics hard to come by. But by 1970 it was not unusual to find towns with fifteen to twenty per cent of the population enrolled in one course or another. A Council of Europe survey taking in Sweden and Denmark reported that enthusiasm for adult education was 'quite simply staggering in comparison with other European countries and might even be disbelieved had it not been confirmed by two independent methods of research'.

The expansion of further and adult education undoubtedly established a powerful counter-attraction to the universities. The trend was most apparent in Norway, where for more than a century the widely dispersed teachers' colleges had attracted local students who might otherwise have gained a place at the University of Oslo. Now, the setting up of regional colleges to cater for a wide range of educational needs helped further to diminish the appeal of moving to the city to take a degree. But in scholastic terms, the status of adult education benefited from the awareness that in a rapidly changing society the schools and colleges could no longer hope to predict the future roles of young people or determine with any accuracy the kind of knowledge they would need in later years. The alternative strategy was to think in terms of recurrent or life-long education: a shift of emphasis away from child-based institutions towards learning centres catering for all ages and providing a range of courses – short, long, full-time or part-time – adapted to the vocational, intellectual and leisure needs of the individual.

By the late sixties the main international educational agencies led by UNESCO and the Council of Europe had accepted the principles of recurrent education, the aims of which, to quote a Canadian commission, were to encourage personal self-fulfilment, enable the individual to cope with an increasingly complex society, improve motivation, develop a more adaptable system of career choice and increase personal freedom of choice between work and study. Sweden and Norway were among the first countries to promote these articles of faith into practical policies. The Norwegian commission on post-secondary education, reporting in 1968, made recommendations for integrating education with the workplace as the first step towards creating a system of life-long learning, and in the same year the Swedish education bill acknowledged that opportunities for adults to keep pace with the expansion of knowledge were high on the list of priorities for government expenditure.

The other Nordic countries, however, were more cautious. There was concern in Finland that scarce resources should not be diverted from the school modernization programme. But as a matter of principle, there was less interest in the purely intellectual aspects of recurrent education. As late as 1978, plans for taking more account of changes in working life concentrated almost exclusively on the provision of advanced vocational training. Political and economic uncertainties prevented the Danes from giving wholehearted support to recurrent education, though it was recognized as an important element within the existing adult-education system. As a measure of the difficulties, modest proposals for making study grants available to adults had to be set aside to pacify the critics of government spending at a time when Sweden was declaring paid educational leave to be the legal right of all employees.

The risk attached to recurrent learning was that it would follow the development pattern of other forms of education, serving best those who were socially and economically advantaged. It was quickly noticed that even where the unions organized courses it was nearly always the shop stewards or other officials who participated, hardly ever the unskilled workers. Yet if democracy was to mean anything it was those with the poorest upbringing who were most in need of education, not least as a boost to their self-confidence. A Norwegian study showed that fifty-eight per cent of early leavers believed they could have no influence whatsoever on political decisions beyond the effect of their vote. For those who had stayed on to upper-secondary level the proportion fell to twenty-five per cent. Not surprisingly it was found that individuals with an education of more than average length were represented far beyond their number in all areas of decision-making and so were able to bring about changes in society which accorded with their priorities.

Discrimination in favour of those groups with least education called for an out-going or out-reaching policy, as the Swedes called it. The first experiments showed just how difficult this was going to be in practice. FÖVUX, the Swedish commission set up to consider new methods in adult education, came in for criticism for its attempts to recruit students at their workplace. There was nothing wrong with the principle, and the incentives – time off for study or an addition to wages – were suitably realistic, but the range of subjects on offer was said to be too narrow and the methods of teaching too formal.

To find ways of recreating the excitement of learning for those who had long departed the classroom – and might not have enjoyed their time there anyway – required of teacher and student a whole new relationship which as yet barely figured in the imagination of the educational establishment. There were implications too for industrial policy, in so far as it was argued that fulfilment of intellectual potential could never be achieved unless structural and organizational changes in the working environment allowed for greater individual initiative and responsibility. Thus further advances in education, recurrent or otherwise, were closely tied to the outcome of the debate on industrial democracy, a subject to which we will return after considering changes in the interpretation of democracy as it was applied to the broader and more elusive theme, the popularization of culture.

In the sixties mood of economic well-being the principle of the state's taking more responsibility for stimulating cultural awareness was shared by governments of all persuasions. Culture was departmentalized, usually as an annex to the education ministry, and a small part of the tax revenue was set aside to protect artists against the flood of cheap commercialism and to encourage a wider interest in their work. Libraries were expanded; musty art galleries and museums were redesigned and brightened up to attract the passer-by; theatre companies and orchestras were encouraged to tour the provinces; and the arts centre, with its piece of modern sculpture in the forecourt, became the prestige symbol for any major enterprise in civic planning.

It is easy now to judge the inadequacy of a movement which, parading under a banner calling for the democratization of culture, was constrained by the customs and values of the establishment. Subsidies to the arts largely benefited those who were already consumers of high culture and, though ambitious efforts were made to broaden the interests of young people, those who controlled the resources too often behaved like missionaries stretching out the hand of salvation. It was an approach calculated to appeal neither to the culturally uninitiated, who needed more gentle encouragement to give up the inhibitions of a lifetime, nor to the radicals, among whom the students were pre-eminent, who equated official cultural policy with conservative propaganda. Marcuse taught that the true strength of opposition to the settled order was to be found in subversive art, and another Marxist critic, T. W. Adorno, went so far as to claim that art had to be unpopular to be taken seriously. Only when an artist's work was no longer suitable for immediate consumption, when it set itself against society, he claimed, could it be said to achieve any real significance.

On a broader political front, inquiries into the excesses of the pulp-culture industry and the mass media raised more questions than they answered. Controls on advertising were largely ineffectual, while the freedom of the press and broadcasting to report objectively on current events were shown to hold true only within the context of established middle-class values. But the biggest failure of cultural policy was not taking early note of the excesses of the urban planners. However serious the housing shortage, its solution did not require the wholesale destruction of established communities to make way for tower blocks and estates of concrete boxes. The growth of the environmentalist and conservationist movements was probably the most significant cultural development of the sixties.

The student revolt confirmed the widespread suspicion that cultural unity could not be achieved by a single transmission of ideas and interests from the élite to the masses. But what was the alternative? One response was to redefine culture so that it lost its élitist connotations. 'While civilization characterizes man's relationship to his surroundings, to nature,' wrote Johannes Sløk, the Danish theologian and historian of ideas, 'culture designates man's relationship to himself, his interpretation of what it means to be human.' André Malraux put it more succinctly: 'Culture is the answer to man's question, why am I here?' To equate culture with the grand sweep of human knowledge and experience was to argue that every individual had something to contribute to the common identity, whether it was intellectual, artistic, social or practical in character. The responsibility of the state was to awaken its citizens to the possibilities of achieving a more rewarding life and then to create the conditions in which they could make best use of their creative talents.

The ultimate objective, according to a background paper for the 1976 Oslo conference of ministers of culture, was a participating democracy,

in which there is a multiplicity of free dialogue on the basis of genuine equality of esteem transcending differences of income, profession, intelligence, personality, manners and tastes; where the opinions and convictions of the bus driver and the surgeon and the hippy and the industrialist and the immigrant worker and the old-age pensioner on the park bench are all given the same courteous and serious consideration.

This declaration of the ideal was immediately followed by a confession from the author, a British sociologist, that the closest he had come to the cultural environment of his dreams was 'in the boy society of public school and in one or two London clubs', both among the more élitist institutions where encounters with bus drivers or immigrant workers were likely to be rare. The suggestion here of a confusion of ideas, or perhaps simply an inability to cut loose from élitist traditions, extended to the conference itself, where delegates wrestled with the problem of trying to create a living cultural environment without putting at risk the values associated with high culture.

The Nordic representatives at the Oslo conference stood alone as avowed supporters of cultural democracy as the natural extension of political democracy. 'Social security is not worth much unless it gives us guarantees for human growth and development,' argued the Swedish minister, endorsing the Finnish view that 'by removing the obstacles caused by educational, economic, social and regional inequalities we also create the real preconditions for developing cultural democracy'. The Danish representative called for '... an active cultural policy as an instrument to consolidate and develop the democratic form of government', and his Norwegian colleague could '... see no conflict between individual activity and amateur culture on one hand and high regard for an official support of professionalism on the other'.

That the Scandinavians were less fearful of the consequences of cultural democracy than their European colleagues was evidence of how far they had already moved towards that objective. As small, homogeneous societies rich in folk traditions which overrode intellectual and class barriers, they had obvious advantages. Institutions normally associated with high culture were sometimes found to enjoy a wide appeal. The theatre, for example, which in European capitals (including those of Scandinavia) qualified as an élitist pastime, unexpectedly came into its own on Tampere, the heavily industrialized second city of Finland. A population of less than two hundred thousand supported two major theatres, an opera company, an experimental theatre and seven amateur societies. Sixty per cent of the people of Tampere visited the theatre at least once a year, a level of involvement which Council of Europe researchers attributed to the foundation of a workers' theatre early in the century and the consequent abatement of working-class antipathy to drama.

Danish enthusiasm for culture centres, otherwise known as people's houses to avoid élitist connotations, owed much to the traditions of the folk high school movement. One of the much-publicized successes of the sixties was the centre at Billund, in Jutland, a town of no more than four thousand including the farming community. The project was criticized by many as overwhelming in its boldness. It was certainly mounted on a grand scale, with library, church, cinema, theatre, meeting rooms and kindergarten brought together in a single horse-shoe-shaped building. But fears that it was too large and forbidding to attract popular support were groundless. The response proved an unsatisfied demand for cultural facilities which cut clear across social and economic divisions. There was more to it than providing the accommodation, of course. It needed gifted organizers to keep up the momentum, and even then things could go badly wrong: in its heyday the people's house in Magstræde, Copenhagen, could attract two to three thousand young people in an evening, but it was closed in 1971 when the authorities decided that with no identifiable control the enterprise had got out of hand.

The people's houses were destined to be an important part of Nordic cultural policy for the seventies, not least in Norway and Sweden where, in the absence of pubs and even cafés, there was a shortage of meeting places. Cushioned by state grants and loans, local authorities in need of cultural centres could afford to plan ambitiously.

Of all élitist cultural institutions the art gallery must count among the most exclusive. Tourists in the big capitals patronize the most famous permanent exhibitions where instantly familiar pictures are on display, but anything more adventurous – the work of younger artists, for example – rarely attracts the crowds. The Swedes tried to break through this cultural barrier as early as the 1930s, when the first travelling exhibitions were organized. Originally dependent on the co-operation of local authorities, the schools and later the trade unions took an interest, with the result that by the fifties national artists could count their viewing public in hundreds of thousands. That pictures were on sale at many of these exhibitions meant that creative skills were frequently rewarded with more than admiration. In most countries this would have been accepted as entirely fair – even generous – since it is an established belief that exhibiting an artist's work is as much a service to the artist as to the public who come to view. But the Swedes were soon questioning this convention, arguing that artists were entitled to be paid for the pleasure they gave to those who were not potential clients. By 1960 it was common practice for the sponsor of an exhibition to offer a display free, and this led eventually to the adoption of an agreed scale of rates. In 1971 a central fund was established from which payments could be made to artists where sales from their exhibitions failed to provide a reasonable margin on costs. A Council of Europe report declared that

Sweden was one of the first countries in which government, the general public and the majority of artists all accepted the idea that artists were not deviants engaged in luxury pursuits reserved for the privileged few, but socially productive workers who should be part of society instead of living on the fringes of it.

The remuneration of artists came to be accepted in principle throughout Norden, though methods of payment varied from country to country. More teaching posts were put on offer, galleries took to arranging lecture programmes and art societies were active in promoting the sale of paintings. A Swedish study of the possibility of paying recognized artists a minimum salary met with opposition from those who thought the money would be better spent if it was allocated to public institutions for buying works of art. More fruitful was an 'art to the people' scheme adopted in Finland, where local authorities were encouraged to offer one-year consultancy contracts to artists – and not just painters but to writers, directors, musicians who could advise on a wide range of cultural activities while continuing with their own creative work.

If the policy of widening the access to professional art was interpreted more imaginatively and constructively in Norden than in Europe as a whole, the Scandinavians diverged more spectacularly in their disregard for liberal conjecture that state intervention in cultural affairs forewarned the state control of ideas. The wave of newspaper failures in Sweden in the fifties and sixties attracted government aid to the industry in the form of cheap loans for modernization programmes and concessional postal rates. These measures were accepted as within the bounds of legitimate state involvement, even though some critics wondered if the social-democrat government would have acted in the same way if the crisis had not caused greatest damage to the left-wing press.

Then in the early seventies, as production costs continued to rise and more closures were threatened, another more controversial support scheme was mooted. The idea was to draw money off the successful papers and periodicals by a tax on advertising revenue which could then be used to subsidize ailing competitors. To those who argued that the freedom of the press was thereby put at risk (what editor would dare to criticize his paymaster?) the government countered that an editor out of a job because his paper had folded was even less likely to be an effective watchdog for the public interest. In any case, what difference in principle was there between state support for the written word and the central funding of broadcasting? The weakness here was that many believed that television and radio *were* too gentle on the government, though less for strictly financial reasons than because most of the leading appointments were held by social democrats.

Initial reaction abroad was, if anything, more critical, but as Swedish journalists and other newspaper workers settled down to the scheme there came the grudging admission that state backing had revived the confidence and fighting spirit of the industry. Conversion to the new technology proved manageable without the labour conflicts experienced elsewhere and the search for new forms of cost saving led to some original exercises in collaboration, such as the production of two more editions of the same paper with advertising, sports coverage and some other non-controversial items in common but with different editorial slants in news and comment.

At first it looked as if Finland would follow Sweden's example on press subsidies. A bill was introduced in the mid-sixties, but even with several newspaper closures, opposition from those who were to be the immediate beneficiaries, the journalists and their employers, led to its defeat. Instead, the money was channelled to the political parties to enable them to get their views across to the public by whatever means available to them, including support for papers sympathetic to their cause. After 1971 the press benefited from reduced charges for telex and postage facilities.

The press was not alone in its financial troubles. By 1978 the national council for cultural affairs in Sweden was underwriting the nation's literary heritage at the rate of fourteen million Kronor a year. This was to keep in print at reasonable prices a good selection of Swedish classics which might otherwise have been swept under in the tide of fiction, good and bad alike, from the English-language market. Concern for the future of a minority culture was at the basis of state support for book publishing, which started in 1962 with payments to authors for loans of their books from libraries.

The scope for subsidized publishing widened significantly in 1974 when new quality fiction became eligible for grants. There was some nervousness that a government agency would take upon itself the right to define 'quality', but the rules were made wide enough to accommodate anything that could reasonably be counted as good fiction. In representing the state, the most important decision to come from the national council for cultural affairs was the price of a book. To be eligible for grants, publishers had to accept that they were no longer free to charge high and print low, relying on the libraries to clear their stock. If literature was to be promoted to the general public it had to be at prices the average citizen could afford. Other areas of publishing to benefit from state munificence included children's literature, where a production subsidy was offered on books normally too expensive to publish, such as Swedish picture stories. The state could also step in with a purchase order for one thousand copies of a title for free distribution to libraries and youth organizations.

Any suggestion that the government might be trying to manipulate the industry to suit its own ideas of the sort of books people should be encouraged to read was contradicted by efforts to combat the concentration of publishing to a few large houses. There were loans and credit guarantees for those wanting to strike out on their own as small independent publishers, a state investment which soon paid good literary dividends. Some of the most exciting and original work to appear in Sweden in recent years has come from outside the big publishing combines.

Defence of the national language, or rather, languages, ranked high on the priorities of the Norwegian culture fund. Any new literary work published in Norwegian, irrespective of merit, qualified for a state purchase of one thousand copies for library use. But to cater specifically for the home market was also a guarantee of grants or loans to cover the production costs of a book, say, or to supplement an author's income. It was a system much admired by publishers and writers in Iceland where, for a quarter of a million population, up to six hundred titles appeared annually with the help of only small grants, mostly paid directly to authors. That further subsidies were not forthcoming was partly the result of the country's economic problems but was also a tribute to the Icelanders' reputation as some of the most enthusiastic book-buyers in the world.

As with publishing, so with film. It was an undercapitalized industry up against strong foreign competition, chiefly from America. But the cinema had the added problem of trying to match the appeal of television which, even in Norden with its tight restrictions on viewing output, was by far the most popular leisure activity. In the 1940s, Sweden produced about forty films a year; by 1960 the figure had dropped to twenty or less. To stop further decline the Swedes set up a Film Institute financed by a levy on the sale of cinema tickets to stimulate production and distribution. Part of its operation was a film school for training directors, producers and technicians. The Institute came in for conflicting criticism with purists, who thought that too much weight was given to commercial interests, battling against those who believed that film-makers were allowed excessive freedom to indulge their often weirdly idiosyncratic philosophies. But with the almost total absence of censorship there was no complaint that the state was trying to limit the expression of ideas. In its first five years the Institute produced less than a dozen films, but by the mid-seventies, with state grants supplementing the ticket levy, it had come to dominate the industry. Competition from television was cushioned by a government-inspired agreement with Swedish Broadcasting on the joint financing of films for which the cinema distributors had exclusive rights for eighteen months. Afterwards they could be shown on television.

The Danish Film Foundation, created in 1964, just one year later than the Swedish Institute, started with a weaker base. Apart from some outstanding documentaries the home industry had produced little of artistic merit since the pioneering days of the silent movies. But the new-wave cinema of the fifties, which showed that the future of the medium did not lie exclusively with the blockbusters, encouraged writers and directors to try their hand at reviving Danish films. The Foundation was less generously financed than its Swedish counterpart and the distribution of limited funds was closely tied to the fashionable concept of 'quality film making'. But confidence increased with output to the point where a film school was set up on the Swedish model. By the seventies, when the Foundation was succeeded by the Danish Film Institute, enthusiasm was strong enough to win financial backing for a people's workshop, which was soon turning out fifty to a hundred films a year.

Norwegian output peaked in the sixties at a modest ten films a year, nearly all of them aimed exclusively at the home market. With such a small potential audience the industry was totally dependent on state finance, which met up to fifty-five per cent of production costs. There was a tougher line on censorship than in Sweden or Denmark. The relaxed attitude to sex for which Scandinavia had an unrivalled reputation did not extend to the Norwegian cinema.

Even though the subsidy channelled to the Finnish Film Foundation amounted to only a tenth of that allocated to the theatre, film-making came out of the doldrums in the sixties with some notable triumphs in the international market. But shortage of funds pointed up the attraction of the more plentifully endowed Swedish cultural scene, with the result that some of the most talented film-makers went into exile.

It was not until the seventies that Icelandic film came out of the doldrums. The incentive to young movie-makers was the setting up of a Film Fund supported by a tax on cinema tickets. The challenge was to produce films capable of drawing into the cinemas at least twenty per cent of the population, an extraordinary target actually recorded by recent full-length features.

Ten years ago no one in Scandinavia would have suggested that state involvement in cultural affairs was anything but imperfect. As one critic put it, too little money was tied to too much bureaucracy. But the record of support for the arts was better than that achieved by most other European countries, and there was certainly no feeling of élitism in the way that the money was distributed.

Nordic politicians and cultural administrators were therefore hurt and surprised by the growing chorus of criticism that much of what they were trying to achieve with the dissemination of art and literature could be interpreted as serving the interests of a minority. But evidence showing that frequently it was the professionals and their cultural peers, not the ordinary consumers, who gained most from government handouts was difficult to refute. The efforts the Norwegians put into decentralizing cultural institutions by supporting nation-wide concert and theatrical tours and travelling art exhibitions and by setting up an Authors' Centre to help popularize modern Norwegian literature probably went furthest in trying to find points of contact with those who, for one reason or another, were outside the cultural mainstream. Yet large sections of the population were not reached, and this was not because of geographical barriers (even the most remote community figured in someone's schedule of cultural events) but because social inhibitions kept away many who resented what they saw as the imposition of the values of the outsider.

Registering cultural achievement in figures, the Swedes were justifiably proud that average attendances at state-run or state-supported theatres reached three million annually between 1970 and 1975, that twelve thousand concerts were given each year and that museum visits passed the six and a half million mark every December. And yet, reporting on his long-term research into the sociology of culture, Harold Swedner observed the antagonism of a large section of the Swedish people to theatres, concerts and exhibitions – all the paraphernalia of what they saw as high culture.

The mistake had been to think that the working class, because of late development, had escaped the worst influences of European industrialization. The consolation was in knowing that the divisions opening up between classes had not grown so wide as to be impossible to bridge. While resenting élitism, the mass of the people did not seek independence from established culture but showed every indication of wanting to divest it of some of its more distinctive bourgeois characteristics.

The subsequent reform of cultural policy was not confined to tinkering with the distribution of state aid. It had a far-reaching influence on government thinking on a range of issues – most significantly, regionalism and Nordic co-operation.

In the subdued political mood of the seventies it was generally acknowledged that centralization had seriously put at risk the social cohesion of the Nordic countries. One side of the problem was the flood of workers to the urban areas, mostly in the south in times of rapid economic growth. Employers, unions and governments had unanimously assumed that the free mobility of labour was essential to the efficiency and profitability of industry and so to the survival of those firms capable of paying the highest wages. But the rise in material standards was achieved at the cost of the social impoverishment of the outlying regions. Resentment at what was seen as blatant discrimination was compounded by the knowledge that real political power was concentrated in the capitals. This was the other aspect of the problem, that successive governments, determined to implement their version of the welfare society, had taken every opportunity to reduce local political initiative to a level where it could not possibly threaten the central bureaucracy.

The plight of the regions was a major factor in the revival of the fortunes of the centre parties, who campaigned successfully for greater autonomy for the provincial authorities. The pressure to revive local democracy, combined with the emotional appeal of doing something for the rural communities with whom even the most urbanized Scandinavian closely identified, was irresistible to the left-wing parties in power. Along with economic aid went the independence to determine how the money should be spent. In cultural affairs the emphasis shifted from the exercise of heavy-handed bureaucracy to the encouragement of local initiative, starting in education.

Denmark led with legislation entitling local authorities to decide their own school curricula. In 1976 the Swedish parliament allocated to the municipalities a no-strings-attached block grant for education amounting to twenty-five per cent of the salary bill for teachers. Cultural budgets were increased substantially – in Norway from a few hundred thousand dollars in the sixties to five million in 1975, with a commitment to exceed twenty million by 1980. Most of the extra money went to regional institutions and voluntary organizations including adult study groups.

After years of gathering in power to the state politicians and administrators, centralization was associated with the post-war social reforms to such a degree that its rejection raised unwarranted fears of a return to conservative principles and the surrender of hard-won causes. No such anxieties attended the updating of Nordic co-operation to take account of the new ideas of cultural democracy. On this front change could only be for the better, since prior to the seventies activity had been restrained to the point of indolence.

The immediate post-war years witnessed the setting up of the Nordic cultural commission, a committee of worthy part-timers whose reports were much respected but seldom read outside establishment circles. After 1952, however, a sense of urgency was inspired by the Nordic Council, the first institution to be able to put some political muscle behind recommendations for co-operative action. The commission was split into three sections – higher education and research; schools; and the arts, adult education and general cultural activities. Each country appointed a senior civil servant to each of the sections, and direct lines of communication were opened to the relevant ministries.

The style of the commission was more informal than that usually associated with official bodies. Writers, academics, teachers, publishers, artists and others deemed to be culturally aware came together in a multiplicity of committees to urge support – invariably financial – for their pet causes. The schools were invited to play their part by offering instruction in the languages and culture of all the Nordic countries, an aspiration most teachers approved more in spirit than in practice. A start was made on co-ordinating public examinations and the qualifications they conferred and encouragement given to student exchange programmes.

The general view that this was about all any Nordic agency could reasonably expect to achieve was confirmed by the 1962 Helsinki Agreement, which made only passing reference to cultural matters. There was special mention of the need to make better use of research funds by setting up joint institutions, but more effort was applied and certainly more publicity was given to the institution of Nordic prizes for literature and music. By the late sixties, however, opinion on the best way of handling cultural co-operation had changed dramatically. Arguments about the extension of democracy revealed the limitations of the cultural commission. It enjoyed the status of a high-ranking advisory body, but without adequate backing services or resources of its own it was bound to appear élitist in character. Moreover, where an effort was being made to reach out to ordinary people, as in the campaign to stimulate Nordic studies in the schools and colleges, it was clear that little if anything had been achieved.

All the evidence suggested that fewer, not more, youngsters were capable of reading a second Nordic language, and that inland from the borders children had a better general know ledge of America than of neighbouring countries. Yet the education system could not be held solely responsible. At government behest, the main effort had gone into teaching English as a second language, a sensible decision economically but one which had attendant dangers for the long-term survival of a distinct Nordic culture. If an American TV movie and the Nordic literature prize were to compete in capturing the popular imagination, few would pause to predict the winner. In terms of Nordic co-operation, therefore, cultural democracy made a double impact. The prospect of extending the boundaries of political democracy had an immediate appeal but the need to protect Nordic culture by reawakening popular awareness of the common heritage was an additional powerful motive for change.

By 1968 the future structure of cultural co-operation was the first item on the agenda for the Nordic ministers of education. The priority was for a decently funded permanent staff backed by a responsible sector of the administration in each of the five countries. It was a proposal easy enough to make but less easy to implement, given the long-standing suspicion of supranational authorities. Fortunately the cultural debate followed hard on the abortive negotiations for Nordek. Following the precedent of 1952, when the Nordic Council was built on the ruins of the defence treaty, the politicians of 1970 looked for some means of recovery after the disappointment of their hopes for economic union. As part of a general restructuring of Nordic institutions, a cultural agreement was signed in Helsinki in 1971. Soon afterwards the staff of the new secretariat for Nordic cultural co-operation moved into offices in Copenhagen.

Reporting directly to the council of ministers, its brief was to raise the level of communication between countries by initiating co-operative ventures in television, radio and film, to bolster the cultural efforts of voluntary organizations like youth and sports clubs, and generally to help create opportunities for artistic and creative expression. Even assuming the ready assistance of the national governments, it was a tall order for a staff of less than fifty operating on a budget of seven million dollars. In the early years, the secretariat kept to the tradition of playing safe, devoting its resources to such worthy projects as a study of adult education facilities throughout Norden and the potential of multi-media instruction for older students, and a programme to inform teachers of curricula developments in English and mathematics in the five countries.

The most newsworthy event was the opening in 1973 of the Nordic Same Institute on the Norwegian–Finnish border to act as a central agency for economic and cultural support for the Lapp population. This followed the success of a Nordic culture house in Reykjavik and led to the promise of another culture centre, this one to be built on one of The Faeroe islands. In most other respects achievements of the secretariat were over-shadowed by what was happening at national level, as for example the remarkable increase in the number of summer festivals in Finland, from three hundred in 1970 to over a thousand within five years, a cultural phenomenon which at-tracted interest well beyond Norden.

But the settling-in period for the cultural secretariat was not a long one. In 1977 it pitched into controversy with a report on the inter-Nordic exchange of television and radio programmes by satellite. It had been known for some time that the transmis-sion of the television and radio output of all five countries to the entire Nordic area was technically feasible. What had stopped the plan from getting any further than the drawing board was the enormous, some said prohibitive, cost. There were other problems. For example, only Finland and Iceland had com-mercial television; the others were strongly against further busi-ness encroachment on the media. And there was no easy way of resolving the heated arguments about the relative quality of programmes put out by the various networks.

But it was the expense that was the real killer of any further initiative – until, that is, the Swedish Space Corporation de-clared that a satellite system could be achieved more economic-ally and within a shorter time than earlier investigations had suggested. This led to another committee and the 1977 report, which estimated a total cost in the region of 150 million dollars, a large investment but one which could be supported by the knowledge that sooner or later the Germans would put up a satellite capable of beaming programmes over Scandinavia, and that quite possibly a business consortium would start an English-language service. In either event, the national broad-casting authorities might find it hard to compete and Nordic culture would suffer accordingly.

The opponents of what soon became known as Nordsat failed to see how it would neutralize competition from foreign stations. Over half the programmes shown on the Scandinavian net-works were bought overseas, mostly from the United States and

Britain. There was no suggestion that the proportion would change if Nordsat got off the ground. A Swedish civil servant dismissed the whole enterprise as 'an expensive way of seeing Kojak with four sets of subtitles'. A cheaper alternative was to extend the well established practice of programme exchange between the Nordic countries while trying to initiate an international agreement on television coverage.

Though at the time of writing the question is still undecided it has opened up a debate which is central to Nordic cultural development. Hitherto the Scandinavians or, to be more precise, those in control of public funds, have not given the impression of thinking too deeply about the social impact of television. While recognizing that television plays a dominant role in leisure activities the tendency has been to resist its influence by restricting viewing time and resources to a point where home-produced quality programmes are thin in the schedules. The virtue of Nordsat, even if it never becomes a reality, is that it has turned the discussion towards the positive contribution of broadcasting to the advance of cultural democracy. The prospects, for instance, for offering an improved service to minority groups including immigrants, for developing local radio and television, for producing more adventurous programmes for schools and adult education groups and for pooling resources to make programmes that would be too costly for a single broadcasting authority are now better than ever before.

The television debate put real life into all those involved in cultural co-operation. Having realized the existing possibilities in one direction, they sought other avenues to explore. In 1978 the secretariat produced an action programme in which better linguistic understanding between Nordic countries, help for the voluntary movements and youth unemployment figured among the subjects needing urgent attention. The reference to youth unemployment made an interesting link across to policies at national level, where increasingly it was argued that cultural fulfilment could only be achieved in an environment which gave full scope to the value and dignity of labour. In the state support for the devolution of authority at the place of work, paid study leave for employees and company-based adult education, the twinning of cultural democracy and industrial democracy was emerging as a principal political theme for the eighties.

*   *   *   *   *   *

The West can expect another industrial revolution within the decade. Price competition from the developing countries where labour is cheap will press hard on old-established industries in high-wage countries, while microchip technology must hasten the shift from mass production to specialist high-value items which cannot easily be created in third-world factories. Part of the process of change will be the increased demand for skilled labour and a corresponding drop in employment opportunities for the untrained and less well educated.

To venture beyond these bland predictions is to invite disagreement on the likely impact of the new order; whether, for example, it will lead to a real improvement in living standards. So much is open to choice, and the hazards of forecasting are magnified in this case by the apparent disinterest among politicians and voters in the ways in which society could be shaped by the end of the century. A long period of recession seems to have stultified the western political imagination. As a result the initiative has passed to the enemies of change, those who for whatever motives find their inspiration in trying to contain the impact of the knowledge explosion. Often the ecologists, conservationists and other 'trend reversers and system haters', as their opponents call them, have acted as a valuable corrective to the insensitivity of planners and bureaucrats. Perhaps also they are justified in fearing that society is as yet poorly equipped to deal with the uncertainties of technological change. But where is the positive side to this argument? How is society to be prepared to make best use of its opportunities and to rediscover the excitement of widening the boundaries of knowledge and experience?

The Nordic countries are better placed than most to break out of this intellectual straitjacket. Though by no means isolated from the vicissitudes of world trade they have a strong economic base. Their long-standing reputation for high-quality, high-technology products should make the decline of uncompetitive industries like shipbuilding and some sectors of forestry easier to bear. Educational standards are high, and though currently there is some dispute as to the teaching priorities in schools and colleges, the commitment to life-long learning is virtually unchallenged. Society is stable, and while problems remain, like the inadequacy of help to maladjusted young people, immigrant families or the elderly, it would be churlish to argue the generalization that Norden has eradicated poverty.

The tendency to try to put back the clock has been evident in recent years, but for all those in politics on left or right who have taken a depressing view of the future there are an equal or greater number who look forward to creating an environment in which the individual can find greater satisfaction and fulfilment. The lessons of an over-centralized and over-systematized administration have been learned. The possibilities for extending the role of the individual and his capacity for deciding how he wants to lead his life are contained in embryo in the proposals for industrial and cultural democracy discussed earlier. There is a long way to go, but at the beginning of the eighties the best guess is that Norden will long retain its reputation as the social laboratory of the Western world.

Select bibliography

General

Connery, Donald, *The Scandinavians* (Eyre and Spottiswoode, London, 1966)

Fullerton, Brian and Williams, Alan, *Scandinavia* (Chatto and Windus, London, 1975)

Scott, Franklin D., *Scandinavia* (Harvard University Press, Cambridge, Mass., 1975)

Countries

Hertling, Knud (ed.) *et al.*, *Greenland, Past and Present* (Edvard Henriksen, Copenhagen)

Ingold, Tim, *The Skolt Lapps Today* (Cambridge University Press, Cambridge, 1976)

Mead, W. R. and Smeds, Helmer, *Winter in Finland* (Hugh Evelyn, London, 1967)

Nickels, Sylvie (ed.) *et al.*, *Finland* (Allen and Unwin, London, 1973)

Nordal, Johannes and Kristinsson, Valdimar (eds.), *Iceland 874–1974* (Central Bank of Iceland, Reykjavík, 1974)

Tomasson, Richard F., *Iceland* (University of Minnesota Press with Icelandic Review, Reykjavík, 1980)

Turner, Barry, *Sweden* (Batsford, London, 1976)

Wadensjö, Gösta, *Meet Sweden* (Liber Hermods, Stockholm, 1979)

West, John F., *Faeroe* (Hurst, London, 1972)

History

Andersson, Ingvar, *A History of Sweden* (Weidenfeld and Nicolson, London, 1970)

Brøndsted, Johannes, *The Vikings* (Penguin, London, 1973)

Graham-Campbell, James and Kidd, Dafydd, *The Vikings* (British Museum, London, 1980)

Jones, W. Glyn, *Denmark* (Ernest Benn, London, 1970)

Kerry, T. K., *A History of Scandinavia* (University of Minnesota Press, Minneapolis, 1979)

Select bibliography

Kirby, D. G., *Finland and Russia 1808-1920* (Macmillan, London, 1975)
Kirby, D. G., *Finland in the Twentieth Century* (Hurst, London, 1979)
Kobbisk, Steven (ed.), *Sweden's Development from Poverty to Affluence 1750-1970* (University of Minnesota Press, Minneapolis, 1975)
Lauring, Palle, *A History of Denmark* (Høst, Copenhagen, 1960)
Moberg, Wilhelm, *A History of the Swedish People* (2 vols.) (Heinemann, London, 1971 and 1972)
Oakley, Stewart, *The Story of Sweden* (Faber, London, 1966)
Oakley, Stewart, *The Story of Denmark* (Faber, London, 1972)
Popperwell, Ronald G., *Norway* (Ernest Benn, London, 1972)
Puntila, L. A., *The Political History of Finland 1809-1966* (Otava, Helsinki, 1975)
Roberts, Michael, *Essays in Swedish History* (Weidenfeld and Nicolson, London, 1966)
Roberts, Michael (ed.), *Sweden's Age of Greatness* (Macmillan, London, 1973)
Samuelsson, Kurt, *From Great Power to Welfare State: 300 years of Swedish social development* (Allen and Unwin, London, 1968)
Scobbie, Irene, *Sweden* (Ernest Benn, London, 1972)
Vloyantes, John P., *Silk Glove Hegemony, Finnish-Soviet Relations 1944-74* (Kent State University Press, Kent, 1975)
Wilson, William H., *Folklore and Nationalism in Modern Finland* (Indiana University Press, Bloomington, 1976)

Politics and economics

Allen, Hilary, *Norway and Europe in the Seventies* (Universitetsforlaget, Oslo, 1979)
Berglund, Sten and Lindström, Ulf, *The Scandinavian Party Systems* (Studentlitteratur, Stockholm, 1978)
Cerny, Karl, H. (ed.), *Scandinavia at the Polls* (American Enterprise Institute for Public Policy Research, Washington, 1977)
Edgren, Gösta *et al.*, *Wage Formation and Economy* (Allen and Unwin, London, 1973)
Hancock, M. Donald, *Sweden: the Politics of Postindustrial Change* (Dryden Press, Hinsdale, 1972)
Helco, Hugh, *Modern Social Politics in Britain and Sweden* (Yale University Press, New Haven, 1974)
Holst, Johan Jørgen, *Five Roads to Nordic Security* (Universitetsforlaget, Oslo, 1973)
Huntford, Roland, *The New Totalitarians* (Allen Lane, London, 1971)
Korhonen, Keijo (ed.), *Urho Kekkonen* (Otava, Helsinki, 1975)
Korpi, Walter, *The Working Class in Welfare Capitalism* (Routledge and Kegan Paul, London, 1978)

299

Lindbeck, Assar, *Swedish Economic Policy* (Macmillan, London, 1975)
Maude, George, *The Finnish Dilemma* (Oxford University Press, Oxford, 1976)
Meidner, Rudolf, *Employee Investment Funds* (Allen and Unwin, London, 1978)
Miljan, Toivo, *The Reluctant Europeans* (Hurst, London, 1977)
Myrdal, Alva, *Towards Equality* (Prisma, Stockholm, 1971)
Nousiainen, Jaakko, *The Finnish Political System* (Harvard University Press, Cambridge, Mass., 1971)
Scase, Richard, *Socialist Democracy in Capitalist Society* (Rowman and Littlefield, Totowa, 1977)
Solem, Erik, *The Nordic Council and Scandinavian Integration* (Praeger, New York, 1977)
Stephens, John D., *The Transition from Capitalism to Socialism* (Macmillan, London, 1979)

Social

Dahlström, Edmund, *The Changing Roles of Men and Women* (Duckworth, London, 1967)
Husén, Torsten, *The Learning Society* (Methuen, London, 1974)
Linnér, Birgitta, *Sex and Society in Sweden* (Jonathan Cape, London, 1968)
Myrdal, Alva, *Nation and Family* (Massachusetts Institute of Technology Press, Cambridge, Mass., 1968)
Myrdal, Alva and Klein, Viola, *Women's Two Roles* (Routledge and Kegan Paul, London, 1968)
Ramsøy, Natalie Rogoff (ed.), *Norwegian Society* (Universitetsforlaget, Oslo, 1974)

English-language journals

Scandinavian Review, Swedish Journal of Economics, Scandinavian Political Studies, Sweden Now, News from Iceland, Icelandic Review

Publications of the Nordic Council (including *The Yearbook of Nordic Statistics*), Nordic Cultural Secretariat, Swedish Institute, Danish Institute, Norwegian Ministry of Foreign Affairs, Council of Europe, OECD.

Index

Index

304